JIM MANTHORPE began his exploration of wild places and developed wanderlust the moment his father armed him with a stick and a rucksack on the first of several childhood trips to Wales and Scotland. He later became an integral member of Stirling University Mountaineering Club. Since then he has explored almost every glen, peak and bothy in the Scottish Highlands and has found himself windswept and soaked through in Scandinavia, the Alps, the Himalaya, the Pyrenees and Patagonian Chile.

Articles for *High Magazine* on the mountains of Scotland and the Pyrenees soon opened the door to guidebook writing; he recently researched and updated the *Trans-Canada Rail Guide* and *Trekking in Ladakh* for Trailblazer, and he is the author of the forthcoming *South Downs Way* guide, also in this British Walking Series.

Jim's enthusiasm for writing, photography, and his love of wild places have never waned despite experiences such as nearly losing his hair to an exploding gas stove in a Pyrenean mountain hut. He now divides his time between working in London at Stanfords, the travel bookshop, and travel writing.

Pembrokeshire Coast Path
First edition: 2004

Publisher
Trailblazer Publications
The Old Manse, Tower Rd, Hindhead, Surrey, GU26 6SU, UK
Fax (+44) 01428-607571, info@trailblazer-guides.com
www.trailblazer-guides.com

British Library Cataloguing in Publication Data
A catalogue record for this book is available from the British Library

ISBN 1-873756-56-9

© **Trailblazer 2004**
Text and maps

Editor: Henry Stedman
Series editor: Charlie Loram
Typesetting: Henry Stedman
Layout: Bryn Thomas, Henry Stedman and Anna Jacomb-Hood
Illustrations: © Nick Hill (pp58-61); Rev CA Johns (p62)
Photographs: ppC1-3: centre photo C2 © Henry Stedman, all others © Bryn Thomas
Photographs opposite p49 (top) and opposite p65 (bottom right) © Bryn Thomas
All other photographs: © Jim Manthorpe 2004
Cartography: Nick Hill
Index: Jane Thomas

The maps in this guide were prepared from out-of-Crown-
copyright Ordnance Survey maps amended and updated by Trailblazer.

Warning: coastal walking can be dangerous
Please read the notes on when to go (p18) and health and safety (pp46-8).
Every effort has been made by the author and publisher to ensure that the information
contained herein is as accurate and up to date as possible. However, they are unable
to accept responsibility for any inconvenience, loss or injury sustained by anyone
as a result of the advice and information given in this guide.

Printed on chlorine-free paper by
D²Print, Singapore

PEMBROKESHIRE COAST PATH

AMROTH TO CARDIGAN
planning, places to stay, places to eat,
includes 96 large-scale walking maps

JIM MANTHORPE

TRAILBLAZER PUBLICATIONS

Para Nuria
Gracias por todo

Acknowledgements

This book would not have been possible without the patience and support of Charlie Loram and Bryn Thomas. Thanks to them for helpful guidance, assistance and for imparting their invaluable knowledge and expertise. Also at Trailblazer, thanks to Henry Stedman for all his hard work editing the text, Nick Hill for the maps and bird illustrations and Jane Thomas for the index.

Special thanks must also go to Amy and Ian McLaughlin. Suffice to say that without them I would never have put pen to paper or digit to keyboard.

I am also indebted to the support of Tommy McManmon and Richard Deighton, the former for accompanying me on the final few miles and claiming all the glory at the finish and the latter for his Yorkshire wit. Thanks also to María José Salmeron who, despite the blisters, managed to hobble her way as far as Trefin yet still kept a smile on her face.

Special thanks are due to my Mum and Dad who have always supported me despite some of my hare-brained ideas and ventures and also to my brothers, Sam and Jack, for their encouragement and help. I'm very grateful to Lucy Spratling and Tim Dwelly for their kind friendship through the years and for helping me with liquid refreshments.

Finally a big hello to all the people I met in Pembrokeshire especially the friendly folk in the Castle Hotel, Newport.

A request

The author and publisher have tried to ensure that this guide is as accurate and up to date as possible. However, things change even on these well-worn routes. If you notice any changes or omissions that should be included in the next edition of this guide, please email or write to Trailblazer (address on p2). You can also contact us via the Trailblazer website at 🖳www.trailblazer-guides.com). Those persons making a significant contribution will be rewarded with a free copy of the next edition and an acknowledgement in the front of that edition.

Updated information will shortly be available on:
🖳 **www.trailblazer-guides.com**

Front cover: Newgale Sands
© Jim Manthorpe 2004

CONTENTS

PART 4: ROUTE GUIDE AND MAPS

Using this guide

Pembrokeshire Coast Path

INDEX

INTRODUCTION

I must go down to the sea again, for the call of the running tide,
Is a wild call and a clear call that may not be denied;
... And all I ask is a windy day with the white clouds flying,
And the flung spray and the blown spume, and the seagulls crying.

I must go down to the sea again, to the vagrant gypsy life,
To the gull's way and the whale's way where the wind's like a whetted knife;
... And all I ask is a merry yarn from a laughing fellow-rover,
And quiet sleep and a sweet dream when the long trick's over.
Sea Fever (selected lines, post-1902 version) – **John Masefield** (1878–1967)

The Pembrokeshire coast is not generally well known yet in its obscurity it is outstanding. More and more people, however, are discovering this magnificent coastline on the extreme western point of Wales. What better way to explore it than to pull on your boots and walk the cliff tops and beaches of this superb 186-mile (299km) route.

The Pembrokeshire Coast Path begins in the seaside village of Amroth and takes you across the contorted sandstone cliffs of south Pembrokeshire past the colourful houses set above Tenby harbour and on to the dramatic limestone cliffs at Stackpole. Around every corner the cliffs surprise you with blowholes, sea caves and spectacular natural arches such as the famous Green Bridge of Wales.

Then it's on across the immaculate sands of Freshwater West and through the patchwork fields around the lazy waters of the Daugleddau estuary to the town of Pembroke with its Norman castle and ancient town walls. North of the estuary everything changes. The scenery is wilder and the walking tougher. The path leaves the Norman south and enters true Welsh country crossing spectacular beaches at Broad Haven and Newgale to reach the beautiful village of Solva, its busy little harbour tucked in a fold in the cliffs.

Next is St David's, the smallest city in Britain, where you can hear the bells of the cathedral echoing across the wooded valley while paying homage to the patron saint of Wales. Leading towards the most westerly point at St David's Head the path takes you past Ramsey Island, a haven for dolphins and seals, and up the rugged heathery coastline to the curious little fishing village of Porthgain. At Fishguard you can learn about the Last Invasion of Britain, or catch a ferry over to Ireland.

The final stretch takes you beneath the shadow of the Preseli Hills, bluestone country, the source of some of the raw material for Stonehenge. Continuing over the highest, most spectacular cliffs in West Wales brings you to the end of the path at St Dogmaels near Cardigan. The Pembrokeshire coast has everything – from endless, sandy beaches and rugged cliffs festooned with wild flowers to lonely hills and sleepy waterways; a beautiful blend of sand, sea and scents.

About this book

This guidebook contains all the information you need. The hard work has been done for you so you can plan your trip from home without the usual pile of books, maps, guides and tourist brochures. It includes:

● All standards of accommodation from campsites to luxurious guesthouses
● Walking companies if you want an organized tour
● A number of suggested itineraries for all types of walkers
● Answers to all your questions: when to go, degree of difficulty, what to pack and how much will the whole walking holiday cost me?

When you're all packed and ready to go, there's detailed information to get you to and from the coast path and 96 detailed maps (1:20,000) and town plans to help you find your way along it. The route guide section includes:

● Walking times in both directions
● Reviews of campsites, bunkhouses, hostels, B&Bs and guesthouses
● Cafés, pubs, tea shops, takeaways, restaurants and shops for buying supplies
● Rail, bus and taxi information for all the villages and towns along the coast path
● Street maps of the main towns: Saundersfoot, Tenby, Pembroke, Pembroke Dock, Milford Haven, St David's, Fishguard, Newport and Cardigan
● Historical, cultural and geographical background information

Minimum impact for maximum insight

Everybody needs a break; climb a mountain or jump in a lake. **Christy Moore**

Why is walking in wild and solitary places so satisfying? Partly it is the sheer physical pleasure: sometimes pitting one's strength against the elements, sometimes relaxing on the springy turf or sand. The beauty and wonder of the natural world restore our sense of proportion, freeing us from the stresses and strains of everyday life.

All this the countryside gives us and the least we can do is to safeguard it by supporting rural economies, local businesses and environmentally-sensitive forms of transport, and low-impact methods of farming and land use. In this book there is a detailed and illustrated chapter on the wildlife and conservation of Pembrokeshire and a chapter on minimum impact walking with ideas on how to tread lightly in this fragile environment. By following these principles we can help to preserve our natural heritage for future generations.

About the Pembrokeshire Coast Path

HISTORY

It was in 1952 that the Pembrokeshire coast received national park status. At the same time naturalist Ronald Lockley proposed a long-distance footpath that would provide an uninterrupted walking route through the length of the national park. But it was not until 1970 that the coast path was finally opened.

A number of problems arose when choosing the best route for the path, particularly around the, quite frankly, ugly industrial stretches among the power stations and oil refineries on either side of the Milford Haven estuary. It is hard to avoid these eyesores, but the path designers have done a good job in choosing a route that keeps the chimneys and towers out of sight for as long as possible. In many places trees and shrubs have been planted alongside the perimeter fences to act as a screen. At times it is only by looking at the map or sensing the acrid smell that you realize you are walking right next to a major refinery.

Nevertheless many walkers quite justifiably choose to leave out this uninspiring section between Angle and Milford Haven. For the rest of its length the path hugs the coastline where possible but inland diversions are inevitable to avoid private land, geographical obstacles and the artillery range at Castlemartin.

The official length of the path has changed over the years. It presently stands at 186 miles (299km) but the distance that any one person walks really depends on how many detours or shortcuts they choose to take.

HOW DIFFICULT IS THE PEMBROKESHIRE COAST PATH?

This is not a technically difficult walk and most reasonably fit people should be able to tackle it without any problems. However, the distance should not be underestimated; although it is not a mountainous path there are many steep up-and-down sections. On completion you will have ascended more than the height of Everest.

The southern section is tamer than the northern stretch with its mighty cliffs where the sense of exposure is more marked and the distances between villages are greater. Always be aware of the ever-present danger of the cliff edge. Accidents often happen late in the day when fatigue sets in and people lose their footing. Be aware of your capabilities and limitations and plan each day accordingly. Don't try to do too much in one day: taking it slowly allows you to relax, see a lot more and you'll enjoy the walk without becoming exhausted or fed up.

Waymarker

Route finding

This should not be a problem since the path is well trodden and obvious. The entire length is waymarked with 'finger-posts' marked with an acorn symbol. For the most part the path hugs the coastline, although detours are sometimes necessary due to erosion of the cliff. Every year at least one large cliff section gives way but the park authorities are usually very quick to realign the path.

Check the tide times (see p47) to avoid lengthy detours around bays and estuaries. You will need to carefully plan crossing the river mouths at Sandy Haven and The Gann, just to the north of Dale, as they are flooded at high tide. If you time it right you will be able to cross them both in the same day (see p121 for further details). One other area for confusion is the Castlemartin MoD range. When firing is taking place a detour must be taken along the road (see p94).

HOW LONG DO YOU NEED?

This depends on your fitness and experience. Do not try to do too much in one day if you are new to long-distance walking. Most people find that two weeks is enough to complete the walk and still have time to look around the villages and enjoy the views along the way. Alternatively the entire path can be done in eleven days or less if you are fit enough.

If you're camping don't underestimate how much a heavy pack laden with camping gear will slow you down. It is also worth bearing in mind that those who take it easy on the path tend to see a lot more than those who sweat out long days and only ever see the path in front of them. When deciding how long you need remember to allow a few extra days for side trips or simply to rest. On pp25-7 there are some suggested itineraries covering different walking speeds.

If you have only a few days available concentrate on the best parts of the coast path; there is a list of recommended day and weekend walks on pp20-1.

Practical information for the walker

ACCOMMODATION

Most of the coast path is well served with accommodation for all budgets from campsites to luxurious hotels. The route guide (Part 4) lists a selection of places to stay along the full length of the trail. It's advisable to book all accommodation in advance, particularly during the high season (Easter to August). The most barren area for accommodation is from Manorbier to Pembroke where pre-planning is even more crucial. Remember that the advantages of walking at less busy times are countered by the fact that many places are closed during the winter months.

Camping

Wild camping is not strictly allowed in the national park but a kind landowner may let you camp in a field (see p42). There are a number of official campsites with basic facilities such as toilets and the all-important showers with prices ranging from £2–£7 per person making this the cheapest accommodation option.

In the summer there are usually plenty of places to camp along the length of the coast path, but if you are planning short days you may have to find alternative accommodation on two or three nights. This is particularly true around Bosherston and the Dale peninsula where you can stay in bed and breakfasts instead (see box p27). Those hardy souls who plan to walk in winter (November to Easter) will find many of the campsites closed, although there are a few that remain open all year; check the details in Part 4.

Camping is like being a snail; carrying your home on your back, and travelling at a similar speed. However, there is great satisfaction to be had from spending not just the day but the night in the great outdoors, watching the stars and witnessing the sunset and sunrise. Those who shy away from tented travel because of its perceived disadvantages really miss out on an enlightening experience.

Hostels and bunkhouses

Hostels are cheap (£8–£12) and allow you to travel on a budget without having to carry cumbersome camping equipment. They are also good places to meet fellow walkers and in many cases are just as comfortable as B&Bs. However, there is a problem. With the exception of Manorbier Youth Hostel there aren't any other hostels or bunkhouses for the first 70 miles or so between Amroth and Marloes Sands. Depending on your speed, you will need to use B&Bs for the first 3-7 nights and again in St David's if you plan to stop there (see box p26).

On the positive side, there are eight youth hostels conveniently spaced a day apart from Marloes Sands to the end of the coast path at St Dogmaels. All the youth hostels on the coast path provide bedding so there is no need to carry a sleeping bag. Additionally they all have self-catering kitchens, while some of the more upmarket ones will actually cook you a hot dinner for a small fee. A few also have a small shop for emergency groceries.

Youth hostels (YHAs) are, despite their name, for anyone of any age as long as you are a member. You can join the **Youth Hostels Association of England and Wales** (☎ 0870-870 8808, 🖳 www.yha.org.uk) at any of the hostels, or over the phone, for £15 per year. They vary greatly in style. The one at Whitesands Bay is an old farmhouse while the one at Manorbier is a converted NATO warehouse. Most youth hostels will only save your booked bed until 6pm which puts you in an uncomfortable rush if you have a lot of walking to do. It's worth phoning ahead to let them know if you're going to arrive later.

In addition to the youth hostels there are also two **independent hostels** on the route, one near Trefin and one at Fishguard. These are privately owned so you do not need to be a member of any association and they also have the welcome advantage of having few rules and no curfew, unlike youth hostels. Otherwise they are similar to YHAs with accommodation in small dormitories with bed linen provided and fully equipped self-catering kitchens.

Finally you could try one of the **bunkhouses** on the coast path (at Cyffredin (near Abereiddy) and Newport) which provide more basic accommodation. They are full of character and eccentricity and are well worth visiting, if only for one night. The drawback is that you need your own sleeping bag to stay there. By using youth hostels and the independent hostels on the northern half of the walk and bed and breakfasts on the southern half you can cut out the need to pack a sleeping bag altogether, thus significantly lightening your load.

If you are planning to walk in **winter** you should bear in mind the following hostels/bunkhouses are closed between November and Easter: Manorbier Youth Hostel, Lydstep; Marloes Sands Youth Hostel; Broad Haven Youth Hostel; St David's Youth Hostel, Whitesands Bay; Pwll-caerog Bunk Barn, Cyffredin (Abereiddy); Trefin Youth Hostel; Pwll Deri Youth Hostel; Trefdraeth Youth Hostel, Newport and Poppit Sands Youth Hostel near St Dogmaels.

Bed and breakfast
Anyone who has not stayed in a bed and breakfast (B&B) has missed out on something very British. They vary greatly in quality, style and price but usually consist of a bed in someone's house and a big cooked British breakfast in the morning. For visitors from outside Britain it can provide an interesting insight into the Welsh way of life as you often feel like a guest of the family.

What to expect All the coastal walker wants is a warm bed and a hot bath. For this reason most B&Bs listed in this guide are recommended because of their usefulness to the walker and their proximity to the path.

Many bed and breakfasts offer en-suite rooms or at least have the choice. However, for a few pounds less you can usually get a standard room and it's never far to the bathroom. Anyone walking alone may find it hard to find establishments with **single** rooms. **Twin** rooms and **double** rooms are often confused but a twin room usually comprises two single beds while a double room has one double bed. **Family** rooms are for three or more people.

All B&Bs provide a hefty cooked breakfast as part of the room price. Some will also cook an evening meal but you will need to give them advance warning. Most, however, are close enough to a pub or restaurant and if they are not, the owner may sometimes give you a lift to and from the nearest eating place.

Prices B&Bs in this guide vary in price from £12 per person for the most basic accommodation to over £30 for the most luxurious en-suite places. Most charge around £20 per person. Remember that many places do not have single rooms and will usually charge a supplement of between £5 and £10 for a single person in a double or twin room. Prices can be substantially lower during the winter months and if you are on a budget you could always ask to go without breakfast which will usually result in a lower price.

Booking You should always book your accommodation. In summer there can be stiff competition for beds and in winter there's the distinct possibility that the place could be closed. Always let the owner know if you have to cancel your booking so they can offer the bed to someone else.

Guesthouses, hotels, pubs and inns

Guesthouses and hotels are usually more sophisticated than bed and breakfasts offering evening meals and a lounge for guests. Pubs and inns offer bed and breakfast of a medium to high standard and have the added advantage of having a bar downstairs, so it's not far to stagger back to bed. However, the noise from tipsy punters might prove a nuisance if you want an early night. Prices usually range from £20 to £30 per person per night.

Hotels are usually aimed more for the motoring tourist rather than the muddy walker and the price (£30 to £50 per person) is likely to put off the budget traveller. A few hotels have been included in the trail guide for those feeling they deserve at least one night of luxury during their trip.

Holiday cottages

Self-catering cottages are ideal for small groups who want to base themselves in the same place for a week or more. This can be a good way to walk parts of the coast path using public transport to travel to and from each day's stage. A good base for a week's walking in south Pembrokeshire would be in the seaside town of Tenby which has good public transport links. If you prefer something quieter you could try Freshwater East which has lots of holiday cottages.

St David's, or somewhere close to Fishguard, would be a convenient place to base yourself for walks in north Pembrokeshire. Try the tiny holiday village of Cwm-yr-eglwys which has a good bathing beach. One particularly good place to stay is Brynawel Country House (see p175) near Goodwick. They specifically cater for walkers planning multi-day trips, picking you up and dropping you off each day anywhere between St David's and Cardigan.

Prices for holiday cottages usually start at £100 for the week based on four to six people sharing. Cottages haven't been listed in this book; contact the tourist information centre in the area you want to stay for details (see p33).

FOOD AND DRINK

Drinking water

Depending on the weather you will need to drink as much as two to four litres of water a day. If you're feeling lethargic it may well be that you haven't drunk enough, even if you're not feeling particularly thirsty.

Drinking directly from streams and rivers is tempting, but is not a good idea. Streams that cross the path tend to have flowed across farmland where you can be pretty sure any number of farm animals have relieved themselves. Combined with the probable presence of farm pesticides and other delights it is best to avoid drinking from these streams. Drinking-water fountains are marked in the trail guide. Where these are thin on the ground you can usually ask a friendly shopkeeper or pub barman to fill your bottle for you, from the tap of course.

Buying camping supplies

If you are camping, fuel for your stove, outdoor equipment and food supplies are important considerations. The best places for outdoor gear are the TYF outdoor adventure shops in Tenby and St David's. In the summer many of the campsites have shops that sell fuel as do most of the general stores along the route but remember that in the winter months many of the smaller ones open for a shorter time or not at all. Check the services details in Part 4 for more detailed information. Particularly barren areas for supplies of any kind are from Tenby to Pembroke and St David's to Fishguard.

Breakfast and lunch

If staying in a B&B or hotel you can be sure to enjoy a full Welsh cooked breakfast which may be more than you are used to. Ask for a lighter continental breakfast if you'd prefer. Many B&Bs and youth hostels can also provide you with a packed lunch at an additional cost.

Alternatively breakfast and packed lunches can be bought and made yourself. There are some great cafés and bakers along the way which can supply both

---

❑ **Local food and drink**

Many of the pubs promote **real ales**. There are plenty of the well-known brands from across the border but for a Welsh ale try Brains SA, Buckley's, Cousin Jack or Reverend James.

As for food, it would be easy to walk the entire coast path surviving on a diet of fish and chips and junk food and, like the rest of Britain, West Wales seems to have claimed Indian food as its own. All of the towns have at least one curry house, many of them of very high quality. Even the old traditional pubs have got in on the act with chicken tikka masala ever present on the menu.

But Welsh cuisine should not be overlooked, as it so often is. The coast path gives you the perfect opportunity to try it for yourself. Unsurprisingly seafood is a speciality in these parts with many restaurants and pubs serving local **cockles** and **mussels**, **sea trout** and **pints of prawns**. If this is not your thing there is always the famous **Welsh lamb**. Here are some other Welsh delicacies:

● **Laver bread** Has been described as Welsh caviar but equally as a seaweed pancake. Take your pick. It is certainly seaweed based and is mixed with oatmeal and fried in fat. Even supermarkets stock it now.

● **Bara brith** A rich fruity bread made by soaking fruit in tea and then adding marmalade, spices and other ingredients.

● **Welsh cakes** Tasty cakes full of currants and sultanas. You can find them in supermarkets and in most tea shops and cafés.

● **Welsh rarebit** Melted cheese with a hint of mustard poured over buttered toast.

● **Leek and parsley broth** (*Cawl cennin a phersli*) A soup full of vegetables with beef and lamb.

● **Tregaron granny's broth** (*Cawl mamgu Tregaron*) Another soup full of vegetables with beef and bacon.

● **Stuffed leek with cheese and mustard sauce** Leeks stuffed with sausagemeat.

● **Miner's delight** (*Gorfoledd y glowyr*) A rabbit casserole dish.

● **Preseli cheese** Goat's cheese, two soft cow cheeses and smoked cheese are all made at Pant Mawr Farm (☎ 01437-532627, 🖳 pantmawr_jennings@hotmail.com), Rosebush, in the Preseli Hills. All the cheeses carry the Pembrokeshire Produce seal of approval and are made from pasteurized milk with vegetarian rennets.

eat-in or takeaway. Remember that stretches of the walk are devoid of anywhere to eat so check the information in Part 4 to make sure you don't go hungry.

Pubs

The Pembrokeshire coast is blessed with some outstanding pubs and inns. There is nothing quite like the lure of a pint to get you through those last few miles of the day. Most pubs offer lunch and evening meals and usually have some vegetarian options. The standard varies from basic pub grub from the bar menu to à la carte restaurant food. Most walkers will be happy with whatever is put in front of them after working up an appetite.

Other places to eat out

There are some quality restaurants in most of the towns with menus varying from French and Italian to the ubiquitous seafood. In addition most towns and some of the larger villages are riddled with cheap takeaway joints offering kebabs, pizzas, Chinese and fish 'n chips. They can come in handy if you finish your walk late in the day since they usually stay open until at least 11pm.

MONEY

On some sections of the coast path there is a distinct lack of banks. There are no banks along the 53-mile (85km) stretch between Tenby and Pembroke, for example, and there is only one between Milford Haven and St David's, a distance of 47 miles (76km). It is a good idea to carry plenty of cash with you, maybe keeping it in a money belt for security. Small independent shops rarely accept payment by card and will require you to pay in cash or by cheque, as will most B&Bs, bunkhouses and campsites. Shops that do take cards, such as supermarkets, will sometimes advance cash against a card as long as you buy something at the same time. **Travellers' cheques** can only be cashed at banks, foreign exchange offices and some large hotels.

Using the post office for banking Several banks in Britain now have agreements with the Post Office allowing customers to make cash withdrawals using a debit card or chequebook and card at post offices throughout the country. As there are plenty of post offices along the coast path this is a useful facility for the walker.

OTHER SERVICES

Most villages and all the towns have at least one public **telephone**, a small **shop** and a **post office**. Post offices can be used for receiving mail if you know where you are going to be from day to day or for sending unnecessary equipment home which may be weighing you down. In Part 4 special mention is given to other services that may be of use to the walker such as **banks**, **cash machines** (cashpoints), **outdoor equipment shops**, **laundrettes**, **internet access**, **pharmacies** and **tourist information centres** which can be used for finding and booking accommodation among other things.

WALKING COMPANIES

For walkers wanting to make their holiday as easy and trouble free as possible there are several specialist companies offering a range of services from accommodation booking to fully-guided group tours.

Baggage carriers

● **Pembrokeshire Discovery – Baggage and People Transfer** (☎ 01437-710720, ☐ www.pembrokeshirediscovery.co.uk) Specifically aimed at coast path walkers who need a hand carrying their rucksacks or a lift back to base.

Some of the **taxi** firms listed in this guide (see Part 4) can provide a similar service within a local area. See also Self-guided holidays below.

Self-guided holidays

The following companies provide all-in customized packages for walkers which usually include detailed advice and notes on itineraries and routes, maps, accommodation booking, daily baggage transfer and transport arrangements at the start and end of your walk. If you don't want the whole all-in package some of the companies will gladly arrange the **accommodation booking** or **baggage carrying** services on their own.

● **Celtic Trails** (☎ 0800-970 7585 or 01600-860846, ☐ www.walking-wales.com) PO Box 11, Chepstow, NP16 6DZ.
● **Contours Walking Holidays** (☎ 01768-867539, ☐ www.contours.co.uk) Smithy House, Stainton, Cumbria, CA11 0ES.
● **Explore Britain** (☎ 01740-650900, ☐ www.xplorebritain.com) 6 George St, Ferryhill, Co Durham, DL17 0DT.
● **Greenways – Pembrokeshire Walking Breaks** (☎ 01834-860965, ☐ www.southpembrokeshire-holidays.co.uk) Freepost, SWC 1331, The Old School, Station Rd, Narberth, SA67 7DU.
● **Pembrokeshire Walking Holidays** (☎ 01437-760075, ☐ www.pembrokeshire-walking-holidays.co.uk) c/o Tourist Information Centre, 19 Old Bridge, Haverfordwest, SA61 2EZ.
● **Sherpa Expeditions** (☎ 020-8577 2717, ☐ www.sherpa-walking-holidays.co.uk) 131a Heston Rd, Hounslow, Middlesex, TW5 0RF.

Group/guided walking tours

Fully guided tours are ideal for individuals wanting to travel in the company of others and for groups of friends wanting to be guided. The packages usually include meals, accommodation, transport arrangements, minibus back-up, baggage transfer, as well as a qualified guide. Companies' specialities differ widely with varying size of groups, standards of accommodation, age range of clients, distances walked and professionalism of guides.

● **Avalon Trekking** (☎ 01889-575646, 0777-596 7644, ☐ www.avalontrekking.co.uk) 40 Waverley Gardens, Etching Hill, Rugeley, Staffordshire, WS15 2YE.
● **Pembrokeshire Walking Holidays** (see above).

Budgeting

The amount of money you take with you depends on your accommodation plans and how you're going to eat. If you camp and cook your own meals your expenses can stay very low but most people prefer to have at least some of their meals cooked for them and even the hardy camper may be tempted into the occasional B&B when the rain is falling.

CAMPING

You can survive on as little as £8 per person if you use the cheapest sites and cook all your own food from staple ingredients. Nevertheless, most people find that the best laid plans to survive on the bare minimum soon fall flat after a couple of hard days' walking. Always budget for unforeseen expenses as well as for the end-of-day pint of beer which costs around £2. Assuming such liquid treats and the occasional takeaway or pub meal a budget of £10–£15 per day is more realistic.

❏ **Information for foreign visitors**

● **Currency** The British pound (£) comes in notes of £100, £50, £20, £10, £5 and coins of £2 and £1. The pound is divided into 100 pence (usually referred to as 'p', pronounced 'pee') which comes in silver coins of 50p, 20p, 10p and 5p and copper coins of 2p and 1p.

● **Rates of exchange** Up-to-date rates of exchange can be found at 🖳 www. xe.com/ucc.

● **Business hours** Most **shops** and main **post offices** are open at least from Monday to Friday 9am–5pm and Saturday 9am–12.30pm. Many choose longer hours and some open on Sundays as well. **Banks** are usually open 10am–4pm Monday to Friday. **Pubs** are usually open 11am–11pm although some close for the afternoon.

● **National holidays** Most businesses in Wales are shut on 1 January, Good Friday (March/April), Easter Monday (March/April), first and last Monday in May, last Monday in August, 25 December and 26 December.

● **Weights and measures** Britain is attempting to move towards the metric system but there is much resistance. Most food is now sold in metric weights (g and kg) but most people still think in the imperial weights of pounds (lb) and ounces (oz). Milk is sold in pints as is beer in pubs, yet most other liquid is sold in litres. Road signs and distances are always given in miles rather than kilometres and the population remains split between those who are happy with centimetres and metres and those who still use inches, feet and yards.

● **Telephone** The country code for Britain is ☎ 44, followed by the area code minus the first 0, and then the number you require. To make a local call you can omit the area code. It is cheaper to ring at weekends and after 6pm and before 8am on weekdays.

● **Emergency services** For police, ambulance, fire brigade and coastguard dial ☎ 999.

BUNKHOUSES AND HOSTELS

Hostels charge between £8 and £12 per person per night and most places have a self-catering kitchen allowing you to survive on cheap food from the supermarket or local shop. Now and then, however, you will need to eat out which adds to your daily costs. Around £20 per day should be enough to cover the cost of accommodation while still allowing for the occasional bar meal and end of day tipple. If you are planning on eating out most nights you should clearly increase your budget to around £25 per day.

B&BS

B&B prices can be as little as £12 per night but are usually almost twice this. Add on the price of a pub meal, beer and other expenses and you can expect to need around £30–£50 per day.

EXTRAS

Don't forget all those little things that secretly push up your daily bill: postcards, stamps, beer, camera film, buses here, buses there, more beer and getting back to Amroth; it all adds up!

When to go

SEASONS

Pembrokeshire is subjected to the full force of the weather sweeping in from the Atlantic so you can expect rain and strong winds at any time of year. Equally you can be blessed with blazing sunshine; the climate is unpredictable. The **main walking season** in Pembrokeshire is from Easter to the end of September.

Spring

Walking in Pembrokeshire from March to June has many rewards, the greatest of which is the chance to appreciate the spectacular wild flowers which come into bloom at this time. Spring is also the time of year when you are most likely to have dry weather. Easter can be a busy time since it is the first major holiday of the year but at other times the path is relatively quiet.

Summer

Unsurprisingly, summer is when every man and his dog descend on the countryside with July and August, when the heather colours the hillsides purple, being the busiest months. At this time many of the beaches are packed and the coast path too. This isn't always a bad thing. Part of the enjoyment of walking is meeting like-minded people and there are plenty of them about. However, accommodation can be hard to come by, so do book well in advance.

Summer weather in west Wales is notoriously unpredictable. One day you can be sweating in the midday sun, the next day battling against the wind and rain. Remember to take clothes for any eventuality.

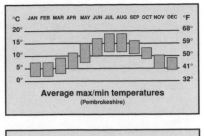

Average max/min temperatures
(Pembrokeshire)

Autumn

Come September the tourists return home. Autumn can be wild with the first storms of winter arriving towards the end of September. Don't let this put you off. Although the likelihood of rain and wind increases as winter approaches, sunny days are still possible and the changing colours of the hillsides make the coastline spectacular.

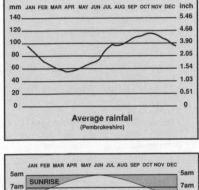

Average rainfall
(Pembrokeshire)

Winter

There are a number of disadvantages of walking the coast path in winter; winter storms are common, daylight hours are short and many of the places to stay are closed until spring. Experienced walkers who are not afraid of getting wet may appreciate the peace and quiet and may be rewarded with one of those beautifully crisp, clear winter days.

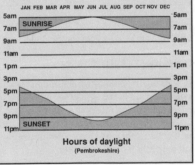

Hours of daylight
(Pembrokeshire)

TEMPERATURE

The Welsh climate is temperate and even in winter the air temperature is relatively mild thanks to the warm Gulf Stream sea current. Consequently the temperature is usually quite comfortable at any time of year although on rare occasions in summer it can get a little too hot for walking.

RAINFALL

Pembrokeshire bears the brunt of the violent weather systems that sweep in from the North Atlantic. As a result, the rainfall is usually higher here than in the more sheltered areas further east. The total annual rainfall for west Wales

❏ **Highlights – the best day and weekend walks**
If you don't have the time to walk the whole trail the following day and weekend walks highlight the best of the coast path and all are well served by public transport (see p37). For the more experienced walker many of the weekend walks suggested here can be completed in a day.

Day walks
● **Amroth to Tenby** 7 miles/11km (see pp71-7). An easy day passing through beautiful coastal woodland culminating in one of the prettiest seaside towns in Wales.
● **Freshwater East to Bosherston** 6.5 miles/10km (see pp86-95). A short day, passing from a twisting sandstone coastline to spectacular limestone cliffs ending at the banks of the wooded lily ponds at Bosherston.
● **Freshwater West to Angle** 8 miles/13km (see pp96-101). Starting at a wonderful beach this is one of the quietest stretches of the coast path.
● **Dale to Marloes Sands (Marloes)** 8 miles/13km (see pp127-33). Varied scenery around the Dale peninsula, beginning with gentle wooded slopes leading to wild scenery around the vast sands of Marloes.
● **Musselwick Sands (Marloes) to Little Haven** 8 miles/13km (see pp134-7). An easy start to this walk but a strenuous finale over high wooded cliffs with spectacular views over St Bride's Bay.
● **Nolton Haven to Solva** 8.5 miles/14km (see pp142-7). A short day, taking in the fantastic Newgale Sands, passing through spectacular coastal scenery and finishing at the prettiest village on the coast.   (*continued opposite*)

is 1000mm with most of it falling from late summer through into the winter with spring being the driest period.

DAYLIGHT HOURS

If walking in autumn, winter and early spring, you must take account of how far you can walk in the available light. The sunrise and sunset times in the table on p19 are based on information for Milford Haven on the first of each month. This gives a rough picture for the rest of Pembrokeshire. Also bear in mind that you will get a further 30-45 minutes of usable light before and after sunrise and sunset depending on the weather.

ANNUAL EVENTS

The free national park newspaper *Coast to Coast* has a comprehensive 'What's On' page updated annually. Check with tourist information centres for details and times. Here is a taster of what can be found to distract you along the way.
● **Fishguard Folk Festival** Fiddles and bodhrans fill the town in the last weekend of May. Concerts and workshops. The main venue is The Royal Oak Inn in Market Square (☎ 01348-872514).
● **Fishguard International Music Festival** Lots of strings and brass in the last week of July. A number of orchestras perform during the week (☎ 01348-873612, 🖳 www.fimf.supanet.com).

❏ **Highlights – the best day and weekend walks (cont'd)**
● **Caerfai Bay to St Justinian's (St David's)** 6.5 miles/10km (see pp153-7). Wild scenery and wildlife on this short stretch with views of Ramsey Island, starting and finishing in the tiny cathedral city of St David's.
● **St Justinian's (St David's) to Abereiddy** 9.5 miles/15km (see pp157-61). A beautiful stretch around the wild St David's peninsula passing Whitesands Bay and St David's Head.
● **Newport to Poppit Sands** 14 miles/23km (see pp185-94). The toughest and most spectacular stretch of the coast path with the highest cliffs.

Weekend walks
● **Amroth to Freshwater East** 21.5 miles/35km (see pp77-84). Easy walking passing through woodland with tiny hidden beaches and pretty villages in the coves.
● **Freshwater East to Angle** 27 miles/43km (see pp84-100). A long stretch which takes in the spectacular limestone scenery around St Govan's and Castlemartin and the wonderful beach at Freshwater West.
● **Dale to Broad Haven** 20.5 miles/33km (see pp127-37). Fantastic beaches and cliffs with the potential to include a trip over to Skomer Island to see the puffins.
● **Newgale to Trefin** 29 miles/47km (see pp142-63). Wild and rugged scenery around the St David's peninsula with a useful halfway point at the tiny cathedral city of St David's.
● **Trefin to Fishguard** 20 miles/32km (see pp163-76). Pwll Deri and its jaw-dropping cliff scenery make a good halfway point on this beautiful stretch that takes in the rugged coast around Strumble Head.

● **St David's Cathedral Festival** Nine days of music in the wonderful St David's Cathedral, beginning the last weekend of May. Widely considered to be one of the best music festivals in Wales (☎ 01437-720271, 🖳 www.stdavid scathedral.org.uk/festivals).
● **Tenby Arts Festival** Exhibitions in various venues around town in the last week of September. Dance workshops, kite-flying competitions, music and drama (☎ 01834-842404, 🖳 www.tenbyartsfest.com).

Itineraries

This guidebook has not been divided up into rigid daily stages. Instead, it's structured to make it easy for you to plan your own itinerary. The Pembrokeshire Coast Path can be tackled in any number of ways, the most challenging of which is to do it all in one go. This does require around two weeks, time which some people just don't have. Most people walk it over a series of short breaks coming back year after year to do a bit more. Others just walk the best bits, avoiding the ugly industrial stretches around the Milford Haven estuary and others use the path for linear day-walks using public transport there and back.

VILLAGE AND

Place name Places in (brackets) are a short walk off the coast path	Distance from previous place approx miles/km	Cash Machine	Post Office	Tourist Information Centre (or Point)
(Kilgetty)		✓	✓	✓
Amroth	3/5		✓	
Wiseman's Bridge	2/3			
Saundersfoot	1/1.5	✓	✓	✓
Tenby	4/6.5	✓	✓	✓
Penally	2.5/4		✓	
Lydstep	4/6.5			
Manorbier	4/6.5			
Freshwater East	4/6.5			
Bosherston	6.5/10.5			
Castlemartin	10/16		✓	
Angle	10.5/17		✓	
Hundleton	9/14.5			
Pembroke	2.5/4	✓	✓	✓
Pembroke Dock	3/5	✓	✓	✓
Neyland & Hazelbeach	4/6.5		✓	
Milford Haven	5.5/9	✓	✓	✓
Sandy Haven (& Herbrandston)	4/6.5		✓	
Lindsway Bay (for St Ishmael's)	2.5/4		✓	
Dale	3/5		✓	
Marloes Sands (& Marloes)	8/13		✓	
Little Haven	12/19.5		✓	
Broad Haven	0.5/1	✓	✓	
Nolton Haven	3.5/5.5			
Newgale	3.5/5.5			
Solva	5/8		✓	
Caerfai Bay	4/6.5			
(St David's)	(1)/(1/5)	✓	✓	✓
Whitesands Bay	8.5/13.5			
Abereiddy	7.5/12			
Porthgain	2/3			
Trefin	2/3		✓	
Pwll Deri & Strumble Head	9.5/15.5			
Goodwick & Fishguard	10.5/17	✓	✓	✓
Pwllgwaelod (& Dinas Cross)	4.5/7		✓	
Newport	7/11	✓	✓	✓
Ceibwr Bay (for Moylgrove)	9/14.5			
Poppit Sands	5/8			
St Dogmaels	2/3		✓	
(Cardigan)	(1)/(1.5)	✓	✓	✓
TOTAL DISTANCE	186 miles (299km)			

TOWN FACILITIES

Eating Place	Food Store (F)= seasonal only	Campsite	Hostels*	B&Bs 1=one F=a few M=many	Place name Places in (brackets) are a short walk off the coast path
✓	F	✓		1	(Kilgetty)
✓	(F)			F	Amroth
✓				F	Wiseman's Bridge
✓	F	✓		M	Saundersfoot
✓	F	✓		M	Tenby
✓	F	✓		F	Penally
✓		✓	YHA		Lydstep
✓		✓		F	Manorbier
✓				F	Freshwater East
✓	(F)			F	Bosherston
✓		✓		F	Castlemartin
✓	F	✓		F	Angle
✓		✓		F	Hundleton
✓	F	✓		M	Pembroke
✓	F			M	Pembroke Dock
✓	F			F	Neyland & Hazelbeach
✓	F			M	Milford Haven
✓	F	✓		F	Sandy Haven (& Herbrandston)
✓				F	Lindsway Bay (for St Ishmael's)
✓	(F)			F	Dale
✓		✓	YHA	F	Marloes Sands (& Marloes)
✓	F	✓		F	Little Haven
✓	F		YHA	F	Broad Haven
✓				F	Nolton Haven
✓		✓	YHA	1	Newgale
✓	F	✓		M	Solva
✓	(F)	✓		1	Caerfai Bay
✓	F			M	(St David's)
✓		✓	YHA	F	Whitesands Bay
✓		✓	B	F	Abereiddy
✓				1	Porthgain
✓		✓	YHA & H	F	Trefin
		✓	YHA		Pwll Deri & Strumble Head
✓	F	✓	H	M	Goodwick & Fishguard
✓	F			F	Pwllgwaelod (& Dinas Cross)
✓	F	✓	YHA & B	M	Newport
				1	Ceibwr Bay (for Moylgrove)
	(F)	✓	YHA	F	Poppit Sands
✓	F			F	St Dogmaels
✓	F			M	(Cardigan)

Hostels* YHA = Youth Hostel, H = Independent Hostel, B = Bunkhouse

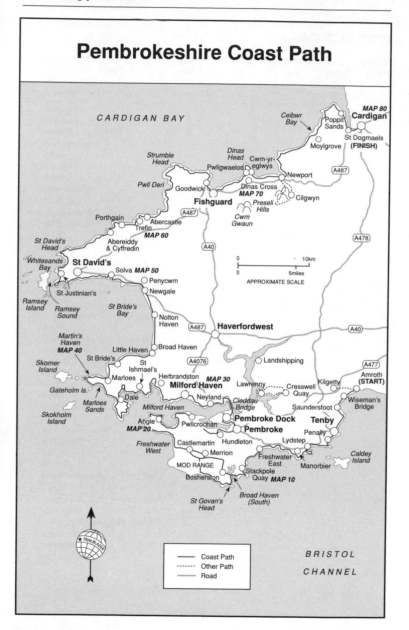

Pembrokeshire Coast Path

CARDIGAN BAY

Ceibwr Bay

MAP 80

Poppit Sands

Cardigan

St Dogmaels (FINISH)

Moylgrove

Dinas Head

Cwm-yr-eglwys

Strumble Head

Pwllgwaelod

Newport

A487

Dinas Cross

MAP 70

Goodwick

Cilgwyn

Pwll Deri

Preseli Hills

Fishguard

A487

Cwm Gwaun

Porthgain

Abercastle

Trefin

MAP 60

A478

St David's Head

Abereiddy & Cyffredin

St David's

A40

Whitesands Bay

Solva MAP 50

St Justinian's

Penycwm

10km

Newgale

5miles

APPROXIMATE SCALE

Ramsey Island

Ramsey Sound

St Bride's Bay

Nolton Haven

A487

Haverfordwest

A40

Martin's Haven

MAP 40

Little Haven

Broad Haven

A4076

Landshipping

A477

Skomer Island

St Bride's

St Ishmael's

Amroth (START)

Kilgetty

Marloes

Herbrandston

MAP 30

Lawrenny

Cresswell Quay

Gateholm Is.

Dale

Milford Haven

Neyland

Cleddau Bridge

Saundersfoot

Wiseman's Bridge

Marloes Sands

Milford Haven

Pembroke Dock

Tenby

Skokholm Island

Angle

MAP 20

Pwllcrochan

Pembroke

Penally

Freshwater West

Castlemartin

Hundleton

Lydstep

Caldey Island

Merrion

Freshwater East

Manorbier

MOD RANGE

Stackpole Quay MAP 10

Bosherston

St Govan's Head

Broad Haven (South)

★ TRAILBLAZER

Coast Path
Other Path
Road

BRISTOL CHANNEL

To help you plan your walk the **planning map** (opposite) and **table of village/town facilities** on pp22-3 gives a run down on the essential information you will need regarding accommodation possibilities and services. You could follow one of the suggested itineraries (below, and pp26-7) which are based on preferred type of accommodation and walking speeds. There is also a list of recommended linear day and weekend walks on pp20-1 which cover the best of the coast path, all of which are well served by public transport. The **public transport map** is on p37.

Once you have an idea of your approach turn to **Part 4** for detailed information on accommodation, places to eat and other services in each village and town on the route. Also in Part 4 you will find summaries of the route to accompany the detailed trail maps.

CAMPING

Night	Relaxed pace Place	Approx. Distance miles/km	Medium pace Place	Approx. Distance miles/km	Fast pace Place	Approx. Distance miles/km
0	Amroth		Amroth		Amroth	
1	Penally	9.5/15	Penally	9.5/15	Swanlake Bay (Nr Manorbier)	20/32
2	Swanlake Bay (Nr Manorbier)	10.5/17	Swanlake Bay (Nr Manorbier)	10.5/17	Castlemartin	18/29
3	Bosherston*	8/13	Castlemartin	18/29	Hundleton	19.5/31
4	Castlemartin	10/16	Angle	10.5/17	Sandy Haven	19/31
5	Angle	10.5/17	Pembroke	11.5/19	Martin's Haven (Nr Marloes Sands)	16/26
6	Pembroke	11.5/19	Sandy Haven	16.5/27	Newgale	17/27
7	Sandy Haven	16.5/27	Martin's Haven	16/26	Whitesands Bay (Nr Marloes Sands)	17.5/28
8	Dale*	5.5/9	Newgale	17/27	Strumble Head	23.5/38
9	Martin's Haven (Nr Marloes Sands)	10.5/17	Whitesands Bay	17.5/28	Newport	19.5/31
10	Little Haven	9.5/15	Trefin	11.5/18	Poppit Sands	14/23
11	Newgale	7.5/12	Strumble Head	12/19	St Dogmaels*	2/3
12	Caerfai Bay	9/14	Fishguard Bay (Nr Fishguard)	10/16		
13	Whitesands Bay	8.5/14	Newport	9.5/15		
14	Trefin	11.5/18	Poppit Sands	14/23		
15	Strumble Head	12/19	St Dogmaels*	2/3		
16	Fishguard Bay (Nr Fishguard)	10/16				
17	Newport	9.5/15				
18	Poppit Sands	14/23				
19	St Dogmaels*	2/3				

* There are no campsites at places marked with an asterisk but there is alternative accommodation available

STAYING IN BUNKHOUSES/HOSTELS

Relaxed pace		Medium pace		Fast pace	
Place	**Approx. Distance**	**Place**	**Approx. Distance**	**Place**	**Approx. Distance**
Night	miles/km		miles/km		miles/km
0 Amroth		Amroth		Amroth	
1 Lydstep	13.5/22	Lydstep	13.5/22	Lydstep	13/22
2 Freshwater East*	8/13	Bosherston*	14.5/23	Castlemartin*	24.5/39
3 Bosherston*	6.5/10	Castlemartin*	10/16	Pembroke*	22/35
4 Castlemartin*	10/16	Angle*	10.5/17	Sandy Haven*	16.5/27
5 Angle*	10.5/17	Pembroke*	11.5/19	Marloes Sands	13.5/22
6 Pembroke*	11.5/19	Milford Haven*	12.5/20	Newgale	19.5/31
7 Milford Haven*	12.5/20	Marloes Sands	17.5/28	Whitesands	17.5/28
8 Dale*	9.5/15	Broad Haven	12.5/20	Pwll Deri	21/34
9 Marloes Sands	8/13	Newgale	7/11	Newport	22/35
10 Broad Haven	12.5/20	Whitesands Bay	17.5/28	Poppit Sands	14/23
11 Newgale	7/11	Trefin	11.5/18	St Dogmaels*	2/3
12 St David's*	9/14	Fishguard	20/32		
13 Whitesands Bay	8.5/14	Newport	11.5/18		
14 Trefin	11.5/18	Poppit Sands	14/23		
15 Pwll Deri	9.5/15	St Dogmaels*	2/3		
16 Fishguard	10.5/17				
17 Newport	11.5/18				
18 Poppit Sands	14/23				
19 St Dogmaels*	2/3				

*No bunkhouses or hostels but alternative accommodation is available

SUGGESTED ITINERARIES

The itineraries in the boxes on pp25-7 are based on different accommodation types – camping, hostels and B&Bs – with each one divided into three alternatives depending on your walking speed. They are only suggestions, feel free to adapt them to your needs. **Don't forget** to add your travelling time before and after the walk.

WHICH DIRECTION?

There are a number of advantages in tackling the path in a south to north direction. An important consideration is the prevailing south-westerly wind which will, more often than not, be behind you, helping rather than hindering you. On a more aesthetic note the scenery is tamer in the south, while more dramatic and wild to the north, so there is a real sense of leaving the best until last. In addition a south to north direction allows you to get used to the walking on easier ground before confronting the more strenuous terrain further north.

Some may choose to walk in the opposite direction, perhaps preferring to

STAYING IN B&Bs

	Relaxed pace		Medium pace		Fast pace
Night	Place	Approx. Distance miles/km	Place	Approx. Distance miles/km	Place	Approx. Distance miles/km
0	Amroth		Amroth		Amroth	
1	Tenby	7/11	Penally	9.5/15	Manorbier	17.5/28
2	Manorbier	10.5/17	Freshwater East	12/19	Castlemartin	20.5/33
3	Bosherston	10.5/17	Castlemartin	16.5/27	Pembroke	22/35
4	Castlemartin	10/16	Angle	10.5/17	Herbrandston	16.5/27
5	Angle	10.5/17	Pembroke	11.5/19	Marloes	13.5/22
6	Pembroke	11.5/19	Milford Haven	12.5/20	Solva	24.5/39
7	Milford Haven	12.5/20	Marloes	17.5/28	Trefin	24/39
8	Dale	9.5/15	Broad Haven	12.5/20	Fishguard	20/32
9	Marloes	8/13	Solva	12/19	Newport	11.5/18
10	Broad Haven	12.5/20	Whitesands Bay	12.5/20	St Dogmaels	16/26
11	Solva	12/19	Trefin	11.5/18		
12	St David's	4/6	Fishguard	20/32		
13	Whitesands Bay	8.5/14	Newport	11.5/18		
14	Trefin	11.5/18	St Dogmaels	16/26		
15	Pwll Deri	9.5/15				
16	Fishguard	10.5/17				
17	Newport	11.5/18				
18	Poppit Sands	14/23				
19	St Dogmaels	2/3				

get the hard stuff out of the way at the beginning. The maps in Part 4 give timings for both directions so the guide can easily be used back to front, or for day trips.

SIDE TRIPS

The coast path gives a fairly thorough impression of what the national park has to offer. However, there are some other hidden gems to be discovered both inland and off-shore for those with some time to spare.

One of the wildest and most beautiful places is the Preseli Hills (see pp185-6) rising above Newport offering extensive views over the whole peninsula with gentle walks in the Cwm Gwaun valley. Closer to Tenby are the Bosherston Lily Ponds (see p94) for short woodland walks; a great place to spot otters. Over on the islands of Skomer, Skokholm and Grassholm (see p132) and Ramsey (see p153) gannets, gulls and puffins festoon the cliffs while the lazy creeks of the Daugleddau estuary (see pp109-11) make a relaxing change from the seething Atlantic surf. It is worth planning a few extra days on your trip to take in one or two, if not all of these side trips. A boat trip to one of the islands makes for a good day off since it is not too strenuous.

TAKING DOGS ALONG THE COAST PATH

The national park trail officers have been working hard recently to make the path more dog friendly. Dog stiles, or doggy stile as they are affectionately known, are being installed all along the path to prevent damage to the fences caused by dogs squeezing their way through. This acceptance shown towards the dog-walking fraternity is thanks in part to the responsible attitude that they have shown.

Dogs should always be kept on leads while on the footpath to avoid disturbing wildlife, livestock and other walkers. Dog excrement should be cleaned up and not left to decorate the boots of other walkers. Bear in mind that dogs are not allowed between 1 May and 30 September on certain parts of the following seven beaches; Amroth, Saundersfoot, Tenby Castle, Tenby South, Lydstep, Newgale and Poppit Sands. Between the same dates complete bans exist on Tenby's North Beach and at Whitesands Bay. However, these restrictions do not pose any great obstacle to coast path walkers with dogs since the path only occasionally crosses a beach and where it does there is always an alternative route a short way inland.

Remember when planning and booking your accommodation you will need to phone ahead to check if your dog will be welcome. Some inns and hotels charge extra (up to £7 or £8) for a dog.

What to take

Deciding how much to take with you can be difficult. Experienced walkers know that you should take only the bare essentials but at the same time you must ensure you have all the equipment necessary to make the trip safe and comfortable.

KEEP IT LIGHT

Carrying a heavy rucksack really can ruin your enjoyment of a good walk and can also slow you down, turning an easy seven-mile day into an interminable slog. Be ruthless when you pack and leave behind all those little home comforts that you tell yourself don't weigh that much really. This advice is even more pertinent to campers who have added weight to carry.

HOW TO CARRY IT

The size of your **rucksack** depends on where you plan to stay and how you plan to eat. If you are camping and cooking you will probably need a 65- to 75-litre rucksack which can hold the tent, sleeping bag, cooking equipment and food.

Make sure your rucksack has a stiffened back and can be adjusted to fit your own back comfortably. This will make carrying the weight much easier. When packing the rucksack make sure you have all the things you are likely to need during the day near the top or in the side pockets. This includes water bottle,

❏ **Disabled access**

Taking the coast path's undulating and rough terrain into account, it may come as a surprise to learn that short sections of it are accessible by wheelchair. The National Park Authority was awarded the BT Access for All Award in 2000 and their guide *Easy Access Routes in the Pembrokeshire Coast National Park* (£2.95) details over 20 routes for wheelchair users ranging from 600m to 3km. Some of these routes include: Tenby South beach to Penally (pp74-80), St Govan's car park to St Govan's Head (pp88-90), Abereiddy to The Blue Lagoon (pp160-1) and Pwllgwaelod to Cwm-yr-eglwys (pp177-81).

packed lunch, waterproofs and this guidebook (of course). Make sure the hip belt and chest strap (if there is one) are fastened tightly as this helps distribute the weight with most of it being carried on the hips. Rucksacks are decorated with seemingly pointless straps but if you adjust them correctly it can make a big difference to your personal comfort while walking. Consider taking a small **bum bag** or **daypack** for your camera, guidebook and other essentials for when you go sightseeing or for a day walk.

Hostellers should find a 40- to 60-litre rucksack sufficient. If you have gone for the B&B option you will find a 30- to 40-litre day pack is more than enough to carry your lunch, warm and wet weather clothes, camera and guidebook.

A good habit to get into is to always put things in the same place in your rucksack and memorize where they are. There is nothing more annoying than pulling everything out of your pack to find that lost banana when you're starving, or your camera when there is a seal basking on a rock ten feet away from you. It's also a good idea to keep everything in **canoe bags**, **waterproof rucksack liners** or strong plastic bags. If you don't it's bound to rain.

FOOTWEAR

Boots

Your boots are the single most important item of gear that can affect the enjoyment of your trek.

In summer you could get by with a light pair of trail shoes if you're only carrying a small pack, although this is an invitation for wet, cold feet if there is any rain and they don't offer much support for your ankles. Some of the terrain can be quite rough so a good pair of walking boots is a safer bet. They must fit well and be properly broken in. It is no good discovering that your boots are slowly murdering your feet three days into a two-week trek. See p47 for more blister-avoidance advice.

Socks

The traditional wearing of a thin liner sock under a thicker wool sock is no longer necessary if you choose a high-quality sock specially designed for walking. A high proportion of natural fibres makes them much more comfortable. Three pairs are ample.

Extra footwear

Some walkers have a second pair of shoes to wear when they are not on the trail. Trainers, sport sandals or flip flops are all suitable as long as they are light.

CLOTHES

Experienced walkers will know the importance of wearing the right clothes. Don't underestimate the weather: Pembrokeshire pokes its nose into a wet and windy Atlantic so it's important to protect yourself from the elements. The weather can be quite hot in the summer but spectacularly bad at any time of the year. Modern hi-tec outdoor clothes can seem baffling but it basically comes down to a base layer to transport sweat from your skin; a mid-layer or two to keep you warm; and an outer layer or 'shell' to protect you from the wind and rain.

Base layer

Cotton absorbs sweat, trapping it next to the skin and chilling you rapidly when you stop exercising. A thin lightweight **thermal top** of a synthetic material is better as it draws moisture away keeping you dry. It will be cool if worn on its own in hot weather and warm when worn under other clothes in the cold. A spare would be sensible. You may also like to bring a **shirt** for wearing in the evening.

Mid-layers

In the summer a woollen jumper or mid-weight polyester **fleece** will suffice. For the rest of the year you will need an extra layer to keep you warm. Both wool and fleece, unlike cotton, have the ability to stay reasonably warm when wet.

Outer layer

A **waterproof jacket** is essential year-round and will be much more comfortable (but also more expensive) if it's also 'breathable' to prevent the build up of condensation on the inside. This layer can also be worn to keep the wind off.

Leg wear

Whatever you wear on your legs it should be light, quick-drying and not restricting. Many British walkers find polyester tracksuit bottoms comfortable. Poly-cotton or microfibre trousers are excellent. Denim jeans should never be worn; if they get wet they become heavy, cold and bind to your legs. A pair of **shorts** is nice to have on sunny days. Thermal **longjohns** or thick tights are cosy if you're camping but are probably unnecessary even in winter. **Waterproof trousers** are necessary most of the year. In summer a pair of windproof and quick-drying trousers are useful in showery weather. **Gaiters** are not really necessary but may come in useful in wet weather when the vegetation around your legs is dripping wet.

Underwear

Three changes of what you normally wear is fine. Women may find a **sports bra** more comfortable because pack straps can cause bra straps to dig painfully into your shoulders.

Other clothes

A **warm hat** and **gloves** should always be kept in your rucksack, all year round. You never know when you might need them. In summer you should also carry a **sun hat** with you, preferably one which also covers the back of your neck. Another useful piece of summer equipment is a **swimsuit**. Some of the beaches are irresistible on a hot day. Also consider a small **towel** especially if you are camping or staying in hostels.

TOILETRIES

Only take the minimum: a small bar of **soap** in a plastic container (unless staying in B&Bs) which can also be used instead of shaving cream and for washing clothes; a tiny tube of **toothpaste** and a **toothbrush**; and one roll of **loo paper** in a plastic bag. If you are planning to defecate outdoors you will also need a lightweight **trowel** for burying the evidence (see p41 for further tips). In addition a **razor**; **deodorant**; **tampons/sanitary towels** and a high-factor **sun screen** should cover all your needs.

FIRST AID KIT

Medical facilities in Britain are excellent so you only need a small kit to cover common problems and emergencies; pack it in a waterproof container. A basic kit should contain **aspirin** or **paracetamol** for treating mild to moderate pain and fever; **plasters/Band Aids** for minor cuts; **Moleskin, Compeed**, or **Second Skin** for blisters; a **bandage** for holding dressings, splints or limbs in place and for supporting a sprained ankle; elastic knee support (tubigrip) for a weak knee; a small selection of different sized **sterile dressings** for wounds; **porous adhesive tape**; **antiseptic wipes**; **antiseptic cream**; **safety pins**; **tweezers** and **scissors**.

GENERAL ITEMS

Essential

The following should be in everyone's rucksack: a one-litre **water bottle**; a **torch** (flashlight) with spare bulb and batteries in case you end up walking after dark; **emergency food** which your body can quickly convert into energy; a **penknife**; a **watch** with an alarm; and a **plastic bag** for packing out any rubbish you accumulate. A **whistle** is also worth taking; although you are very unlikely to need it you may be grateful of it in the unlikely event of an emergency.

Useful

Many would list a **camera** as essential but it can be liberating to travel without one once in a while; a **notebook** can be a more accurate way of recording your impressions. Other things you may find useful include a **book** to pass the time on train and bus journeys; a pair of **sunglasses** in summer; **binoculars** for observing wildlife; a **walking stick** or pole to take the shock off your knees and a **vacuum flask** for carrying hot drinks. Although the path is easy to follow a 'Silva' type **compass** and the knowledge of how to use it is a good idea in case the sea mist comes in or for any side trips in the Preseli Hills.

SLEEPING BAG

A sleeping bag is only necessary if you are camping or staying in one of the bunkhouses on the route. Campers should find that a two- to three-season bag will cope but obviously in winter a warmer bag is a good idea.

CAMPING GEAR

Campers will need a decent **tent** (or bivvy bag if you enjoy travelling light) able to withstand wet and windy weather; a **sleeping mat**; a **stove** and **fuel** (there is special mention in Part 4 of which shops stock fuel); a **pan** with frying pan that can double as a lid/plate is fine for two people; a **pan handle**; a **mug**; a **spoon**; and a wire/plastic **scrubber** for washing up.

MONEY

There are not many banks along the coast path so you will have to carry most of your money as **cash**. A **debit/credit card** is the easiest way to draw money from banks or cash machines and can be used to pay in larger shops, restaurants and hotels. A **cheque book** is very useful for walkers with accounts in British banks as a cheque will often be accepted where a card is not.

TRAVEL INSURANCE

Members of the EU should complete form E111 which entitles them to medical treatment under the National Health Service. However, this is no substitute for proper medical cover on your travel insurance for unforeseen bills and getting you home should that be necessary. Also consider cover for loss and theft of personal belongings, especially if you are camping or staying in hostels, as there will be times when you'll have to leave your belongings unattended.

MAPS

The hand-drawn maps in this book cover the trail at a scale of 1:20,000; plenty of detail and information to keep you on the right track. For side trips to the Preseli Hills, the Daugleddau estuary or anywhere else in the national park you will need an Ordnance Survey map (☎ 0845-200 2712, 🖳 www.ordsvy.gov.uk). There are two excellent maps of the national park available: OS Outdoor Leisure Maps (yellow cover) Nos 35 and 36 for North and South Pembrokeshire at a scale of 1:25,000 (£6.50 each).

Enthusiastic map buyers can reduce the often considerable expense of purchasing them: members of the **Ramblers' Association** (see opposite) can bor-

❑ FURTHER INFORMATION

Trail information
● **The Pembrokeshire Coast National Park** (☎ 01437-764636, 🖳 www.pembro keshirecoast.org.uk) Winch Lane, Haverfordwest, Pembrokeshire, SA61 1PY. The park authority provides a wealth of useful information about the area from specific information about the coast path and outdoor activities to wildlife and beaches. The website is very informative and has a detailed section on the coast path.

Tourist information
● **Tourist information centres** TICs are based in towns throughout Britain and provide all manner of locally specific information and an accommodation booking service. There are eleven centres relevant to the coast path with the ones at St David's and Newport doubling up as national park information centres. The centres are in **Kilgetty** (see p66), **Saundersfoot** (p72), **Tenby** (p74), **Pembroke** (p107), **Pembroke Dock** (p111), **Milford Haven** (p117), **St David's** (p150), **Goodwick** (p173), **Fishguard** (p175), **Newport** (p181) and **Cardigan** (p195).
● **Wales Tourist Board** (☎ 029-2049 9909, 🖳 www.visitwales.com) Brunel House, 2 Fitzalan Rd, Cardiff, CF24 0UY. The tourist board oversees all the local tourist information centres. It's a good place to find general information about the country and information on outdoor activities and local events. They can also help with arranging holidays and accommodation.

Organizations for walkers
● **The Backpackers' Club** (🖳 www.backpackersclub.co.uk, 29 Lynton Drive, High Lane, Stockport, Cheshire, SK6 8JE). A club aimed at people who are involved or interested in lightweight camping through walking, cycling, skiing, canoeing, etc. They produce a quarterly magazine, provide members with a comprehensive advisory and information service on all aspects of backpacking, organize weekend trips and also publish a farm pitch directory. Membership is £12 per year.
● **Friends of Pembrokeshire National Park** FPNP, PO Box 218, Haverfordwest SA61 1WR. Besides arranging walks in which the members are the guides this organization also gives you the opportunity to give something back to the park. They arrange projects which involve repairing footbridges and dry stone walls and clearing overgrown paths. You do not have to be from the local area to join. Annual subscription is £8.
● **The Long Distance Walkers' Association** (🖳 www.ldwa.org.uk) An association of people with the common interest of long-distance walking. Membership includes a journal three times per year giving details of challenge events and local group walks as well as articles on the subject. Information on over 500 long distance paths is presented in the LDWA's Long Distance Walkers' Handbook. Membership is currently £7 per year.
● **The Ramblers' Association** (☎ 020-7339 8500, 🖳 www.ramblers.org.uk) 2nd Floor, Camelford House, 87–89 Albert Embankment, London, SE1 7BR. Looks after the interests of walkers throughout Britain. They publish a large amount of useful information including their *Yearbook* (£4.99 to non-members), a full directory of services for walkers.

row up to 10 maps for a period of six weeks at 30p per map from their library; members of the **Backpackers' Club** (see p33) can purchase maps at a significant discount through their map service.

RECOMMENDED READING

Most of the following books can be found in the tourist information centres.

General guidebooks

The Rough Guide series includes the comprehensive *Wales: The Rough Guide* by Mike Parker.

Walking guidebooks

A couple of books cover day walks away from the coast path that explore the hidden corners of Pembrokeshire. The National Park Authority publish a guide to *Walking in the Preseli Hills* and Abercastle Publications have a *Short Guide to the Best Walks in Pembrokeshire* by A Roberts for just £1.95. Those who like to round off the day with a pint may appreciate *Pub Walks in Pembrokeshire* published by Sigma with a cover price of £6.95. Of course if you are a seasoned

---

❏ GETTING TO BRITAIN

● **Air** Most international airlines serve London Heathrow and London Gatwick. In addition a number of budget airlines fly from many of Europe's major cities to the other London terminals at Stansted and Luton. From London it is five to six hours by train to Pembrokeshire. There are a few flights from Europe to Bristol and Cardiff which are closer to Pembrokeshire than London. Trains from here to Pembrokeshire take about three hours.

● **From Europe by train** Eurostar (☎ 020-7928 5163, 🖳 www.eurostar.com) operates a high-speed passenger service via the Channel Tunnel between Paris and London (2hr 45mins) and Brussels and London (2hr 40mins). Trains arrive and depart London from the international terminal at Waterloo Station. Waterloo has connections to the London Underground and to all other main railway stations in London. There are also various rail/ferry services between Britain and Europe; for more information contact Rail Europe (☎ 08705 848848, 🖳 www.raileurope.co.uk).

● **From Europe by bus** Eurolines (☎ 08705-143219, 🖳 www.eurolines.co.uk) have a huge network of long-distance bus services connecting over 500 cities in 25 European countries to London.

● **From Europe by car** P&O Stena Line (☎ 0870-600 0600, 🖳 www.posl.com) run frequent passenger ferries between Calais and Dover. The journey takes about 75 minutes. Hoverspeed (☎ 0870-240 8070, 🖳 www.hoverspeed.co.uk) offer a faster journey taking 35 minutes between Dover and Calais by hovercraft. Eurotunnel (☎ 08705-353535, 🖳 www.eurotunnel.com) operates a shuttle train service for vehicles via the Channel Tunnel between Calais and Folkestone taking one hour between the motorway in France and the motorway in Britain. There are also countless other ferries plying routes between all the major North Sea and Channel ports of mainland Europe and the ports on Britain's eastern and southern coasts.

long-distance walker or even if you are new to the game and like what you see, check out the other titles in the Trailblazer series; see p208.

Flora and fauna field guides

The National Park Authority publish a small booklet highlighting the more common species along the coastline called *The Birds of the Pembrokeshire Coast* by Peter Knights. It's only 75p and slips easily into a pocket. The Dyfed Wildlife Trust's *Birds of Pembrokeshire* by Donovan and Rees at £17.95 is an expensive yet useful guide but some might prefer a book which is also of use when travelling elsewhere. The AA's *Birds of Britain and Europe* at £9.99 is one of many excellent bird guides that can fit inside a rucksack pocket.

Pembrokeshire is famous for its wild flowers so a guidebook on these may come in handy. At just £3.99 Andrew Branson's *Wild Flowers of Britain and Europe* published by Bounty Books is an excellent pocket-size guide that categorizes flowers according to habitat.

Getting to and from the Coast Path

A glance at any map of Britain gives the impression that Pembrokeshire is a long way from anywhere and hard to get to. In reality road and rail links with the coast path are excellent with Kilgetty, close to the start of the coast path, lying on both the national rail network and the National Express coach network.

Travelling to the start of the coast path by public transport makes sense. There's no need to worry about the safety of your abandoned vehicle while walking, there are no logistical headaches about how to return to your car when you've finished the walk and it's obviously one of the biggest steps you can take towards minimizing your ecological footprint. Quite apart from that, you'll simply feel your holiday has begun the moment you step out of your front door, rather than having to wait until you've slammed the car door behind you.

NATIONAL TRANSPORT

By rail

For those walking the whole path the nearest train stations are Kilgetty (3 miles/5km from the start of the path at Amroth) and Fishguard Harbour (a 50-minute bus ride from the end of the coast path near Cardigan). There are fairly frequent services to these stations from Cardiff and Swansea which in turn are served by trains from all over the country. In addition there are a few direct services from London. Other points of the path can also be reached by train. There are stations at Tenby, Penally, Pembroke, Pembroke Dock and Milford Haven.

All timetable and fare information can be found at **National Rail Enquiries** (☎ 08457-484950, 24hrs; 🖳 www.nationalrail.co.uk).

By coach

National Express (☎ 08705-808080, lines open 8am–10pm daily; 🖥 www.go bycoach.com) is the principal coach (long-distance bus operator) in Britain. Coach travel is generally cheaper but longer than travel by train. Kilgetty, which is just three miles (5km) from Amroth and the start of the coast path, is rather conveniently located on one of the National Express routes. The same coach also makes calls at Tenby, Pembroke and Milford Haven on its way to Haverfordwest.

By car

Pembrokeshire has good links to the national road network with the M4 motorway stretching as far as Swansea. From here Kilgetty, near the southern end of the coast path, can be reached by following the A48 to Carmarthen, A40 to St Clears and finally the A477. From Kilgetty it is a short drive down the lane to Amroth and the start of the path. The National Park Authority have a car park, indicated by a blue 'P' sign, just off the seafront road near the Amroth Arms pub.

The end of the coast path and the northern half of the coast are reached by following the A484 from Carmarthen to Cardigan. The best place to park your car is at the National Park supervised car park at Poppit Sands which is opposite the lifeboat station.

By ferry

Visitors from Ireland are lucky enough to have two ferry services direct to Pembrokeshire. Both Pembroke Dock and Fishguard are served by a daily ferry to and from Rosslare in southern Ireland. Day trips to Rosslare are perfectly feasible for anyone who fancies a break from the coast path. Contact Irish Ferries (☎ 08705-134252, 🖥 www.irishferries.com) at Pembroke Dock or Stena Line (☎ 08705-421107, 🖥 www.stenaline.co.uk) at Fishguard for details.

By air

Air travel is not the best way to get to the coast path: the nearest airport, Swansea, is 45 miles (72km) away. Quite apart from that, it's by far the least environmentally-sound option (see 🖥 www.chooseclimate.org for the true costs of flying).

LOCAL TRANSPORT

Pembrokeshire has an excellent public transport system reaching some of the smallest, most out-of-the-way villages. This is great news for anyone hoping to do any linear day or weekend walks. Of particular interest are the four summer shuttle bus services (see p38) that are designed especially for coast path walkers, serving all the villages along the coast between Milford Haven and St David's.

The public transport map opposite gives an overview of the most useful bus and train routes, approximate frequency of services in both directions and whom you should contact for detailed timetable information. The whole county is covered in the *Pembrokeshire Bus Timetable*, published each year. It can be picked up for free at any of the tourist information centres.

There's also a useful travel information line and website for Wales: ☎ 0870-608 2608, 🖥 www.traveline-cymru.org.uk.

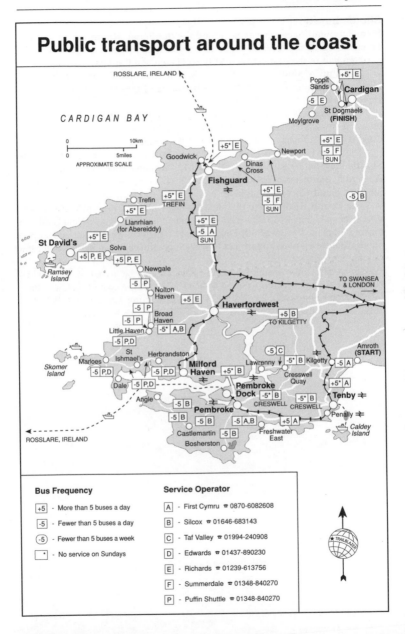

Public transport around the coast

ROSSLARE, IRELAND

CARDIGAN BAY

Poppit Sands

Cardigan

+5* E

-5 E

St Dogmaels
(FINISH)

Moylgrove

Newport

+5* E

-5 F
SUN

+5* E
TREFIN

Trefin

+5* E

Llanrhian
(for Abereiddy)

+5* E

Goodwick

+5* E

Dinas
Cross

Fishguard

+5* E

-5 F
SUN

-5 B

St David's

+5 P, E

Solva

+5 P, E

+5* E

-5 A
SUN

Ramsey
Island

Newgale

-5 P

Nolton
Haven

+5 E

Broad
Haven

-5 P

Little Haven

-5 A,B

TO SWANSEA
& LONDON

Haverfordwest

+5 B
TO KILGETTY

-5 P,D

St
Ishmael's

Herbrandston

-5 P,D

-5 C

Amroth
(START)

Skomer
Island

Marloes

-5 P,D

Dale

-5 P,D

Milford
Haven

Lawrenny

-5* B

Cresswell
Quay

Kilgetty

-5 A

+5* B

+5* A

Angle

Pembroke
Dock

-5* B

-5* B
CRESWELL

CRESWELL

Tenby

+5* B
CRESWELL

Penally

-5 B

Pembroke

-5 B

-5 A,B

+5 A

Caldey
Island

Castlemartin

-5 B

Freshwater
East

Bosherston

ROSSLARE, IRELAND

Bus Frequency

+5 - More than 5 buses a day

-5 - Fewer than 5 buses a day

-5 - Fewer than 5 buses a week

* - No service on Sundays

Service Operator

A - First Cymru ☎ 0870-6082608

B - Silcox ☎ 01646-683143

C - Taf Valley ☎ 01994-240908

D - Edwards ☎ 01437-890230

E - Richards ☎ 01239-613756

F - Summerdale ☎ 01348-840270

P - Puffin Shuttle ☎ 01348-840270

0 10km
0 5miles
APPROXIMATE SCALE

TRAILBLAZER

Shuttle buses

From July until September (year round for the Poppit Rocket) there are four excellent shuttle bus services aimed directly at weary coast path walkers on the northern half of the path between Milford Haven and Cardigan.

The **Puffin Shuttle**, operated by Summerdale (☎ 01348-840270), runs twice daily linking Milford Haven with Herbrandston, Dale, Marloes, Broad Haven, Newgale, Solva and St David's.

The St David's peninsula is served by the hourly **Celtic Coaster** which is powered by eco-friendly liquid petroleum gas. It makes stops at St David's, Caerfai Bay, Porthclais, St Justinian's and Whitesands.

The coast between St David's and Fishguard is covered by the **Strumble Shuttle** operated by Richards (☎ 01239-613756) three times a day stopping at Abereiddy, Porthgain, Trefin, Abercastle, Pwll Deri, the Strumble Head road junction, Goodwick and Fishguard.

The **Poppit Rocket**, also operated by Richards (☎ 01239-613756), shoots its way from Fishguard to the end of the coast path at St Dogmaels and Cardigan making stops at Pwllgwaelod, Dinas Cross, Newport, Moylgrove and Poppit Sands. The Newport to Poppit Sands service continues to run in the winter but on only three days a week.

Up-to-date information for these services can be found at St David's National Park Information Centre (☎ 01437-720392), Newport National Park Information Centre (☎ 01239-820912) or by contacting Traveline (☎ 0870-608 2608, 🖥 www.traveline-cymru.org.uk).

In this chaotic world in which people live their lives at an increasingly frenetic pace, many of us living in overcrowded cities and working in jobs that offer little free-time, the great outdoors is becoming an essential means of escape. Walking in the countryside is a wonderful means of relaxation and gives people the time to think and re-discover themselves.

Of course as the popularity of the countryside increases so do the problems that this pressure brings. It is important for visitors to remember that the countryside is the home and workplace of many others. Walkers in particular should be aware of their responsibilities. Indeed a walker who respects and understands the countryside will get far more enjoyment from their trip.

By following a few simple guidelines while walking the coast path you can have a positive impact, not just on your own well-being but also on local communities and the environment, thereby becoming part of the solution.

ECONOMIC IMPACT

Rural businesses and communities in Britain have been hit hard in recent years by a seemingly endless series of crises. Most people are aware of the country code; not dropping litter and closing the gate behind you are still as pertinent as ever, but in light of the economic pressures that local countryside businesses are under there is something else you can do: buy local.

Buy local

Look and ask for local produce to buy and eat. Not only does this cut down on the amount of pollution and congestion that the transportation of food creates, (the so-called 'food miles'), but also ensures that you are supporting local farmers and producers; the very people who have moulded the countryside you have come to see and who are in the best position to protect it. If you can find local food which is also organic then so much the better.

Support local businesses

If you spend £1 in a local business 80p of that pound stays within the local economy where it can be spent again and again to do the most good for that community and landscape. If, on the other hand, you spend your money in a branch of a national or multinational chain store, restaurant or hotel the situation is reversed; only 20% (mainly the staff wages) stays within the local economy and the other 80% is effectively lost to that community as it's siphoned off to pay for goods, transport and profit. The more money which circulates locally and is spent on local labour and materials the more power the community has to effect the change it wants to see; a world of difference from the corporatism of the countryside which we are currently witnessing.

❏ **Nourishing facts to ponder while walking**

● A supermarket provides one job for every £250,000 spent, compared with a village shop which provides one job for every £50,000 spent.

● The UK earns £630 million a year from meat and dairy exports yet the cost of the foot and mouth epidemic in terms of lost tourism, government compensation etc was estimated to be over £9 billion.

● In 1998 the UK exported 109,533 pigs while importing 203,174 pigs.

● Britain imports 61,400 tonnes of poultry meat from the Netherlands and exports 33,100 tonnes of poultry meat to the Netherlands.

● Britain imports 125,000 tonnes of lamb and exports 102,000 tonnes of lamb.

● In 1997 the UK imported 126 million litres of liquid milk and exported 270 million litres of liquid milk at the same time.

● The distribution of 1kg of apples from New Zealand to a UK consumer results in 1kg of CO_2 emissions compared with less than 50g CO_2 for 1kg of locally-sourced apples from a home-delivery fruit and vegetable box scheme.

Encourage local cultural traditions and skills

No part of the countryside looks the same. Buildings, food, skills, and language evolve out of the landscape and are moulded over hundreds of years to suit the locality. Discovering these cultural differences is part of the pleasure of walking in new places. Visitors' enthusiasm for local traditions and skills brings awareness and pride, nurturing a sense of place; an increasingly important role in a world where economic globalization continues to undermine the very things that provide security and a feeling of belonging.

ENVIRONMENTAL IMPACT

A walking holiday in itself is an environmentally-friendly approach to tourism. The following are some ideas on how you can go a few steps further in helping to minimize your impact on the natural environment while walking the Pembrokeshire Coast Path.

Use public transport whenever possible

Public transport in Pembrokeshire is excellent and in many cases specifically geared towards the coast path walker. By using the local bus you will help to keep the standard high. Public transport is always preferable to using private cars as it benefits everyone: visitors, locals and the environment.

Never leave litter

Leaving litter shows a total disrespect for the natural world and others coming after you. As well as being unsightly litter kills wildlife, pollutes the environment and can be dangerous to farm animals. **Please** carry a plastic bag so you can dispose of your rubbish in a bin in the next village. It would be very helpful if you could pick up litter left by other people too.

● **Is it OK if it's biodegradable?** Not really. Apple cores, banana skins, orange peel and the like are unsightly, encourage flies, ants and wasps and ruin a picnic spot for others. Using the excuse that they are natural and biodegradable just doesn't cut any ice. When was the last time you saw a banana tree in Wales?

● **The lasting impact of litter** A piece of orange peel left on the ground takes six months to decompose; silver foil 18 months; a plastic bag 10 years; clothes 15 years; and an aluminium can 85 years.

Erosion

● **Stay on the main trail** The effect of your footsteps may seem minuscule but when they are multiplied by several thousand walkers each year they become rather more significant. Avoid taking shortcuts, widening the trail or taking more than one path; your boots will be followed by many others.

● **Consider walking out of season** Maximum disturbance by walkers coincides with the time of year when nature wants to do most of its growth and repair. In high-use areas, like that along much of the coast path, the trail never recovers. Walking at less busy times eases this pressure while also generating year-round income for the local economy. Not only that, but it may make the walk a more relaxing experience with fewer people on the path and less competition for accommodation.

Respect all wildlife

Care for all wildlife you come across along the coast path; it has as much right to be there as you. Tempting as it may be to pick wild flowers leave them so the next people who pass can enjoy them too. Don't break branches off or damage trees in any way.

If you come across wildlife keep your distance and don't watch for too long. Your presence can cause considerable stress, particularly if the adults are with young, or in winter when the weather is harsh and food is scarce. Young animals are rarely abandoned. If you come across young birds keep away so that their mother can return. Anyone considering a spot of climbing on the sea cliffs should bear in mind that there are restrictions in certain areas due to the presence of nesting birds. Check with tourist information.

The code of the outdoor loo

'Going' in the outdoors is a lost art worth re-learning, for your sake and everyone else's. As more and more people discover the joys of the outdoors this is becoming an important issue.

In some parts of the world where visitor pressure is higher than in Britain walkers and climbers are required to pack out their excrement. This could soon be necessary here. Human excrement is not only offensive to our senses but, more importantly, can infect water sources.

● **Where to go** Wherever possible **use a toilet**. Public toilets are marked on the trail maps in this guide and you will also find facilities in pubs, cafés and campsites along the coast path.

If you do have to go outdoors choose a site at least **30 metres away from running water**. Carry a small trowel and **dig a small hole** about 15cm (6") deep to bury your excrement in. It decomposes quicker when in contact with the top layer of soil or leaf mould. Use a stick to stir loose soil into your deposit as well as this speeds up decomposition even more. Do not squash it under rocks as this slows down the composting process. If you have to use rocks to cover it make sure they are not in contact with your faeces.

● **Toilet paper and sanitary towels** Toilet paper takes a long time to decompose whether buried or not. It is easily dug up by animals and will then blow into water sources or onto the path.

The best method for dealing with it is to **pack it out**. Put the used paper inside a paper bag which you then place inside a plastic bag (or two). Then simply empty the contents of the paper bag at the next toilet you come across and throw the bag away. You should also pack out **tampons** and **sanitary towels** in a similar way; they take years to decompose and will be dug up and scattered about by animals.

Wild camping

Unfortunately, wild camping is not encouraged within the national park. In any case there are few places where it is a viable option. This is a shame since wild camping is an altogether more fulfilling experience than camping on a designated site. Living in the outdoors without any facilities provides a valuable lesson in simple, sustainable living where the results of all your actions, from going to the loo to washing your plates, can be seen.

If you do insist on wild camping always ask the landowner for permission. Anyone contemplating camping on a beach should be very aware of the times and heights of the tide. Follow these suggestions for minimizing your impact and encourage others to do likewise.

● **Be discreet** Camp alone or in small groups, spend only one night in each place and pitch your tent late and move off early.

● **Never light a fire** The deep burn caused by camp fires, no matter how small, damages the turf which can take years to recover. Cook on a camp stove instead.

● **Don't use soap or detergent** There is no need to use soap; even biodegradable soaps and detergents pollute streams. You won't be away from a shower for more than a day or so. Wash up without detergent; use a plastic or metal scourer, or failing that, a handful of fine pebbles from the beach or some bracken or grass.

● **Leave no trace** Learn the skill of moving on without leaving any sign of having been there: no moved boulders, ripped up vegetation or dug drainage ditches. Make a final check of your campsite before departing; pick up any litter that you or anyone else has left, so leaving the place in a better state than you found it.

ACCESS

Britain is a crowded cluster of islands with few places where you can wander as you please. Most of the land is a patchwork of fields and agricultural land and the Pembrokeshire Coast National Park is no different. However, there are

❏ **Maintaining the Pembrokeshire Coast Path**

Maintenance of the path is carried out by the national trail officers and is funded by the Countryside Council for Wales and European Regional Development Fund. Tasks throughout the year vary. In summer there is the constant battle to cut back vigorous growth which would engulf the path if left alone and repairs need to be carried out on some of the 134 footbridges and 500 stiles. Many of the stiles are now being replaced by kissing gates to make access easier for the less able.

Where erosion of the path becomes a problem wooden causeways or steps are constructed and particularly boggy areas are drained by digging ditches. Occasionally the trail officers will re-route the path where erosion has become so severe as to be a danger to the walker. In the winter some sections of the path slip into the sea necessitating the realignment of the path, often involving the instalment of new stiles or kissing gates in order to run the path through a field.

Take these potential route changes into account when using the maps in Part 4. They usually cover a very short distance but have the potential to cause a little confusion.

countless public rights of way, in addition to the coast path, that criss-cross the land. This is fine, but what happens if you feel a little more adventurous and want to explore the beaches, dunes, moorland, woodland and hills that can also be found within the national park boundaries?

Right to roam

The Countryside & Rights of Way Act 2000, or 'Right to Roam' as dubbed by walkers, was passed by parliament after a long campaign to allow greater public access to areas of countryside in England and Wales deemed to be uncultivated open country. This essentially means moorland, heathland, downland and upland areas.

In the case of the Pembrokeshire Coast National Park this implies the Preseli Hills and the wild country around the St David's peninsula. It does not mean free access to wander over farmland, woodland or private gardens. Indeed the legislation, although passed by parliament, has not yet come into effect and it may be some years before it does. If the urge takes you and you feel like tramping the Preseli Hills or getting lost among the sand dunes check with the tourist information centres first for the latest situation. With more freedom in the countryside comes a need for more responsibility from the walker. Remember that wild open country is still the workplace of farmers and home to all sorts of wildlife. Have respect for both and avoid disturbing domestic and wild animals.

Lambing

Around 80% of the coast path passes through private farmland much of which is pasture for sheep. Lambing takes place from mid-March to mid-May when dogs should not be taken along the path. Even a dog secured on a lead is liable to disturb a pregnant ewe. If you should see a lamb or ewe that appears to be in distress contact the nearest farmer.

Don't disturb farm animals

The Country Code

The countryside is a fragile place which every visitor should respect. The country code seems like common sense but sadly some people still seem to have no understanding of how to treat the countryside they walk in. Everyone visiting the countryside has a responsibility to minimize the impact of their visit so that other people can enjoy the same peaceful landscapes. It does not take much effort; it really is common sense.

● **Enjoy the countryside and respect its life and work** Access to the countryside depends on being sensitive to the needs and wishes of those who live and work there. Being courteous and friendly to those you meet will ensure a healthy future for all based on partnership and co-operation.

● **Leave all gates as you found them** If in doubt close a gate to prevent farm animals straying.

● **Guard against all risk of fire** Accidental fire is a great fear of farmers and foresters. Never make a camp fire and take matches and cigarette butts out with you to dispose of safely.

● **Keep your dog under control** The only place you can safely allow your dog off the lead is along the beaches but there are restrictions in the summer (see p28). Across farmland dogs should be kept on a lead. During lambing time they should not be taken with you at all (see p43).

● **Keep to paths across farmland** Stick to the official coast path across arable or pasture land. Minimize erosion by not cutting corners or widening the path.

● **Use gates and stiles to cross fences, hedges and walls** The coast path is well supplied with stiles where it crosses field boundaries. On some of the side trips you may find the paths less accommodating. If you do have to climb over a gate which you can't open always do so at the hinged end.

● **Leave livestock, crops and machinery alone** Help farmers by not interfering with their means of livelihood.

● **Take your litter home** 'Pack it in, pack it out'. Litter is not only ugly but can be harmful to wildlife. Small mammals often become trapped in discarded cans and bottles. Many walkers think that orange peel and banana skins do not count as litter. Even biodegradable foodstuffs attract common scavenging species such as crows and gulls to the detriment of less dominant species. Carry a plastic bag to put yours and other people's litter and food scraps in and take it home or find a bin. For information on going to the toilet in the outdoors see p41.

● **Help keep all water clean** Leaving litter and going to the toilet near a water source can pollute people's water supplies.

● **Protect wildlife, plants and trees** Care for and respect all wildlife you come across along the coast path. Don't pick plants, break trees or scare wild animals. If you come across young birds that appear to have been abandoned leave them alone. If you visit any of the islands always stick to the designated paths to avoid disturbing nesting seabirds.

● **Take special care on country roads** Cars travel dangerously fast on narrow winding lanes. To be safe walk facing the oncoming traffic and carry a torch or wear highly visible clothing when it's getting dark.

● **Make no unnecessary noise** Enjoy the peace and solitude of the outdoors by staying in small groups and acting unobtrusively.

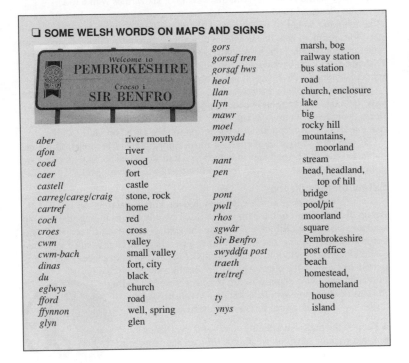

❏ **SOME WELSH WORDS ON MAPS AND SIGNS**

Welsh	English
gors	marsh, bog
gorsaf tren	railway station
gorsaf hws	bus station
heol	road
llan	church, enclosure
llyn	lake
mawr	big
moel	rocky hill
mynydd	mountains, moorland
nant	stream
pen	head, headland, top of hill
pont	bridge
pwll	pool/pit
rhos	moorland
sgwâr	square
Sir Benfro	Pembrokeshire
swyddfa post	post office
traeth	beach
tre/tref	homestead, homeland
ty	house
ynys	island
aber	river mouth
afon	river
coed	wood
caer	fort
castell	castle
carreg/careg/craig	stone, rock
cartref	home
coch	red
croes	cross
cwm	valley
cwm-bach	small valley
dinas	fort, city
du	black
eglwys	church
fford	road
ffynnon	well, spring
glyn	glen

Outdoor safety

AVOIDANCE OF HAZARDS

With good planning and preparation most hazards can be avoided. This information is just as important for those out on a day walk as for those walking the entire coast path.

Ensure you have suitable **clothes** to keep you warm and dry, whatever the conditions (see p18) and a spare change of inner clothes. A compass, whistle, torch and first aid kit should be carried and are discussed further on p31. The **emergency signal** is six blasts on the whistle or six flashes with a torch.

Take plenty of **food** with you for the day and at least one litre of **water** although more would be better, especially on the long northern stretches. It is a good idea to fill up your bottle whenever you pass through a village since stream water cannot be relied upon. You will eat far more walking than you do normally so make sure you have enough for the day, as well as some high-energy snacks (chocolate, dried fruit, biscuits) in the bottom of your pack for an emergency.

Stay alert and know exactly where you are throughout the day. The easiest way to do this is to **regularly check your position** on the map. If visibility suddenly decreases with mist and cloud, or there is an accident, you will be able to make a sensible decision about what action to take based on your location.

If you choose to walk alone you must appreciate and be prepared for the increased risk. It's a good idea to leave word with someone about where you are going and remember to contact them when you have arrived safely.

Safety on the cliff top

Sadly every year people are either injured or killed walking the coast path. Along the full length of the path you will see warning signs urging you to keep well away from the cliff edge. They are there for a reason. Cliffs are very dangerous. In many places it is difficult to see just where the edge is since it is often well hidden by vegetation. Added to this is the fact that, in places, the path is extremely close to the edge. Always err on the side of over-caution and think twice about walking if you are tired or feeling ill. This is when most accidents happen. To ensure you have a safe trip it is well worth following this advice;

● Keep to the path – avoid cliff edges and overhangs.
● Avoid walking in windy weather. Cliff tops are dangerous in such conditions.
● Be aware of the increased possibility of slipping over in wet or icy weather.
● Wear strong sturdy boots with good ankle support and a good grip rather than trainers or sandals.

Take note of signs warning of dangerous cliffs

● Be extra vigilant with children.
● In an emergency dial ☎ 999 and ask for the coastguard.

Safety on the beach

Pembrokeshire's beaches are spectacular in any weather but it's when the sun is shining that the sweaty walker gets the urge to take a dip. The sea can be a dangerous environment and care should be taken if you do go for a swim and even if you're just walking along the beach. Follow this common-sense advice:

● If tempted to take a shortcut across a beach be aware of the tides to avoid being cut off or stranded.
● Do not sit directly below cliffs and do not climb them unless you are an experienced climber with the right equipment, or with someone who has experience.
● Don't swim after eating, or after drinking alcohol.
● Be aware of local tides and currents. Don't assume it is safe just because other people are swimming there. If in doubt consult the tide tables (see below) or check with the nearest tourist information centre.
● Be extra vigilant with children.
● In an emergency dial ☎ 999 and ask for the coastguard.

TIDE TABLES

Tide tables are available from newsagents. Between Easter and the end of October they are also published in the free newspaper, *Coast to Coast*, which you can get from tourist information centres.

WEATHER FORECASTS

The Pembrokeshire coast is exposed to whatever the churning Atlantic can throw at it. Even when it's sunny sea breezes usually develop during the course of the day so it's worth taking weather forecasts with a pinch of salt. A warm day can feel bitterly cold when you stop for lunch on a cliff top being battered by the wind.

Try to get the local weather forecast from the newspaper, TV or radio or one of the telephone forecasts before you set off. Alter your plans for the day accordingly.

Telephone forecasts

These are frequently updated and generally reliable. Calls are charged at the expensive premium rate. **Weather call** ☎ 09068-500414.

BLISTERS

It is important to break in new boots before embarking on a long walk. Make sure the boots are comfortable and try to avoid getting them wet on the inside. Air your feet at lunchtime, keep them clean and change your socks regularly. If you feel any hot spots stop immediately and apply a few strips of zinc oxide tape and leave on until it is pain free or the tape starts to come off. If you have left it too late and a blister has developed you should surround it with 'mole-skin' or any other blister kit to protect it from abrasion. Popping it can lead to infection. If the skin is broken keep the area clean with antiseptic and cover with a non-adhesive dressing material held in place with tape.

HYPOTHERMIA

Also known as exposure, this occurs when the body can't generate enough heat to maintain its normal temperature, usually as a result of being wet, cold, unprotected from the wind, tired and hungry. It is usually more of a problem in upland areas. However, even on the Pembrokeshire coast in bad weather the body can be exposed to strong winds and driving rain making the risk a real one. The northern stretches of the path are particularly exposed and there are fewer villages making it difficult to get help should it be needed. Hypothermia is easily avoided by wearing suitable clothing, carrying and eating enough food and drink, being aware of the weather conditions and checking the morale of your companions. Early signs to watch for are feeling cold and tired with involuntary shivering. Find some shelter as soon as possible and warm the victim up with a hot drink and some chocolate or other high-energy food. If possible give them another warm layer of clothing and allow them to rest until feeling better.

If allowed to worsen, strange behaviour, slurring of speech and poor co-ordination will become apparent and the victim can quickly progress into unconsciousness, followed by coma and death. Quickly get the victim out of wind and rain, improvising a shelter if necessary. Rapid restoration of bodily warmth is essential and best achieved by bare-skin contact: someone should get into the same sleeping bag as the patient, both having stripped to their underwear, any spare clothing under or over them to build up heat. Send urgently for help.

DEALING WITH AN ACCIDENT

● Use basic first aid to treat the injury to the best of your ability.
● Work out exactly where you are. If possible leave someone with the casualty while others go to get help. If there are only two people, you have a dilemma. If you decide to get help leave all spare clothing and food with the casualty.
● Telephone ☎ 999 and ask for the coastguard. They will assist in both offshore and onshore incidents.

(**Opposite**): Bosherston Church (see p88) dates from the 13th century.

PART 3: THE ENVIRONMENT & NATURE

But we, how shall we listen to the little things
And listen to the birds and winds and streams
Made holy by their dreams
Nor feel the heart-break in the heart of things?
WW Gibson 1918

The Pembrokeshire coast is not just about beaches and the sea. The coast path takes you through all manner of habitats from woodland and grassland to heathland and dunes providing habitats for a distinct array of species. This book is not designed to be a comprehensive guide to all the wildlife that you may encounter, but serves as an introduction to the animals and plants that the walker is likely to find within the boundaries of the national park.

Making that special effort to look out for wildlife and appreciating what you are seeing enhances your enjoyment of the walk. To take it a step further is to understand a little more about the species you may encounter, appreciating how they interact with each other and learning a little about the conservation issues that are so essential today. At a time when man seems ever more detached from the natural world it is important to remember that we continue to be a part of this complex web and this brings a responsibility to limit our negative influences.

Conserving Pembrokeshire

Like much of the British Isles, the Welsh countryside has had to cope with a great deal of pressure from the activities of an ever industrialized world. It must have been a fascinating place when the broadleaved forests, home to wolves and wild boar, stretched as far as the eye could see. Today the surviving pockets of forest and heathland are still under threat but thankfully, there is a greater understanding of the value of the natural environment and with it a number of organizations who are actively helping to safeguard what remains of Wales's natural heritage.

As beautiful as the modern-day countryside may be it is sad to note that almost every acre of land has been altered in some way by man. What we have today are fragments of semi-natural woodland and hedgerows stretched across farmland. Aside from the tops of the highest Welsh mountains the only truly untouched land is found on the coast; the cliffs, islands and beaches.

(Opposite) Top: Looking across Pwll Deri to Strumble Head (see p169) on the northern section of the walk. **Bottom**: The translucent waters of Aber Grugog (see p178).

This plundering of the countryside has had a major effect on its biodiversity. Add to the loss of the wolf and wild boar a number of other species lost and others severely depleted in number and one begins to appreciate the influence that man has had over the years.

There is good news, however. In these enlightened times when environmental issues are quite rightly given more precedence, many endangered species, such as the otter, have increased in number thanks to the active work of voluntary conservation bodies. One such success story is the red kite, a beautiful bird of prey which was all but extinct in Britain some ten years ago when just 50 pairs remained in the hills of Mid-Wales. Since then their range has increased to cover greater parts of Wales as well as Scotland and England thanks to an on-going release programme that covers the country.

There is reason to be optimistic. The environment is no longer the least important issue in party politics and this reflects the opinions of everyday people who are concerned about conservation on both a global and local scale. In Wales there are organizations both voluntary and government based dedicated to conserving their local heritage; everything from Norman castles to puffins.

COUNTRYSIDE COUNCIL FOR WALES

This is the main government body concerned with nature conservation and countryside protection in Wales. Previously known as the Nature Conservancy Council it was split into three separate bodies for England, Scotland and Wales. The Countryside Council aims to sustain the natural beauty and wildlife of Wales while promoting the opportunity for public access to, and enjoyment of, the outdoors. The Council manage three national parks in Wales, Pembrokeshire being the only coastal one.

They also manage a number of **National Nature Reserves** (NNR) within the national park including the limestone cliffs of Stackpole estate on the south coast and the **Marine Nature Reserve** (MNR) around Skomer Island. They are also responsible for the conservation of protected plant, bird and animal species and the designation and maintenance of **Sites of Special Scientific Interest** (SSSI). These range in size from tiny patches set aside for an endangered plant or nesting site, to larger expanses of dunes, saltmarsh, woodland and heathland. These SSSIs are some of the best protected areas in Wales.

❑ **Statutory bodies**
● **Countryside Council for Wales** (☎ 08451-306229, 🖳 www.ccw.gov.uk), Maes-y-Ffynnon, Penrhosgarnedd, Bangor, Gwynedd, LL57 2DW. Government body responsible for conservation and landscape protection in Wales, including the maintenance of Wales's three national parks (see p43).
● **Pembrokeshire Coast National Park Authority** (☎ 01437-764636, 🖳 www.pembrokeshirecoast.org), Winch Lane, Haverfordwest, Pembrokeshire, SA61 1PY. Concerned with conserving and managing the national park.

❏ **National Trails**

The Pembrokeshire Coast Path is one of 15 National Trails in England and Wales. These are Britain's flagship long distance paths which grew out of the post-war desire to protect the country's special places, a movement which also gave birth to national parks and AONBs (see below).

National Trails in Wales are designated and largely funded by the Countryside Council for Wales and are managed on the ground by a National Trail Officer. They co-ordinate the maintenance work undertaken by the local highway authority and landowners to ensure that the trail is kept to nationally agreed standards.

Pembrokeshire is not just about the national park. Outside its boundaries the Countryside Council has an array of designations for land of special interest. **Areas of Outstanding Natural Beauty** (AONBs) gives some protection to land, though less than that enjoyed by national parks. In addition, 500km of the Welsh coast, much of it in Pembrokeshire, has been defined as **Heritage Coast**.

These designations aim to give protection from modern development and to maintain the countryside in its present state. An effective plan until the government decides a new road or housing estate needs to be built, ignoring their own legislation. The Countryside Council play an important role in conservation in Wales but at times it seems that the rules of protection are only effective when they do not interfere with more 'important' matters.

The Countryside Council oversees the Pembrokeshire Coast National Park Authority whose wardens and conservation officers work with landowners, encouraging traditional farming and land-use techniques. The aim is to safeguard the local environment, the very features that make the landscape of Pembrokeshire what it is. The stone walls and cliff-top heathland can only survive through careful grazing methods.

They are also responsible for the active protection of endemic species and habitats, as well as geological features, within the national park. If necessary this may involve access restrictions and designating specific areas as Sites of Special Scientific Interest. However, promoting public access and appreciation of Pembrokeshire's natural heritage is also of importance, as is educating locals and visitors about the significance of the local environment.

There is no doubt that the Countryside Council plays a vital role in safeguarding Pembrokeshire for future generations. However, the very fact that we rely on national parks and other such designations for protecting limited areas begs the question: what are we doing to the vast majority of land that remains relatively unprotected? Surely we should be aiming to protect the natural environment outside national parks just as much as within them.

VOLUNTARY ORGANIZATIONS

The Royal Society for the Protection of Birds (RSPB) was the pioneer of voluntary conservation bodies. It began over a hundred years ago when concern

❑ **Sustainability websites**
For lovers of the natural world who have ever asked 'but what can I do', the following websites are a good place to start.
● *The Ecologist Magazine* (💻 www.theecologist.org) Britain's longest-running environmental magazine.
● **Friends of the Earth** (💻 www.foe.co.uk) International network of environmental groups campaigning for a better environment.
● **Greenpeace** (💻 www.greenpeace.org) International organization promoting peaceful activism in defence of the environment.
● **International Society for Ecology and Culture** (💻 www.isec.org.uk) Promoting locally-based alternatives to globalization to protect biological/cultural diversity.
● **Permaculture Magazine** (💻 www.permaculture.co.uk) Explains the principles and practice of sustainable living.
● **Resurgence Magazine** (💻 www.gn.apc.org/resurgence) 'The flagship of the green movement'.

was raised about the use of feathers in ladies' hats. Since then voluntary conservation and environmental organizations have flourished both on a local and global scale. They play a vital role in education, conservation and campaigning and many of the local organizations in Wales are also some of the most significant landowners in the national park. The **RSPB** manage a number of nature reserves including the islands of Ramsey and Grassholm, as does the **Wildlife Trust West Wales** who manage Skokholm Island and Skomer Island on behalf of the Countryside Council for Wales. The **National Trust** meanwhile, owns many stretches of the mainland coast.

The large lobbying groups such as **Friends of the Earth** and the **World Wide Fund for Nature** have an important influence over government environmental policy but also appreciate the importance of local environmental issues.

BEYOND CONSERVATION

Pressures on the countryside grow year on year. Western society, whether directly or indirectly, makes constant demands for more oil, more roads, more houses, more cars. At the same time awareness of environmental issues increases and the knowledge that our unsustainable approach to life cannot continue. Some governments appear more willing to adopt sustainable ideals, others less so.

Yet even the most environmentally positive of governments are some way off perfect. It's all very positive to classify parts of the countryside as national parks and Areas of Outstanding Natural Beauty but it will be of little use if we continue to pollute the wider environment; the seas and skies. For a brighter future we need to adopt that sustainable approach to life. It would not be difficult and the rewards would be great.

The individual can play his or her part. Walkers in particular appreciate the value of wild areas and should take this attitude back home with them. This is

❏ **Conservation organizations**

● **Campaign for the Protection of Rural Wales** (☎ 01938-552525, 🖥 www. cprw.org.uk) Ty Gwyn, 31 High St, Welshpool, Powys, SY21 7YD. Organization campaigning over a number of local issues from sustainable development to conservation of landscape, historic sites and local traditions.

● **Friends of the Pembrokeshire National Park** (🖥 www.home.freeuk.com/fpnp) PO Box 218, Haverfordwest, Pembrokeshire, SA61 1WR. Conservation charity dedicated to protecting, conserving and enhancing the national park.

● **Marine Conservation Society** (☎ 01989-566017, 🖥 www.mcsuk.org.uk) 9 Gloucester Road, Ross-on-Wye, Herefordshire, HR9 5BU. Aims to protect Britain's marine environment and its wildlife and promote global marine conservation. Lots of voluntary projects such as beach cleans and species surveys.

● **National Trust** (☎ 01558-822800, 🖥 www.nationaltrust.org.uk) The King's Head, Bridge St, Llandeilo, Dyfed, SA19 6BB. Conservation charity that owns and protects countryside and historic buildings.

● **Royal Society for the Protection of Birds (RSPB)** (☎ 01767-680551, 🖥 www. rspb.org.uk) The Lodge, Sandy, Bedfordshire, SG19 2DL. The largest voluntary conservation body in Europe.

● **Wildlife Trust West Wales** (☎ 01437-765462, 🖥 www.wildlife-wales.org.uk) 7 Market St, Haverfordwest, Pembrokeshire, SA61 1NF. Actively promotes and protects the area's wildlife. Organizes marine and coastal wildlife watching events.

● **Woodland Trust** (☎ 01476-581111, 🖥 www.woodland-trust.org.uk) Autumn Park, Dysart Rd, Grantham, Lincs, NG31 6LL. Restores woodland throughout Britain for its amenity, wildlife and landscape value.

● **World Wide Fund for Nature (WWF)** (☎ 01483-426444, 🖥 www.panda.org) Panda House, Weyside Park, Godalming, Surrey, GU7 1XR. One of the world's largest conservation organizations.

not just about recycling the odd green bottle or two and walking to the corner shop rather than driving, but about lobbying for more environmentally-sensitive policies in local and national government.

The first step to a sustainable way of living is in appreciating and respecting this beautiful complex world we live in and realizing that every one of us plays an important role within the great web. The natural world is not a separate entity. We are all part of it and should strive to safeguard it rather than work against it. So many of us live in a world that does seem far removed from the real world, cocooned in centrally-heated houses and upholstered cars. Rediscovering our place within the natural world is both uplifting on a personal level and important regarding our outlook and approach to life.

Walkers are in a great position to appreciate this, yet some people still find it difficult to shake off the chaos of modern life even when they are in the countryside. When you are out on the coast path don't just look at the view. Slow down and use all your senses. Listen, smell and touch everything you see.

Flora and fauna

REPTILES

The only poisonous snake in Wales is the **adder** (*Vipera berus*) which can be identified by its dark colouring, the zigzagging down its back and a diamond shape on the back of its head. Common on heathland, it can be seen basking in the sun on rocks or on the path during warm spring and summer days. If you see one consider yourself lucky and don't frighten it. Despite their reputation adders are not as fearsome as you might think. Their venom is designed to kill small mammals, not humans and they only bite if provoked. However, in the unlikely event of a bite, stay still and send someone else to get medical attention. Deaths in humans are extremely rare but the bite is unpleasant and can be dangerous to children, the elderly and pets.

The **grass snake** (*Natrix natrix*) is an adept swimmer and is a much longer, slimmer snake with a yellow collar around the neck. It's non-venomous but does emit a foul stench should you attempt to pick one up. It's much better for you and the snake to leave them in peace.

The **common lizard** (*Lacerta vivipara*) is a harmless creature often seen basking in the sun on rocks and stone walls. However, you are more likely to hear them scuttling away through the undergrowth as you approach.

MAMMALS

The Pembrokeshire coast is a stronghold for marine mammals and no trip to the region is complete without spotting a **grey seal** (*Halichoerus grypus*). From late August to October the downy white pups can be seen in the breeding colonies hauled up on the rocks. The best places to spot them are around the Skomer Marine Nature Reserve and in Ramsey Sound and your chances of a sighting increase should you take a boat trip to one of the islands. Look out too for schools of **common porpoise** (*Phocoena phocoena*), a small slate-grey dolphin which can be seen breaking the surface as they head up Ramsey Sound, and the

---

❏ The Skomer vole

The island of Skomer is famous for its puffins and shearwaters but is also home to a diminutive character perhaps deserving of a little more attention. The Skomer vole (*Clethrionomys glaeolus skomerensis*) is a sub-species of the bank vole. An estimated 20,000 of the little rodents inhabit the island, playing an important role in the diet of the resident short-eared owls. Unique to the island, the Skomer vole is larger than its mainland cousin and is a perfect example of Darwin's evolutionary theory, evolving differing characteristics from its mainland cousin due to its geographic isolation.

bottle-nosed dolphin (*Tursiops truncatus*) which can be found in Cardigan Bay.

Further inland in the woodland and on the farmland, particularly around the Preseli Hills, are a number of common but shy mammals. One of the most difficult to see is the **badger** (*Meles meles*), a sociable animal with a distinctive black and white striped muzzle. Badgers live in family groups in large underground setts coming out to root for worms on the pastureland after sunset. Unfortunately the most common way of seeing them is as a bloody mess on the road: they are one of the most frequent animal road casualties.

The much maligned **fox** (*Vulpes vulpes*) inhabits similar country to the badger. Despite relentless persecution it is a born survivor, even having adapted to life in cities where they are quite tolerant of human presence. In Pembrokeshire the fox is far more wary and any sightings are likely to be brief. Keep an eye out for one crossing fields or even scavenging on the beach. They are not exclusively nocturnal. In fact where they are least disturbed they are more likely to be active during the day.

The cliff tops are home to the **rabbit** (*Oryctolagus cuniculus*) where their warrens can prove to be quite a safety hazard to the careless walker. They come out both during the day and at night.

The **otter** (*Lutra lutra*) is a rare native species which is slowly increasing in numbers thanks to long-running conservation efforts. It's at home both in salt and fresh water, although here in Pembrokeshire they are more likely to inhabit rivers and lakes. The otter is a good indicator of a healthy unpolluted environment and it's encouraging to see their numbers increasing not only in Wales but across the British Isles. A good place to see an otter is at the Bosherston lily ponds, where a walk at dawn or dusk may reward the patient and quiet watcher with a sighting.

If you are serious about otter watching take binoculars and choose a good vantage point above the lake, making sure the wind is blowing into your face. A calm evening or morning is best as it is easier to spot the wake of a swimming otter on a still lake surface rather then a choppy one.

In the woodlands you may be lucky enough to spot the native **red squirrel** (*Sciurus vulgaris*). Persecuted to extinction in other parts of the British Isles, here in west Wales they are making a comeback thanks in part to the efforts of local conservationists. In some parts of Wales grey squirrels, which are seen to be one of the main causes of the reds' decline, have been trapped. The effect has been a marked increase in red numbers. No one is entirely sure why reds suffer in the presence of greys but it seems clear that the red revival accelerates when greys are removed. Particularly good places to see reds are in the wooded sections on the south coast such as Rhode Wood north of Tenby and in the forested Cwm Gwaun valley in the Preseli Hills.

The **grey squirrel** (*Sciurus carolinensis*) on the other hand was introduced from North America at the turn of the century. Its outstanding success in colonizing Britain is very much to the detriment of other native species including songbirds and, most famously, the aforementioned red squirrel. Greys are bigger and stockier than reds and to many people the reds, with their tufted ears, bushy tails and small beady eyes are the far more attractive of the two.

The **roe deer** (*Capreolus capreolus*) is a small native species of deer that tends to hide in woodland. They can sometimes be seen alone or in pairs on field edges or clearings in the forest but you are more likely to hear its sharp dog-like bark when it smells you coming. On Ramsey Island there is a famous herd of **red deer** (*Cervus elaphus*), the largest land mammal in Britain. They have adapted successfully to open country due to the loss of their natural habitat of deciduous woodland and can be spotted quite easily on Ramsey's windswept slopes.

At dusk **bats** can be seen hunting for moths and flying insects along hedgerows, over rivers and around street lamps. Bats have had a bad press thanks to Dracula and countless other horror stories but anyone who has seen one up close knows them to be harmless and delightful little creatures. As for their blood-sucking fame, the matchbox-sized species of Britain would not even be able to break your skin with their teeth let alone suck your blood. Their reputation is improving all the time thanks to the work of the many bat conservation groups around the country and all fourteen species in Britain are protected by law. The commonest species in Britain, and likewise in Pembrokeshire, is the **pipistrelle** (*Pipistrellus pipistrellus*).

Some other small but fairly common species which can be found in the scrubland and grassland on the cliff tops include the carnivorous **stoat** (*Mustela erminea*), its smaller cousin the **weasel** (*Mustela nivalis*), the **hedgehog** (*Erinaceus europaeus*) and a number of species of **voles**, **mice** and **shrews**.

BIRDS

Without doubt Pembrokeshire is a hot spot for ornithologists. The cliffs, and more especially the islands, are important breeding grounds for a number of species such as the razorbill which has been adopted as the symbol of the national park authority. Away from the rolling waves other species, adapted to completely different habitats, can be spotted in the woodland, farmland and heathland that covers the cliff tops and valleys.

Islands and cliffs

The islands of Skomer and Skokholm are home to the **manx shearwater** (*Puffinus puffinus*) which lives in huge colonies of thousands, breeding in burrows along the cliff top. They can be identified by their dark upperside and paler underside with slender pointed wings and a fast swerving flight across the surface of the sea. Boat trips at dusk can be taken to watch the spectacular displays as the birds leave their burrows to look for food (see p132).

Grassholm Island is one of the world's most important breeding sites for the **gannet** (*Morus bassanus*), a large bird with a wing span of 175cm. They are easily identified by their size and white plumage, with a yellow head and black wing tips. In winter they spend most of their time over the open sea, returning in summer to breed in huge colonies on offshore rocky outcrops such as Grassholm. They catch fish by folding their wings back and diving spectacularly into the water.

❏ The *Sea Empress* disaster and other threats

Ever since the 1960s the oil industry has sat rather uncomfortably on the edge of the national park. A number of small oil spills raised concerns about the potential for a greater accident and on the night of 15 February 1996 those fears were realized. The *Sea Empress* oil tanker ran aground on rocks in the mouth of the Milford Haven estuary near West Angle Bay and began to spill its load. Attempts to refloat the tanker simply caused more damage to the hull releasing more oil into the sea. She was finally towed into Milford Haven six days later but by then the damage had been done.

The consequences were far reaching. Oil was washed up on beaches as far away as Lundy Island in the Bristol Channel and the southern coast of Ireland. The worst damage was in the immediate vicinity of the accident along 200km of the Pembrokeshire coast. The principal victims were the seabirds. Over 7000 dead or dying birds were recovered, with the actual total of affected birds estimated at ten times that number, making this one of the worst-ever bird kills due to oil in Europe.

The greatest victims were the common scoter and guillemot. An estimated 4700 and 1100 of these species were killed respectively along with cormorants, razorbills and even the rare red-throated diver. In total 25 species of seabird were hit. The birds were affected in a number of ways from direct contact with the oil to contaminated food supply; the invertebrate populations in the sand of the beaches were decimated and the oiled invertebrates that remained were eaten by the birds.

Volunteers worked hard to clean the oiled birds as well as the sandy beaches and rocks and after two months there was no visible sign of oil on the shoreline. However, during the storms of the following autumn oil reformed on the surface of the sea and once again washed up on the beaches and rocks.

The birds were not the only victims. Local fishing communities suffered greatly as a result of depleted fish stocks and the tourism industry also suffered. Although many of the beaches were relatively clean by the summer many tourists had already decided to go elsewhere having seen the news pictures. The money-hungry oil industry should feel responsible for this damage to both the local environment and the local economy due to its reluctance to pay for improved accident prevention measures.

It is hard to gauge the long-term effects of the disaster but there is no doubt that seabird populations have been reduced. This of course has implications for the whole food chain; if you alter one part of the chain it has a knock-on effect for other species eventually affecting local economies. Yet more worryingly is the potential for it all to happen again.

Since this disaster oil tankers have continued to enter Milford Haven harbour and the accident contingency plans have not been changed. The threat of a repeat incident always looms over the beaches of Pembrokeshire. Indeed new threats emerged, quite incredibly, just a few months after the *Sea Empress* incident. In 1997 there were proposals for oil and gas exploration off the Pembrokeshire coast. The consequences of this would be brightly-lit oil rigs decorating the view from the national park's cliff tops, seismic tremors from the drilling that would disturb marine and terrestrial life and emissions of toxic waste. Thankfully nothing has come of this frightening proposal.

Around the same time the Milford Haven Port Authority put forward another proposal to burn orimulsion imported from Venezuela at Pembroke Power Station. This controversial and dirty chemical releases a toxic dust when burnt that is purported to have gender bending potential.   (*continued overleaf*).

❏ The *Sea Empress* disaster and other threats

(*Continued from p57*) Unsurprisingly the local population and Friends of the Earth asked for an inquiry. Thankfully common sense seems to have prevailed over the clamour for more money and the issue has, for the time being, gone quiet.

It seems incredible that a national park can sit in the shadow of oil refineries and a power station which operate to the detriment of the local environment and the health of local inhabitants. National park status is supposed to afford protection from such damaging influences and yet here is an example of conflicting policies. We have to ask ourselves if the pursuit of money is really more important than our health and the health of the world around us.

Puffin

There are three species of auk in Pembrokeshire, the most famous and popular of which has to be the **puffin** (*Fratercula arctica*) with its lavishly-coloured square bill. Like the manx shearwater, puffins breed in burrows or under boulders. They can often be seen with a bill full of fish on their way back to their burrows. Skomer Island is Puffin Central but remember that they come to the island only during the breeding season (April to early August), spending the winter out at sea. You are far less likely to spot a puffin on the mainland.

The **razorbill** (*Alca torda*) is another auk that breeds on the cliff tops. It is black with a white belly and has a distinctive white stripe across the bill to the eye.

Similar in appearance to the razorbill but with a much more slender bill is the **guillemot** (*Uria aalge*). It stands more upright than the razorbill and is less stocky. They nest in huge colonies on cliff-face ledges and are often seen in small groups flying close over the surface of the sea with very fast wing beats.

The **storm petrel** (*Hydrobates pelagicus*) spends most of the time over the open sea. It has an erratic flight pattern often just skimming the surface. It can be identified by the square tail, white rump and a white band on the underside of the wings which contrasts with the dark body. They also have strange tube-like nasal implements on a hooked beak.

Looking something like a medium-sized gull, the **fulmar** (*Fulmarus glacialis*) can also be seen far out to sea but nests on ledges on the cliff face. They vary in appearance from a buff grey to white and can be distinguished from gulls by their gliding flight pattern and occasional, slow, stiff wing beats.

The **cormorant** (*Phalacrocorax carbo*) is a prehistoric-looking bird. It can often be seen perched on rocks, its wings outstretched. Unlike other birds their feathers are not oily and water resistant so this is the only way of drying out. Dark in appearance, often with a white patch around the stocky bill, it swims with an outstretched neck and frequently dives underwater with a little jump as it bobs on the surface. It is commonly seen in estuaries and on more sheltered stretches of water. From the same family as the cormorant is the **shag** (*Phalacrocorax aristotelis*).

The **kittiwake** (*Rissa tridactyla*) spends the winter out at sea where large flocks follow the fishing boats. In the summer they breed in large colonies on the coastal cliffs. It is a small gull with a short yellow bill and short black legs. It has a white plumage except for the light grey wings with black tips. The tail is distinctively square when in flight.

The **common tern** (*Sterna hirundo*) is gull-like but smaller. It is generally white but with grey wings and a black crown. The short legs are red as is the short, pointed bill which usually has a black tip.

The **chough** (*Pyrrhocorax pyrrhocorax*), pronounced 'chuff', is one of the more attractive members of the crow family; slender and elegant in appearance with a deep red curved and pointed bill and legs of the same colour. Choughs are often found in mountainous areas, but in Pembrokeshire they breed on the coast where they can be seen flying acrobatically around the cliffs.

The **peregrine falcon** (*Falco peregrinus*) is a beautiful raptor that can be found nesting on some of the sea cliffs. It is a lean and efficient hunter with slate grey plumage and a white underside with thin black barring. It kills its prey with a spectacular dive known as stooping, in which the bird closes its wings and plummeting from the sky like a small missile, stunning its prey on impact. It's a fantastic sight.

Of the numerous gulls the most common include the **herring gull** (*Larus argentatus*), a large white gull with grey wings tipped with black, a bright yellow bill with a red spot at the end and yellow eyes. It is not a shy bird and can often be seen around harbours where it is something of a scavenger.

Cormorant

It's not difficult to tell cormorants and shags apart. The **cormorant** is larger than the shag and has a bigger bill and head. In the breeding season the cormorant has a white patch on its flank. The **shag** is slimmer, has a more uniform dark plumage with a green glossy sheen. It also has a more slender bill and a pronounced tuft on the top of the head. Shags are often seen in flocks on the coast or out to sea, whereas cormorants are usually found in river estuaries and in pairs or alone except when in nesting colonies.

Shag

Some other gulls which you may spot include the **great black-backed gull** (*Larus marinus*) similar to the herring gull but with black wings and the **lesser black-backed gull** (*Larus fuscus*) which is, not surprisingly, smaller.

Herring gull

The **black-headed gull** (*Larus ridibundus*) spends a lot of time feeding in large flocks on farmland close to the coast. It is a slender gull with a distinctive black head and black wing tips.

Great black-backed gull

The **Herring gull** (above) is the most frequently-seen member of the gull family. It has pink legs and feet and a grey upper body. Largest of the gulls is the **great black-backed gull** (left) which has, as the name implies, a black back. It also has pink legs and feet which distinguish it from the **lesser black-backed gull**, which has yellow legs.

Beaches and mudflats

A distinctive bird that can often be seen running along the shingle and sandy beaches is the **ringed plover** (*Charadrius hiaticula*). This stocky little bird the size of a thrush has a white belly and brown upper-parts with a pair of characteristic black bands across the face and throat. The legs and bill are both orange.

Similar in size is the **common sandpiper** (*Actitis hypoleucos*) a small bird that can be found on rocky shores. It has white under-parts with a light brown breast and upper-parts. White bars can be seen on the wings when it is in flight.

Also to be found on the beach and often feeding on inland fields is the **oystercatcher** (*Haematopus ostralegus*). It is quite common and easily identified by the distinctive black upper-parts and white belly. It has a sharp stabbing orange bill used for probing the ground when feeding and a distinctive shrill call.

The **lapwing** (*Vanellus vanellus*) with its long legs, short bill and distinctive long head crest also feeds on arable farmland. Sadly, this attractive bird is declining in numbers. The name comes from its lilting flight, frequently changing direction with its large rounded wings. It is also identified by a white belly, black and white head, black throat patch and distinctive dark green wings.

Inhabiting the sand dunes, moors and bogs is the **curlew** (*Numenius arquata*) a brown mottled bird with a very long slender bill which curves downwards at the end. It has an evocative far-reaching call that reflects its name; 'Kooor-lee'. In the winter it groups together in large flocks on open ground such as fields and mudflats.

Scrubland and grassland

On open ground you may be lucky enough to see the **short-eared owl** (*Asio flammeus*) which, unlike other owls, often hunts during the day. Skomer is a good place to look out for it. It is quite large with fairly uniform dark streaks and bars over an otherwise golden brown plumage. The pale face is a typical round owl's face with golden eyes ringed by black eye patches.

A more common sight is the **stonechat** (*Saxicola torquata*), a colourful little bird with a deep orange breast and a black head. Its name comes from its call which sounds like the chink of two stones being knocked together. During the summer months you will see it along the coast path flitting from the top of one gorse bush to another.

The **yellowhammer** (*Emberiza citrinella*), a bunting, is not seen quite so much as the stonechat though it has the same habit of singing atop gorse bushes. It has a distinctive call said to sound like 'a little bit of bread and no cheese' according to those with vivid imaginations, although it's certainly no mynah bird.

Less striking in appearance is the **meadow pipit** (*Anthus pratensis*), a rather drab looking small brown bird. It can be identified by white flashes on the edge of its tail as it flies away. Another small brown bird spotted above grassland is the **skylark** (*Alauda arvensis*). It has a distinctive flight pattern rising directly upwards ever higher singing constantly as it goes. It climbs so high that the relentless twittering can be heard while the bird is nowhere to be seen.

Woodland

The **raven** (*Corvus corax*) is so big that it is often mistaken for a buzzard. They have lifelong breeding partners and nest on rocky ledges along the coast and further inland high in the tree tops. In St David's there is a rookery in Cross Square. The raven has all-black plumage, a thick stocky bill and a deep guttural croaking call.

A common raptor that is often heard before being seen is the **buzzard** (*Buteo buteo*), a large broad-winged bird of prey which looks much like a small eagle. It is dark brown in appearance and slightly paler on the underside of the wings. It has a distinctive mewing call and can be spotted soaring ever higher on the air thermals, or sometimes perched on the top of telegraph poles.

Much smaller than the buzzard is the **kestrel** (*Falco tinnunculus*) a small falcon and the most commonly seen bird of prey. It hovers expertly in a fixed spot, even in the strongest of winds, above grassland and road side-verges hunting for mice and voles.

TREES

Before man and his axe got to work there were forests covering 80% of what is now the national park. Sadly this woodland cover has dropped to just 6%, some of which is coniferous plantation. From an ecological perspective the most important forest cover is the ancient semi-natural woodland which covers a mere 1% of the national park area. Twenty of these ancient broadleaved woodlands are designated sites of special scientific interest (SSSI).

Ash (with seeds)

On the Pembrokeshire Coast Path most of the woodland is encountered along the southern section from Amroth to Tenby and on the southern side of the Milford Haven estuary. The windswept northern stretches are more barren although many of the small valleys are wooded. Another good place to find ancient broadleaved woodland is the Cwm Gwaun valley in the Preseli Hills. Look out for lichen on the tree trunks as this is a classic indicator of clean air. Over 300 species of lichen can be found in many of the forests.

Alder (with flowers)

None of the woodland in Pembrokeshire can be described as completely natural as it has all been managed or altered in some way by man. In the past rural communities coppiced the trees and used the wood from hazel for fencing and thatching. Evidence of charcoal burning is also present and oak was grown along sheltered bays and estuaries to provide wood for shipbuilding.

These practices began to die out at the end of the 19th century when cheap coal began to replace coppiced wood and charcoal as fuel. However, there has been a small revival in recent years by aficionados of traditional countryside ways and conservationists who recognize the benefits of coppicing for a number of species, including the endangered dormouse.

Hazel (with flowers)

In Pembrokeshire coppicing can be seen in several places and is a method of woodland management that has been used by the National Park Authority itself.

Predominant tree species

The dominant species in semi-natural broadleaved woodland is the **sessile oak** (*Quercus petraea*) with good examples around the Daugleddau estuary. The sessile oak differs from the English common oak in a number of ways; most notably in having brighter more shapely leaves. The name 'sessile' means 'without stalks' referring to the acorns which grow directly from thin branches. Oak woodland is a diverse habitat and is also home to **downy birch** (*Betula pubescens*), **holly** (*Ilex aquifolium*) and **hazel** (*Corylus avellana*) which has traditionally been used for coppicing.

The **common ash** (*Fraxinus excelsior*) is well adapted to cope with the salt-laden sea winds and can be found on the limestone rich soils in the south of the county, around the Bosherston lily ponds for example. The **common alder** (*Alnus glutinosa*) is often found alone growing by streams.

Perhaps surprisingly the mighty **beech** (*Fagus sylvatica*) is not native to this part of the country but has established itself wherever there is well-drained soil and is surely one of the most beautiful of the broadleaved trees. Other species to look out for include the **aspen** (*Populus tremula*), **hawthorn** (*Crataegus monogyna*) and **rowan** or mountain ash (*Sorbus aucuparia*) with its slender leaves and red berries.

FLOWERS

The coast path is renowned for its wild flowers. Spring is the time to come and see the spectacular displays of colour on the cliff tops while in late summer the heather on the northern slopes turns a vibrant purple.

The coast and cliff-top meadows

The coastline is a harsh environment subjected to strong winds, wind-blown salt and tides. Plants that colonize this niche are hardy and well adapted to the conditions. Many of the cliff-top species such as the pink flowering **thrift** (*Armeria maritima*) and white **sea campion** (*Silene maritima*) turn the cliff tops into a blaze of colour from May to September.

On shingle beaches and dunes you might see the **yellow-horned poppy** (*Glaucium flavum*), but don't think about eating it, it's poisonous. On the cliff top and track sides you might encounter the straggly stems of **fennel** (*Foeniculum vulgare*), a member of the carrot family which grows to over a metre high.

Other plants to look for are **spring squill** (*Scilla verna*) and **scurvygrass** (*Cochlearia officilanis*) and in saltmarshes and estuaries **sea-lavender** (*Limonium vulgare*) and **sea aster** (*Aster tripolium*).

Woodland and hedgerows

The **wood anemone** (*Anemone nemorosa*), the **bluebell** (*Hyacinthoides non-scripta*) and the yellow **primrose** (*Primula vulgaris*) flower early in spring, with the bluebell and wood anemone covering woodland floors in a carpet of white and blue. The bluebell and primrose are also common on open cliff tops. **Red campion** (*Silene dioica*), which flowers from late April, can be found in hedgebanks along with **rosebay willowherb** (*Epilobium augustifolium*) which also has the name fireweed owing to its habit of colonizing burnt areas.

In scrubland and on woodland edges you will find **bramble** (*Rubus fruticosus*), a common vigorous shrub, responsible for many a ripped jacket thanks to the sharp thorns and prickles. The blackberry fruits ripen from late summer to autumn. Fairly common in scrubland and on woodland edges is the **dog rose** (*Rosa canina*) which has a large pink flower, the fruits of which are used to make rose-hip syrup.

Other flowering plants to look for in wooded areas and in hedgerows include the tall **foxglove** (*Digitalis purpurea*) with its trumpet-like flowers, **forget-me-not** (*Myosotis arvensis*) with tiny, delicate blue flowers and **cow parsley** (*Anthriscus sylvestris*), a tall member of the carrot family with a large globe of white flowers which often covers roadside verges and hedgebanks.

Heathland and scrubland

Some of the cliff tops, particularly in the north of the region, are carpeted in heather resulting in a spectacular purple display when it comes into flower in late summer. Heathland is an important habitat for butterflies, snakes and lizards. There are good examples of it on the west side of the Dale peninsula, east of Marloes Sands, on the high slopes north of Newport Sands and most notably on the St David's peninsula.

There are three species of heather. The dominant one is **ling** (*Calluna vulgaris*) which has tiny flowers on delicate upright stems. The other two species are **bell heather** (*Erica cinera*) with deep purple bell-shaped flowers and **cross-leaved heath** (*Erica tetralix*) with similarly shaped flowers of a lighter pink, almost white colour. Cross-leaved heath prefers wet and boggy ground. As a consequence, it usually grows away from bell heather which prefers well-drained soils.

Heathland is also the stronghold of **gorse** (*Ulex europeous*), a dark green bush of sharp thorns with spectacular displays of yellow flowers from February through to June. Not a flower but worthy of mention is the less attractive species **bracken** (*Pteridium aquilinum*), a vigorous non-native fern that has invaded many heathland areas to the detriment of native species.

In more overgrown areas where the heath has reverted to scrubland you invariably find **broom** (*Cytisus scoparius*), a big bushy plant with dark green stalk-like leaves and bright yellow flowers. As its name suggests it looks like a big upturned broom and was indeed used for this purpose. It was also believed to have magical powers and was used as a diuretic. On hot days you can hear the seed pods cracking open, spreading the seeds about.

Foxglove
Digitalis purpurea

Thrift (Sea Pink)
Armeria maritima

Sea Campion
Silene maritima

Common Vetch
Vicia sativa

Bell Heather
Erica cinerea

Heather (Ling)
Calluna vulgaris

Yarrow
Achillea millefolium

Rosebay Willowherb
Chamerion angustifolium

Rowan tree
Sorbus aucuparia

Primrose
Primula vulgaris

Common Ragwort
Senecio jacobaea

Gorse
Ulex europaeus

Birdsfoot-trefoil
Lotus corniculatus

Evening Primrose
Oenothera erythrosepala

Ox-eye Daisy
Leucanthemum vulgare

Tormentil
Potentilla erecta

Scarlet Pimpernel
Anagallis arvensis

Meadow Buttercup
Ranunculis acris

Cornflower
Centaurea cyanus

Common Knapweed
Centaurea nigra

Red Campion
Silene dioica

Germander Speedwell
Veronica chamaedrys

Herb-Robert
Geranium robertianum

Lousewort
Pedicularis sylvatica

Violet
Viola riviniana

Common Fumitory
Fumaria officinalis

Meadow Cranesbill
Geranium pratense

Using this guide

The trail guide and maps have not been divided into rigid daily stages since people walk at different speeds and have different interests. The **route summaries** below describe the trail between significant places and are written as if walking the path from south to north. To enable you to plan your own itinerary **practical information** is presented clearly on the trail maps. This includes walking times for both directions, all places to stay, camp and eat, as well as shops where you can buy supplies. Further service details are given in the text under the entry for each settlement. For an overview of this information see Itineraries, pp21-7.

TRAIL MAPS

Scale and walking times
The trail maps are to a scale of 1:20,000 (1cm = 200m; $3^1/_8$ inches = one mile). Walking times are given along the side of each map and the arrow shows the direction to which the time refers. Black triangles indicate the points between which the times have been taken. **See note below on walking times**.

The time-bars are a tool and are not there to judge your walking ability. There are so many variables that affect walking speed, from the weather conditions to how many beers you drank the previous evening. After the first hour or two of walking you will be able to see how your speed relates to the timings on the maps.

Up or down?
The trail is shown as a dotted line. An arrow across the trail indicates the slope; two arrows show that it is steep. Note that the arrow points towards the higher part of the trail. If, for example, you are walking from A (at 80m) to B (at 200m) and the trail between the two is short and steep it would be shown thus: A— — — >> — — – B. Reversed arrow heads indicate downward gradient.

Accommodation
Apart from in large towns where some selection of places has been necessary, almost every place to stay that is within easy reach of the trail is marked. Details

> ❏ **Important note – walking times**
> Unless otherwise specified, **all times in this book refer only to the time spent walking**. You will need to add 20-30% to allow for rests, photography, checking the map, drinking water etc. When planning the day's hike count on 5-7 hours actual walking.

(Opposite) **Top**: Penllechwen Cliffs (see p158). **Bottom**: Herring gull (l) and puffin (r).

of each place are given in the accompanying text. Unless otherwise specified **B&B prices are summer high-season prices per person** assuming two people sharing a room with a separate bathroom. The number and type of rooms are given after each entry: S = single room, T = twin room, D = double room, F = family room (sleeps at least three people).

Other features

Features are marked on the map when pertinent to navigation. In order to avoid cluttering the maps and making them unusable not all features have been marked each time they occur.

The route guide

KILGETTY (CILGETI)   MAP 1

If you are coming by train or coach Kilgetty is the closest stop to the start of the coast path at Amroth three miles (5km) away. Kilgetty is pleasant enough but there is not much to keep you here so it would be best to head straight to the start of the trail proper.

Services

Everything of importance can be found by turning left out of the train station and walking down the main street.

The **tourist information centre** (☎ 01834-814161, 10am–5pm) is the last building on the left hand side, past the Co-op **supermarket**, which is a good place to get some last minute supplies, as is the smaller **Bridge Stores** which is where the name suggests it is. There is also a **cash machine** at the Co-op and a **post office** just before it. There is no bank at the next port of call, Amroth. If you are already worried about blisters you should head for the chemist near The White Horse.

The **bus stop** for the National Express coach is outside the tourist information centre at the far western end of the village. Bear in mind that the **train station** is a request stop so you will have to let the driver know before you get on otherwise you will end up in Tenby, missing the first seven miles (11km) and that's just cheating.

Alternatively, if you have come by car or have a return bus or train ticket from Kilgetty, you could make your way to Cardigan and do the entire coast path in reverse so that you end up back at your departure point at the end of the walk. There is an infrequent **bus** service from Kilgetty to Cardigan (see public transport map p37).

Where to stay

There are not many places to stay in Kilgetty but if you do decide to spend the first night here rather than at Amroth you could try *Pleasant View* (☎ 01834-814040, 🖳 redford@btinternet.com, Apr–Oct, 8D) with en-suite rooms from £21 per person. You'll find it up Ryelands Lane.

Campers should aim for *Ryelands Park Campsite* (☎ 01834-812369, Apr–Oct) which can be found about half a mile up Ryelands Lane to the north of the village. Prices are £2 per camper. *Stone Pitt Campsite* (☎ 01834-811086, open all year) in Begelly charges £7.50 per tent. Unfortunately, it's in the wrong direction for the coast path lying on the main road towards Narberth.

Better located is *Mill House Caravan Park* (☎ 01834-812069, 🖳 www.millhous ecaravan.demon.co.uk, Mar–Oct) in Stepaside. It's geared more towards caravans and those big tents the size of bungalows

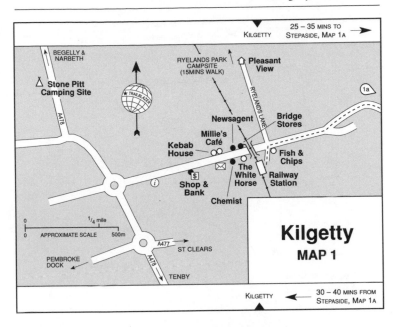

25 – 35 MINS TO
KILGETTY   STEPASIDE, MAP 1a →

BEGELLY & NARBETH

RYELANDS PARK CAMPSITE (15MINS WALK)

⌂ Pleasant View

Stone Pitt Camping Site

★ TRAILBLAZER

A478

RYELANDS LANE

Newsagent

Bridge Stores

1a

Millie's Café

Kebab House

The White Horse

Fish & Chips

Railway Station

Shop & Bank

Chemist

0   ¼ mile
0   APPROXIMATE SCALE   500m

Kilgetty
MAP 1

A477

ST CLEARS

PEMBROKE DOCK ←

A478

TENBY

30 – 40 MINS FROM
KILGETTY ← STEPASIDE, MAP 1a

but they should be able to squeeze in a smaller one. Prices are from £8.50 a pitch. Book well in advance in the summer. It is on the way towards the start of the coast path about a mile east of Kilgetty (see Map 1a).

Unfortunately the youth hostel in the nearby village of Pentlepoir has closed down. It may be worth checking with the YHA (see p11) to see if there are any plans to re-open it.

Where to eat

Next to the exit from the train station is a **fish and chip** shop and just down the road under the railway bridge is *Millie's* (8am–late) which has all-day breakfasts from £3.25 and sandwiches from £1.50.

Next door is the *Kebab House* with kebabs from £2.70 and fish and chips at £2.90. Unfortunately, the *White Horse* by the railway bridge doesn't do food but it's a good place for a tipple before the walk.

KILGETTY TO AMROTH   MAPS 1, 1a and 1b

These **three miles (5km, 1–1½hrs)** provide a pleasant walk to the coast and the start of the path at Amroth but if you are feeling lazy you can catch the bus which leaves opposite the post office (see public transport map p37). The bus drops you at the castle, which is now a holiday park, close to the start of the path at the New Inn.

If you want to limber up for the big trek ahead then you may as well walk to the start of the path by following the lane to **Stepaside**. Take care crossing the main road, the A477. Stepaside received its quirky name thanks, it is said,

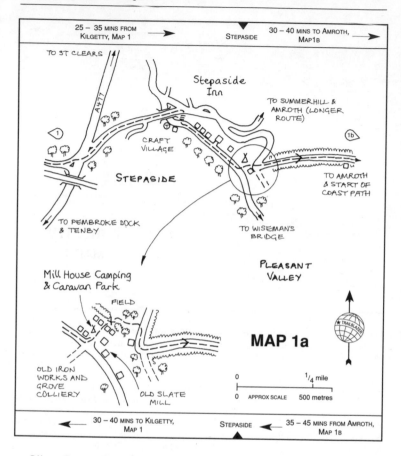

25 – 35 MINS FROM KILGETTY, MAP 1 →   ▼ STEPASIDE   30 – 40 MINS TO AMROTH, MAP 1B →

TO ST CLEARS

Stepaside Inn

TO SUMMERHILL & AMROTH (LONGER ROUTE)

A477

CRAFT VILLAGE

STEPASIDE

TO AMROTH & START OF COAST PATH

TO PEMBROKE DOCK & TENBY

TO WISEMAN'S BRIDGE

PLEASANT VALLEY

Mill House Camping & Caravan Park

FIELD

MAP 1a

TRAILBLAZER

OLD IRON WORKS AND GROVE COLLIERY

OLD SLATE MILL

0   1/4 mile
0   APPROX SCALE   500 metres

← 30 – 40 MINS TO KILGETTY, MAP 1   ▲ STEPASIDE   ← 35 – 45 MINS FROM AMROTH, MAP 1B

to Oliver Cromwell who in 1648, while marching to Pembroke, stopped here and told his men to step aside and take their victuals. At Stepaside you should join the little lane through Pleasant Valley to Mill House Caravan and Camping Site where you can see the old slate mill and the iron works, both dating from the mid-nineteenth century. A path takes you through the caravan site and then you join the lane through Summerhill to **Amroth**.

You are now on the coast path but unfortunately it begins at the northern end of the village, at the New Inn. If you want to say you have done the whole official path you will have to walk to the start and then come back again the way you have just come.

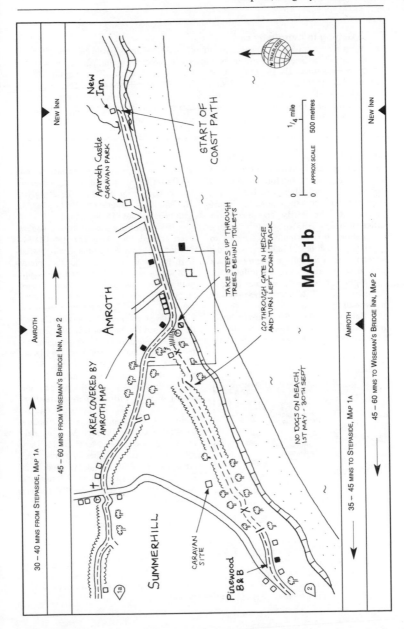

NEW INN

30 – 40 MINS FROM STEPASIDE, MAP 1A

45 – 60 MINS FROM WISEMAN'S BRIDGE INN, MAP 2

AMROTH

New Inn

START OF COAST PATH

Amroth Castle CARAVAN PARK

TAKE STEPS UP THROUGH TREES BEHIND TOILETS

GO THROUGH GATE IN HEDGE AND TURN LEFT DOWN TRACK

AMROTH

AREA COVERED BY AMROTH MAP

MAP 1b

¼ mile
500 metres
0
0
APPROX SCALE

NO DOGS ON BEACH, 1ST MAY – 30TH SEPT

SUMMERHILL

CARAVAN SITE

Pinewood B & B

18

2

NEW INN

AMROTH

45 – 60 MINS TO WISEMAN'S BRIDGE INN, MAP 2

35 – 45 MINS TO STEPASIDE, MAP 1A

❏ **Getting to Amroth by car**

If you are coming by car you need to turn off for Stepaside (opposite the turning for Kilgetty). The lane goes down to the village and then goes uphill. About half way up the hill turn right along a very narrow lane which leads to Summerhill. Go straight over at the crossroads and follow the road downhill to Amroth. The start of the path is at the far eastern end of the village at the New Inn but a better place to leave the car is in the free National Park Authority car park. It is just off the seafront road near Amroth Castle and is indicated by a blue 'P' sign.

AMROTH   MAP 1b

Amroth is stretched out along a single road facing a pretty beach with forested slopes at either end. It's not a big place but being a popular holiday spot there are a few eating places and some B&Bs. The small **post office** (☎ 01834-813310) is half way along the seafront. It is currently up for sale so check to see if it is still in business. At the southern end of the village where the coast path leaves the road there is a **toilet** block and a **phone box**. In the summer there is sometimes a small **shop** through a doorway in the wall by the castle.

Half way along the seafront road, *Beach Haven Guest House* (☎ 01834-813310, 2S/2T) at the post office has beds

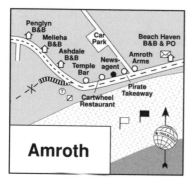

at £15 per night. There are also a few B&Bs on the steep road leading down to the village from Summerhill: *Penglyn*, *Melieha* and *Ashdale* (☎ 01834-813853) with beds around £15 per person.

If you feel like a break before you've even started, the *New Inn* (☎ 01834-812368, 12–2pm, 6–8pm) is ideally placed to distract you from the walk. It's a pretty spot with a garden by a stream at the beginning of the coast path. They have curries from £5.50 or for something less fiery try the soup, roll and cheese for £2.55. It's a good place for a pint but unfortunately they don't do bed and breakfast. On the seafront is the *Temple Bar Inn* with ploughman's for £4, while the *Amroth Arms* (☎ 01834-812480, 12–2pm, 6.30–9pm) has Welsh pork and local fish dishes from £4.95.

At the western end of the village is the award winning *Cartwheel Restaurant* (☎ 01834-812100, 🖳 rjsimpson@LineOne .com, 12– 3pm, 6pm–late) which displays the Pembrokeshire Produce Mark guaranteeing the food to be of local origin. They specialize in seafood dishes with prawn and crab salad for £8.95 and honeyroast duck at £11.95. After such a strenuous half mile it's worth treating yourself. It usually has live music on Saturdays.

For something cheaper try the *Pirate Restaurant and Takeaway*.

❏ **Prices and room types**

Where applicable the number and type of rooms are given after the address of each entry: S = single room, T = twin room (two beds), D = double room (one double bed), F = family room (sleeps at least three people).

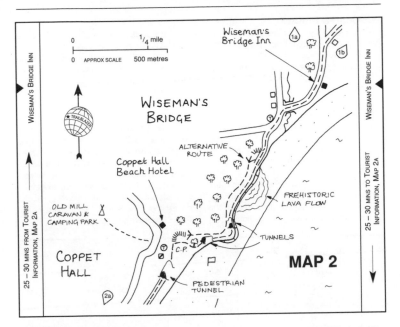

Wiseman's Bridge Inn

WISEMAN'S BRIDGE

ALTERNATIVE ROUTE

Coppet Hall Beach Hotel

OLD MILL CARAVAN & CAMPING PARK

COPPET HALL

PREHISTORIC LAVA FLOW

TUNNELS

MAP 2

C.P.

PEDESTRIAN TUNNEL

0   ¼ mile

0   APPROX SCALE   500 metres

★ TRAILBLAZER

AMROTH TO TENBY

MAPS 1–3, 3a

These first **seven miles (11km, 2½–3½hrs)** pass through beautiful and varied scenery, mixing cool cliff-top woodland with small sandy beaches and coves which can be spied through the trees. Don't underestimate this stretch. Although not as rugged as the coastline further north there is enough up and down to make this a tiring introduction especially if you have been slacking in the training!

The path leaves Amroth at its western end where some steps lead up through the trees taking you into a meadow above the cliffs and along a dirt track to the inn at **Wiseman's Bridge**. From here the main route follows the route of an old colliery railway passing through two old tunnels. The railway dates from 1834 when coal from the Stepaside colliery was transported by horse-drawn trams and later steam engines to Saundersfoot where it was shipped to the continent. As you walk this stretch look out for the fan-shaped rock formation on the beach which is an old lava flow dating from prehistoric times. An alternative path passes through shady woodland above the beach to Coppet Hall, where a third tunnel on the other side of the beach car park leads you into the lively seaside town of **Saundersfoot**.

In Rhode Wood south of Saundersfoot keep an eye out for red squirrels. At Monkstone Point you have the option of a ten-minute detour to the wooded headland. The final stretch takes you through more woodland and fields, eventually entering **Tenby** above the immaculate sands of North Beach.

WISEMAN'S BRIDGE   MAP 2

This is a great spot for a morning break, or lunch if you started from Kilgetty. The hamlet, which hugs a sandy bay, comprises a scattering of houses, a **phone box** and, most importantly, ***Wiseman's Bridge Inn*** (☎ 01834-813236, 1T/1D/1F) which has

beds at £20 per person. It's a good idea to book. They also do good food but are often very busy in the summer. Above the hamlet there is a B&B next to the path: ***Pinewood*** (☎ 01834-811082, Cliff Rd, 2D en suite). Prices start from £19.50.

SAUNDERSFOOT   MAP 2a

This is a typical small seaside town pleasantly free of any tackiness. In fact, despite the hustle and bustle, on a summer day Saundersfoot has a rather lazy, even carefree feel to it.

Somewhat overshadowed by the more famous seaside town of Tenby, many see Saundersfoot as a quieter alternative to the commotion of its southern neighbour.

Services

The **TIC** (☎ 01834-813672) is by the harbour in a small building by the car park. There is also a **newsagent**, a small Spar **supermarket** and **post office**, all of which are scattered around the car park by the harbour. If your feet are not suffering from blisters already there are remedies at the **chemist** on The Strand where you can also find a **bank** with a cashpoint.

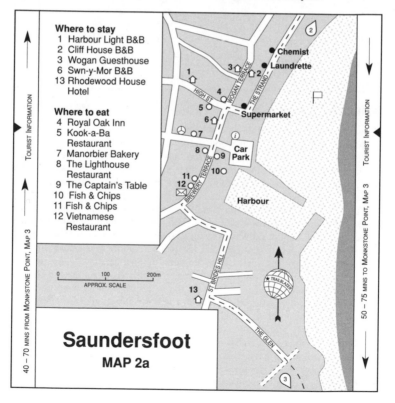

Where to stay
1 Harbour Light B&B
2 Cliff House B&B
3 Wogan Guesthouse
6 Swn-y-Mor B&B
13 Rhodewood House
   Hotel

Where to eat
4 Royal Oak Inn
5 Kook-a-Ba
   Restaurant
7 Manorbier Bakery
8 The Lighthouse
   Restaurant
9 The Captain's Table
10 Fish & Chips
11 Fish & Chips
12 Vietnamese
   Restaurant

Chemist
Laundrette
Supermarket
Car Park
Harbour

HIGH ST
WOGAN TERRACE
THE STRAND
BREWERY TERRACE
ST BRIDES HILL
THE GLEN

0   100   200m
APPROX. SCALE

Saundersfoot
MAP 2a

TOURIST INFORMATION

TOURIST INFORMATION

40 – 70 MINS FROM MONKSTONE POINT, MAP 3

50 – 75 MINS TO MONKSTONE POINT, MAP 3

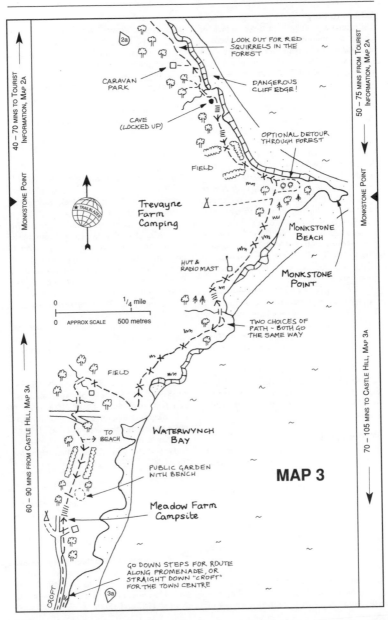

LOOK OUT FOR RED SQUIRRELS IN THE FOREST

CARAVAN PARK

DANGEROUS CLIFF EDGE!

CAVE (LOCKED UP)

OPTIONAL DETOUR THROUGH FOREST

FIELD

Trevayne Farm Camping

MONKSTONE BEACH

MONKSTONE POINT

HUT & RADIO MAST

TWO CHOICES OF PATH – BOTH GO THE SAME WAY

★ TRAILBLAZER

0   1/4 mile
0   APPROX SCALE   500 metres

FIELD

TO BEACH

WATERWYNCH BAY

PUBLIC GARDEN WITH BENCH

MAP 3

Meadow Farm Campsite

GO DOWN STEPS FOR ROUTE ALONG PROMENADE, OR STRAIGHT DOWN "CROFT" FOR THE TOWN CENTRE

CROFT

40 – 70 MINS TO TOURIST INFORMATION, MAP 2A

MONKSTONE POINT

60 – 90 MINS FROM CASTLE HILL, MAP 3A

50 – 75 MINS FROM TOURIST INFORMATION, MAP 2A

MONKSTONE POINT

70 – 105 MINS TO CASTLE HILL, MAP 3A

Where to stay

Unfortunately, there is a distinct lack of cheap accommodation although there is the *Old Mill Caravan and Camping Park* (☎ 01834-812657) which charges £4 per person. It is ten minutes from the coast path near Coppet Hall (see Map 2). There is another **campsite** a mile south of Saundersfoot at *Trevayne Farm* (☎ 01834-813402, Apr–Oct); pitches are £2 per person.

In contrast there are B&Bs aplenty. Before you reach the town, on the other side of the pedestrian tunnel is the *Coppet Hall Beach Hotel* (☎ 01834-814467, 7T/7S) with plenty of rooms at £20 per person.

In the town you could try *Cliff House* (☎ 01834-813931, 🖳 www.smoothhound. co.uk/hotels/cliffhse, Wogan Terrace, 5D) with five en-suite rooms from £25 for a single and £22 for a double. Close by, *Wogan Guest House* (☎ 01834-812473, 🖳 wogansf @talk21.com, Wogan Terrace, 7D) where a single bed will cost you £18. Some of the rooms are en suite.

The Harbour Light (☎ 01834-813496, 🖳 www.users.globalnet.co.uk/~hbrlight, 2 High St, 10D en suite) is a large guesthouse with beds from £23.50 and a £5 single person's supplement. *Rhodewood House Hotel* (☎ 01834-812200, 🖳 www.rhodewood.co. uk) on St Bride's Hill is another big place with 45 en-suite rooms. Prices range from £26 to £35 for a single. Opposite the harbour car park is *Swn-y-mor* (☎ 01834-813201, 10D en suite). A room here works out at £20 per person.

Where to eat

There is a plethora of eating dens here. A fantastic pub to look out for with friendly staff is the *Royal Oak Inn* (☎ 01834-812546, 12–2.30pm, 6–9.30pm) with steak and bacon pie for £7.50, or you can neck a pint of prawns for £4. For a more regular pint they have a selection of real ales including their own Royal Oak ale at £1.80. The cosy bar is a good place to unwind after a hard day.

The *Captain's Table* (☎ 01834-812 435, daily 12–2.30pm, 6.15–9pm) by the harbour does prawn stir-fry for £8.25 and barbecues in the summer.

On Brewery Terrace is the smart *Lighthouse Restaurant* (☎ 01834-811313, 12–2.30pm, 6–late, 7 days), with jacket potatoes from £3.95 and leek and mushroom crumble for £8.95.

Also on Brewery Terrace there is *The Sao Mai Dragon*, a good Vietnamese restaurant (5pm–12am) which is useful if you arrive late with an empty belly. It has curries from £5.80 and seafood dishes from £6.80. Next to it is the *Delight Kebab* (Mon–Thu 4pm–12am, Fri–Sun 2pm–12am) with jacket potatoes, kebabs and fish and chips at down-to-earth prices.

There are a couple of other fish and chip shops by the harbour and a good greasy spoon café next to The Lighthouse Restaurant.

Globalization has reached Saundersfoot in the shape of *Kook-a-ba* (☎ 01834-813814, 6–10pm), a good Australian bar and restaurant with 'Long Neck' ostrich and 'Skippy' kangaroo steaks; something to put a spring in your step for £7.95. Packed lunches can be bought at the *Manorbier Bakery* where you can get filled baguettes for £1.50.

TENBY (DINBYCH Y PYSGOD) MAP 3a

The Little Fort of the Fishes, as it is known in Welsh, has grown from being just a fishing port to a delightful holiday town. In many respects it is typical of the great British seaside resort, yet it retains a certain charm and sophistication, having resisted stumbling down the road to cheap tackiness as some other seaside towns have done.

Immaculate expanses of sand almost surround the town attracting throngs of holidaymakers in the summer. Colourful houses perch above the harbour and South Beach while the wonderfully well preserved **mediaeval town walls** hide a maze of crooked streets.

One of the original three gateways and seven of the original twelve towers which make up the town wall still remain. It was probably built in response to attacks on the town in 1187 and 1260.

In the 12th century the Normans built a **castle** on the promontory but there is little left of it today.

Built into part of the old castle is the **Tenby Museum** (☎ 01834-842809, 10am–5pm daily; Castle Hill) where they have an art gallery and exhibitions covering everything from local maritime and social history to displays on archaeology, geology and natural history. They also trace the history of the town from the tenth century, as well as a 'pirate's cell'. You can even find out if you have any ancestors from the local area by checking out their local family history researcher.

Look out for the National Trust's **Tudor Merchant's House** (☎ 01834-842 279, Mon–Sat 10am–5pm, Sun 12–3pm, admission £1.80 with discounts for members) an old townhouse tucked into tiny Quay St near the harbour. It dates back to the 15th century and still has its original roof beams and a herb garden.

Tenby itself has plenty to keep you busy for a day, even if that means just wandering the streets or exploring the wonderful beaches. It is also the place to catch the boat over to **Caldey Island** and its monastery (see p78).

Services

The **TIC** (☎ 01834-842404) is on your right as you enter the town from the north. It sits on the corner of The Croft and The Norton. Another vital port of call is the **bank** of which there are plenty in the centre. Tenby is the last place to get money until you reach Pembroke 53 miles (85km) away.

It is also worth taking into account that many of the pubs and guesthouses along the path to Pembroke do not take credit cards; another good reason to fill your pockets with cash before you leave town.

Neither are there any shops to speak of until you reach Angle so take a good supply of food unless you plan to eat out every night. For camping supplies head for **TYF Outdoor** (☎ 01834-843488, 💻 www.tyf. com, 16 St Julian's St). They also organize courses in climbing, canoeing, surfing and coasteering (see p82).

The **bus station** is on Upper Park Rd while the **train station** can be found a little further along the same road. Trains run to Pembroke Dock and all the way back to Swansea and London for those who have already had enough. For bad foot problems you can always pay a visit to the **health centre** which is in the north of the town on Narberth Rd. There's a laundrette for your smelly socks on Upper Frog St.

Where to stay

On the path just to the north of town (see Map 3) is *Meadow Farm* (☎ 01834-844829, 💻 adjohn@meadowfarm.ndo.co.uk, Apr–Oct) with camping from £10 per tent.

Like most seaside towns there are countless B&Bs but they do, of course, get very busy at holiday time. As you enter the town from the north, close to North Beach is *Sea Breezes* (☎ 01834-842753, 18 The Norton, 3D) with beds from £18 per person.

There is a cluster of guesthouses around Warren St and Harding St in the centre of the town. *Lyndale Guest House* (☎ 01834-842836, Warren St, 3T/1F) has beds from £18 and *Weybourne Guest House* (☎ 01834-843641, 14 Warren St, 1T/3F) has beds at £16 a night. Slightly more expensive is *Sunny Bank Guest House* (☎ 01834-844034, 💻 www.sunny-bank.co.uk, Harding St, 1S/3T/2F) from £23 a night and the nearby *Ivy Bank Guest House* (☎ 01834-842311, 💻 www.ivybanktenby.co.uk, Harding St) from £25.

Close to the town centre is the *Normandie Inn* (☎ 01834-842227, Upper Frog St, 8T/2F) where all the rooms are en suite and cost £60 for a double room or £45 for a single person. Down by the harbour is *Gwynne House* (☎ 01834-842862, 💻 www. gwynnehouse.com, Bridge St) with views over North Beach and the harbour. Rooms are from £20 to £25 per person. Just off the esplanade is *Glenholme Guesthouse* (☎ 01834-843909, 💻 www.glenholmeguesthouse.co.uk, 18T) with beds from £16.50 and *Lindholme Guesthouse* (☎ 01834-843368, 27 Victoria St, 6D) which can be found near the end of the esplanade by South Beach. It has rooms from £18 per person.

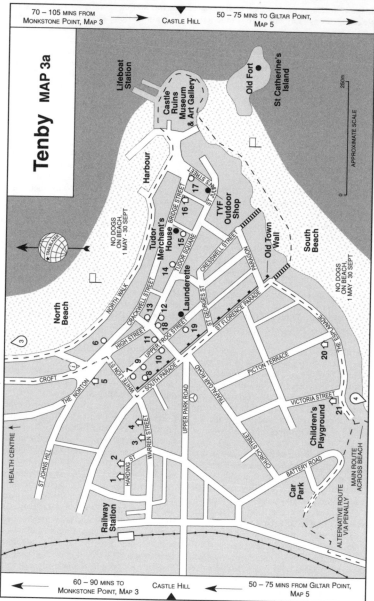

Tenby MAP 3a

70 – 105 MINS FROM MONKSTONE POINT, MAP 3 →

CASTLE HILL

50 – 75 MINS TO GILTAR POINT, MAP 5 →

Lifeboat Station

Castle Ruins Museum & Art Gallery

Old Fort

St Catherine's Island

APPROXIMATE SCALE

250m

0

Harbour

TYF / Outdoor Shop

Old Town Wall

South Beach

NO DOGS ON BEACH 1 MAY - 30 SEPT

NO DOGS ON BEACH 1 MAY - 30 SEPT

North Beach

NORTH WALK

Tudor Merchant's House

BRIDGE STREET

ST JULIAN'S STREET

17

16

15

TUDOR SQUARE

CRESSWELL STREET

PARAGON

14

CRACKWELL STREET

Launderette

13

18 12

19

ST GEORGES ST

ST FLORENCE PARADE

THE ESPLANADE

6

HIGH STREET

11

UPPER FROG STREET

9 10

8

7

SOUTH PARADE

WHITE LION ST

20

PICTON TERRACE

5

THE NORTON

CROFT

1

3

UPPER PARK ROAD

TREFLOYNE ROAD

VICTORIA STREET

21

Children's Playground

CROFT

HEALTH CENTRE ←

ST JOHNS HILL

4

3

WARREN STREET

1 2

HARDING ST

CHURCH STREET

BATTERY ROAD

Car Park

Railway Station

60 – 90 MINS TO MONKSTONE POINT, MAP 3 ←

CASTLE HILL ←

50 – 75 MINS FROM GILTAR POINT, MAP 5 ←

ALTERNATIVE ROUTE VIA PENALLY

MAIN ROUTE ACROSS BEACH

KEY

Where to stay
1 Sunny Bank Guesthouse
2 Ivy Bank Guesthouse
3 Lyndale Guesthouse
4 Weybourne Guesthouse
5 Sea Breezes
16 Gwynne House
20 Glenholme Guesthouse
21 Lindholme Guesthouse

Where to eat
6 Bay of Bengal Indian Restaurant
7 Get Stuffed Pizza
8 Mews Bistro
9 Crumbs & Cream Coffee Shop
10 Normandie Inn
11 Five Arches Tavern
12 The Lamb Inn
13 The Sun Inn
14 Pam Pam Restaurant
15 Plantagenet Restaurant
17 St Julian's Restaurant
18 The Picnic Basket
19 China Town Restaurant

Where to eat

There are some great little restaurants in Tenby, most of them on High St and Tudor Sq or at the top end of Upper Frog St. *Plantagenet Restaurant and Quay Room* (☎ 01834-842350), said to be the oldest house in Tenby, is definitely worth finding. It is on the corner of Tudor Sq with the short and narrow Quay Hill. The menu guarantees local ingredients with the home-made sausages a speciality. The Welsh lamb, parsnip and cashew sausage dish costs £7.25 while the traditional Welsh cawl (a lamb broth) is £5.95.

Mews Bistro (☎ 01834-844068, 12.30–3pm Jul/Aug, 6.30pm–late, all year), set back from Upper Frog St, is something of a Tenby institution and is always busy, so it's worth booking. They specialize in locally caught fish and meat dishes. The Welsh black beef is £12.95.

Closer to the harbour is the very smart *St. Julian's Restaurant* (☎ 01834-845481, St Julian's St) which is possibly too upmarket for sweaty walkers. They are open all day until 8.30pm with crab sandwiches for £3.75, toasties for £3.25 and chicken dishes from £6.25.

Cheaper food can be found in High St at the *Lamb Inn* (☎ 01834-842151, 14 High St) which has a variety of pub food such as jacket potatoes for £2.95 and big breakfasts for £4.50. Close by is *The Sun Inn* (☎ 01834-845941, 11pm–late), a bright and cheerful joint with cheap food such as the 'silly price' sirloin steak at £3.95 and

toasties from £2.10. Full of character and perfectly affordable is *Pam Pam Restaurant* (☎ 01834-842946, 2 Tudor Sq), an interesting place with all manner of dishes. They have everything from all day breakfasts for £3.75 to pizza for £3.95.

For more traditional pub grub try the *Normandie Inn* (see p75, 5.30–10pm) on Upper Frog St which does a tasty steak and mushroom pie for £5.25. They also have live music most nights. Also on Upper Frog St you will find the rustic *Five Arches Tavern* (☎ 01834-842513, 6–9.30pm) with local fish dishes from £6.95.

Those with oriental tastes should head to Crackwell St, just off High St, for the *Bay of Bengal Indian Restaurant* (☎ 01834-843331, 5.30pm–12am, 7 days). They have a typically extensive Indian menu. The chicken curry is £5.50 and the wonderful views over the North Beach are totally free.

Alternatively there is the *China Town Chinese Restaurant* (☎ 01834-843557, Lower Frog St, daily 12–2pm, 5.30–midnight) which has the usual array of rice and sweet and sour dishes.

Slightly less sophisticated food can be found at *Get Stuffed Pizza* (☎ 01834-845945, 10 Upper Frog St, 5pm–12am) and next door at the *Crumbs and Cream Coffee Shop*; a useful stop for a cheap and filling lunch. Likewise *The Picnic Basket* on St Georges St will set you up with a good packed lunch.

❏ **Caldey Island**

The small island of Caldey (☎ 01834-844453/842296) is clearly visible just south of Tenby. Monks have been on the island for around 1500 years and about 20 monks from the Reformed Cistercian Community live on the island currently, attending seven services a day in the private monastery. The first service kicks off at 3.15am!

Boat trips (☎ 01834-844453 and ☎ 01834-842296) to the island run from Easter to October from Tenby (every fifteen minutes, Mon–Fri; also Sat, Jun–Aug). Tickets are sold at the kiosk by Tenby harbour. There are also short **cruises** (☎ 01834-845400) around the island or to a number of other places including neighbouring St Margaret's Island and St Govan's Chapel.

There is a surprising amount to see on the island although tours of the **monastery** itself are available only for men. Everyone is free to explore the island outside of the monastery grounds including **St Illtud's Church** and **Old Priory**. There is also a tea room, small museum, post office (with its own official Caldey stamp) and a good bathing beach at Priory Bay. Look out for seals around the light-house on the southern tip of the island. Services for the public are held in the island's parish church, **St David's**, at 2.30pm on Tuesdays.

The resident monks are a dab hand at farming with many of their dairy products available for sale in the shop. Perhaps more surprising is their range of per-fumes and toiletries available for sale in the **Perfumery Shop**. All the products are based on local flowers, herbs and even prickly gorse.

TENBY TO MANORBIER BAY   MAPS 4–8

These **ten and a half miles (17km, 3–4½hrs)** are reasonably straightforward. The scenery is tamer than before but no less interesting. The path leaves Tenby at the end of the esplanade and drops down onto the vast sands of South Beach. The direct route takes you across the beach to **Giltar Point** in the south. In the unlikely event of an exceptionally high tide or if you are planning on staying in the village of **Penally** you will need to take the alternative and slightly longer path which follows the track between the railway line and the golf course.

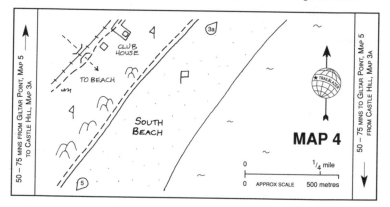

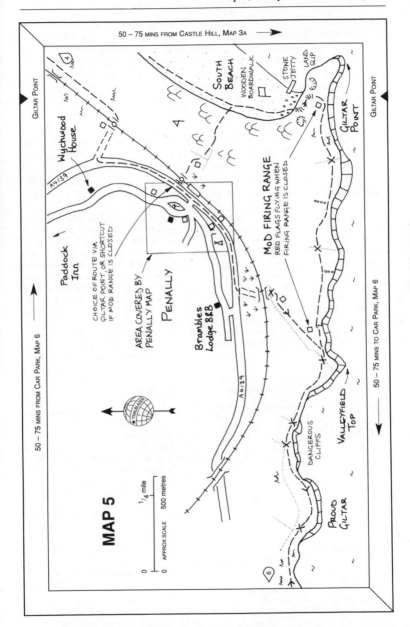

MAP 5

APPROX SCALE
0 — ¼ mile
0 — 500 metres

50 – 75 MINS FROM CASTLE HILL, MAP 3A →

50 – 75 MINS FROM CAR PARK, MAP 6 ↑

GILTAR POINT

4

Wychwood House

A4139

Paddock Inn

SOUTH BEACH

WOODEN BOARDWALK

STONE JETTY

LAND SLIP

GILTAR POINT

GILTAR POINT

CHOICE OF ROUTE VIA GILTAR POINT, OR SHORTCUT IF MOD RANGE IS CLOSED

AREA COVERED BY PENALLY MAP

PENALLY

Brambles Lodge B&B

A4139

MOD FIRING RANGE
RED FLAGS FLYING WHEN FIRING RANGE IS CLOSED

50 – 75 MINS TO CAR PARK, MAP 6 ↓

DANGEROUS CLIFFS

VALLEYFIELD TOP

PROUD GILTAR

6

TRAILBLAZER

Giltar Point is the first of a number of MoD firing ranges and it is occasionally closed to the public (indicated, as with all the firing ranges, by a red flag flying). If it is open you can climb the steps up through the high dunes onto the cliff top. When it is closed you must take the detour from the beach through the dunes to the train station at Penally. From here you must follow the main road a short distance before joining a track that goes under the railway line and back up onto the coast path proper. There is a number you can call to check the times of firing on the range (☎ 01834-845950).

The path continues over low grassy cliff tops, passing the pretty sandy bay of Lydstep Haven. At Lydstep there's an optional 20-minute detour to the open headland of Lydstep Point with views along the coast in both directions. The cliffs up to Skrinkle Haven are impressive but then the path heads inland to avoid another MoD enclosure. The stretch to Manorbier Bay follows some beautiful coast, the path contouring steep heathery slopes that drop straight into the sea.

PENALLY (PENALUN) MAP 5

Apart from a few old cottages around the pretty church, Penally is a less than inspiring place feeling much like a residential arm of Tenby. You should have got all you need in Tenby as there is little on offer here except the **post office** in the centre of the village, which also incorporates a small **shop**.

Should your feet be aching after the first day there are some good places to stay. Campers should head for *Penally Court Farm Campsite* (☎ 01834-845109, open Apr–Oct) at the western end of the village. Pitches currently cost around £4 per person.

There are also a number of good B&Bs on offer. In the centre of the village up the

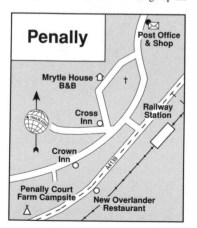

lane behind the church is *Myrtle House* (☎ 01834-842508, 8D) where beds are £24 per person. *Brambles Lodge* (☎ 01834-842393, ✉ gumf@supanet.com, 1S/3T/4F) can be found in the western corner of Penally, just off the main road. It has standard rooms from £18 single or en suite from £23 per person. *Wychwood House* (☎ 01834-844387, 1D/2F en suite) at the other end of the village is a very classy place at a very affordable price. Rooms are en suite with four-poster beds. Prices are from £21 to £25 per person and dinner costs £17; there's no licence so bring your own wine.

There are two pubs in the centre of the village, both serving food. The *Crown Inn* (☎ 01834-844030, 6–9pm) is a traditional pub with good cheap food. Just around the corner you will find another mouthwatering menu at the *Cross Inn* (☎ 01834-844665, 6.30–9pm); they also do breakfasts from 9.30am. On the road north of the village is the *Paddock Inn* (☎ 01834-843783, 6–9.30pm) also with good pub grub.

In the other direction, just outside the village on the main A4139 road is the *New Overlander Restaurant* (☎ 01834-842868, 9.30am–9pm), a smart little place with a garden and lots of clocks for sale on the walls. Try the Welsh lamb for £6.25. For under £2 the garlic mushrooms are fantastic. They also do breakfasts from £3.95.

(**Opposite**): Tenby (see pp74-8).

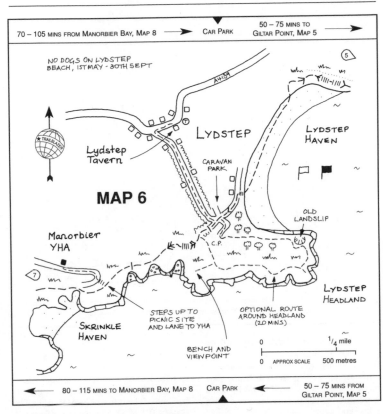

NO DOGS ON LYDSTEP BEACH, 1ST MAY - 30TH SEPT

A4139

LYDSTEP

Lydstep Tavern

CARAVAN PARK

MAP 6

Manorbier YHA

LYDSTEP HAVEN

OLD LANDSLIP

C.P.

LYDSTEP HEADLAND

SKRINKLE HAVEN

STEPS UP TO PICNIC SITE AND LANE TO YHA

OPTIONAL ROUTE AROUND HEADLAND (20 MINS)

BENCH AND VIEWPOINT

0   1/4 mile
0   APPROX SCALE   500 metres

LYDSTEP   MAP 6

Lydstep Haven is dominated by an unattractive caravan park though the village of Lydstep itself is further inland, reached by following the coast path up from the beach and turning right just past the caravan park entrance. It's a small village and unless you are dying for a pint it's really not worth the detour. It has a phone box and a pub but nothing else. The *Lydstep Tavern* (☎ 01834-871521, 12–2pm, 7–9pm) is on the bend of the main road. As well as home cooked pub regulars like chicken curry (£6.25) and vegetable lasagne (£6) they also do baguettes from £2.45.

There is nowhere to stay in the village but budget travellers should head for the *Manorbier Youth Hostel* (☎ 01834-871803, 🖳 manorbier@yha.org.uk, open all year) a little further along the coast path, some 200 metres from the beach at Skrinkle Haven. It has 63 beds but is often full in the summer months. The rather unfortunate sardine tin appearance of the hostel is thanks to its original use as a 1950s NATO storage building. Thankfully the interior is actually quite habitable now. Prices are £11 for members (see p11). You can also **camp** here for half the normal bed price with full use of the hostel facilities.

(Opposite) Top: The Green Bridge of Wales (see p90). **Bottom**: St Govan's Chapel (see p90).

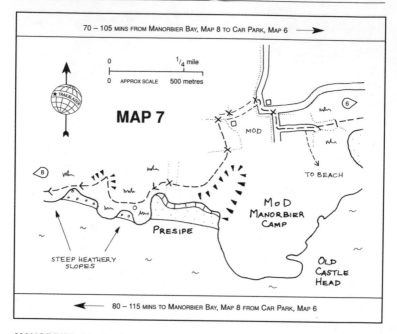

MAP 7

TRAILBLAZER

0 ¼ mile

0 APPROX SCALE 500 metres

MOD

6

TO BEACH

8

PRESIPE

MoD
MANORBIER
CAMP

STEEP HEATHERY
SLOPES

OLD
CASTLE
HEAD

MANORBIER (MAENORBYR) MAP 8a

Pronounced 'manor-bee-er' this village boasts a windswept sandy beach and an impressive, well preserved castle (see p84). It also has a handful of B&Bs and a good pub, which is a saving grace on a rainy day.

Castlemead Hotel (☎ 01834-871358) is the first building on the right as you enter the village by the lane from the beach. This is the most luxurious option and also the

most expensive. B&B is from £35. There are cheaper places to stay: *Fernley Lodge* (☎ 01834-871226, 🖳 fernleylodge@yahoo. co.uk, 3S/2T/1F) is in the centre of the village and has beds from £20. Meanwhile *The Gate* (☎ 01834-871629) has rooms from £25 per person. At the far end of the village in the residential area is *Honeyhill B&B* (☎ 01834 -871906, Warlows Meadow, 4D en suite) with beds from £18 to £20 per person.

❏ Coasteering

Coasteering is a real hands-on approach to exploring the Pembrokeshire coastline but is not a sport that everyone will be familiar with. It involves traversing sheer sea cliffs by scrambling, climbing, jumping off ledges into the churning sea and getting very wet. It makes quite a change from simply walking along the cliff tops and certainly provides more of an adrenaline rush.

For some guidance on how to do it properly **TYF** (01437-721611, 🖳 www.tyf. com), who claim to have invented this fast-growing sport, offer day courses around the cliffs of Lydstep and the St David's peninsula.

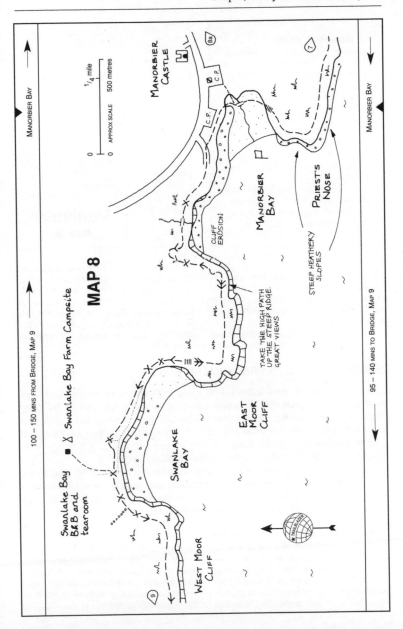

MANORBIER BAY

100 – 150 MINS FROM BRIDGE, MAP 9

Swanlake Bay B&B and tearoom

X Swanlake Bay Farm Campsite

MAP 8

APPROX SCALE

0 ¼ mile

0 500 metres

WEST MOOR CLIFF

SWANLAKE BAY

EAST MOOR CLIFF

TAKE THE HIGH PATH UP THE STEEP RIDGE. GREAT VIEWS

CLIFF EROSION

MANORBIER BAY

STEEP HEATHERY SLOPES

PRIEST'S NOSE

MANORBIER CASTLE

C.P.

C.P.

8a

7

MANORBIER BAY

95 – 140 MINS TO BRIDGE, MAP 9

9

❏ **Manorbier Castle**

History is visible everywhere you go in Pembrokeshire from standing stones and Iron-Age hill-forts to the numerous castles dotted around the countryside.

One of the finest, Manorbier Castle (☎ 01646-621500), can be visited. The birth place of Gerald of Wales, a 12th-century scholar, it stands in a wonderful location close to the beach, just off the coast path.

Visitors can explore the turrets and dungeons from Easter to the end of September, 10.30am–5.30pm. Admission £2.20.

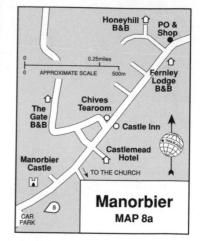

Manorbier
MAP 8a

For hungry tummies, on the right-hand side as you climb up the lane into the village from the beach is the *Castle Inn* (☎ 01834-871268, 12–2pm, 7–9pm). It has an extensive menu, a pool table and a friendly boxer dog.

On the other side of the road is *Chives Tearoom* with sandwiches from £2.25,

baked potatoes from £2.50 and lasagne for £5.50. A mile and a half (2km) further along the coast path, above Swanlake Bay, is B&B from £20 and a tearoom at *Swanlake Bay Farm* (☎ 01834-871204, 🖳 swanlake@pembrokeshire.com, 7D). They also allow **camping** but there are no facilities.

MANORBIER BAY TO FRESHWATER EAST   MAPS 8–9

This short section of **four miles (6km, $1^1/_2$–2hrs)** takes in two wild windswept headlands which sandwich **Swanlake Bay**, a sandy beach backed by steep slopes and farmland. Short but strenuous accurately describes this section. No sooner do you drop down the side of one steep cliff than you find yourself climbing up another. It can make for slow progress if you have a heavy pack. The broad sands of Freshwater East make a welcome sight.

It is worth bearing in mind that budget accommodation is pretty thin on the ground from here until Pembroke and the same can be said for any other services you may be looking for. Forward planning is essential. Book all your accommodation well in advance especially in the high season.

FRESHWATER EAST   MAP 9

Freshwater East is a peculiar place. A number of houses lie scattered among the wooded slopes above the bay while the steep road up from Trewent Park is lined by yet more homes. In fact there is little here other than houses. If you are staying here it is

worth using the footpath that cuts in to the village just before the coast path drops down to the beach. Otherwise you have to walk down and then back up the steep road to reach the village. Just down the hill from the crossroads at the top of the village is

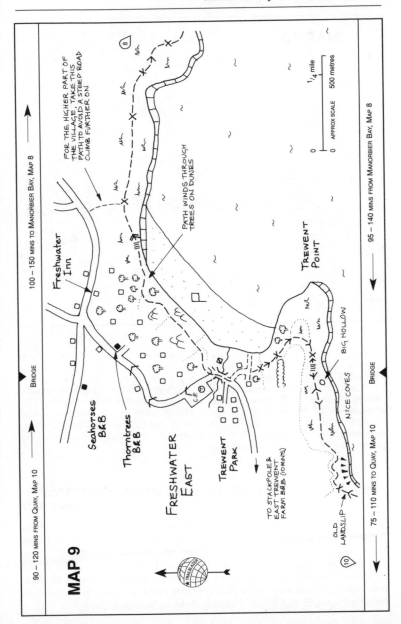

MAP 9

90 – 120 MINS FROM QUAY, MAP 10

BRIDGE

100 – 150 MINS TO MANORBIER BAY, MAP 8

FOR THE HIGHER PART OF THE VILLAGE, TAKE THIS PATH TO AVOID A STEEP ROAD CLIMB FURTHER ON

Freshwater Inn

Seahorses B&B

Thorntrees B&B

FRESHWATER EAST

Trewent Park

C.P.

TO STACKPOLE & EAST TREWENT FARM B&B (10 MINS)

PATH WINDS THROUGH TREES ON DUNES

TREWENT POINT

BIG HOLLOW

NICE COVES

OLD LANDSLIP

BRIDGE

95 – 140 MINS FROM MANORBIER BAY, MAP 8

75 – 110 MINS TO QUAY, MAP 10

APPROX SCALE

0   ¼ mile

0   500 metres

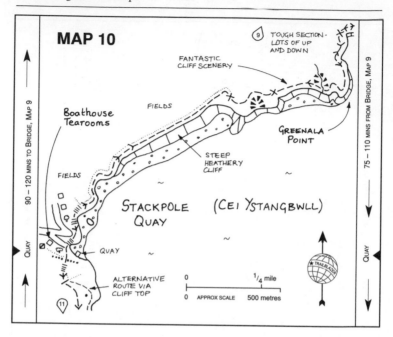

MAP 10

9 TOUGH SECTION - LOTS OF UP AND DOWN

FANTASTIC CLIFF SCENERY

FIELDS

Boathouse Tearooms

GREENALA POINT

STEEP HEATHERY CLIFF

FIELDS

STACKPOLE QUAY (CEI YSTANGBWLL)

QUAY

ALTERNATIVE ROUTE VIA CLIFF TOP

0   1/4 mile
0   APPROX SCALE   500 metres

90 – 120 MINS TO BRIDGE, MAP 9

75 – 110 MINS FROM BRIDGE, MAP 9

QUAY

QUAY

TRAILBLAZER

11

Thorntrees (☎ 01646-672352, 🖥 thorn-trees@hotmail.com, 1S/1D) a smart place with beds from £30 per person.

Further out of the village and away from the coast path is the cheaper option of *Seahorses* (☎ 01646-672405, 1T/1D) on the B4584 Lamphey road. It's open in the summer only with prices at £18 per person. Closer to the path, half a mile west

of Freshwater East, is *East Trewent Farm* (☎ 01646-672127, 1S/2T/1F) with prices at £18 per person, or £22 for en suite.

Well worth the detour from the path, the food at the *Freshwater Inn* (☎ 01646-672828, 12–9.30pm) comes with a wide choice and big helpings. The chicken and chips is £4.95 and the garlic chicken £8.50.

FRESHWATER EAST TO BROAD HAVEN (FOR BOSHERSTON)
MAPS 9–12

The scenery really is spectacular for the next **six and a half miles (10km, 2–3hrs)** to Broad Haven (not to be confused with the village of Broad Haven further north). It begins with more tortuous 'up-and-downs' as the cliffs twist and turn their way west of Freshwater East. Between Trewent Point and Greenala Point there are some fantastic contorted green cliffs, coves and blow-holes lining the coastline. Once past Greenala Point the path follows the high top of a long steep cliff before dropping down to Stackpole Quay.

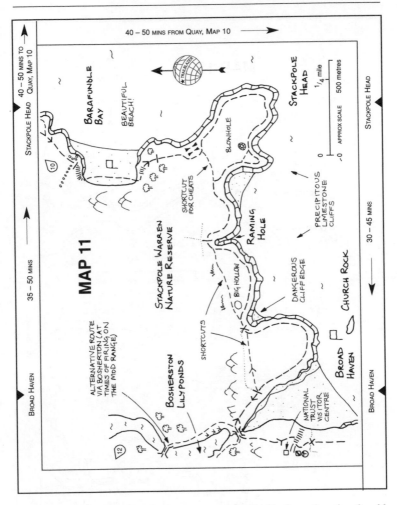

The scenery changes dramatically as you pass Stackpole Quay. Leaving the old red sandstone behind, the path moves into carboniferous limestone country where the cliffs drop precipitously into the sea. Flat grassy tops here make the walking easier on the feet.

Barafundle Bay is probably one of the most beautiful beaches along the entire walk with lush woodland dropping down to its southern edge. It's a great spot for lunch on a nice day. If it's raining you're better off stopping at the tearooms at Stackpole Quay.

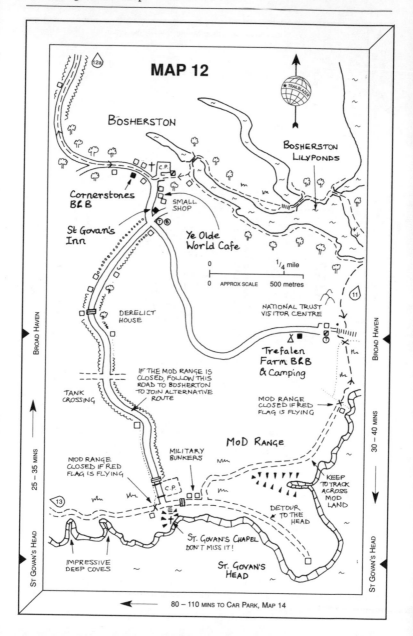

MAP 12

BOSHERSTON

BOSHERSTON LILYPONDS

Cornerstones B&B

St Govan's Inn

SMALL SHOP

Ye Olde World Cafe

0   ¼ mile
0   APPROX SCALE   500 metres

NATIONAL TRUST VISITOR CENTRE

DERELICT HOUSE

Trefalen Farm B&B & Camping

IF THE MOD RANGE IS CLOSED, FOLLOW THIS ROAD TO BOSHERTON TO JOIN ALTERNATIVE ROUTE

TANK CROSSING

MOD RANGE CLOSED IF RED FLAG IS FLYING

MOD RANGE CLOSED IF RED FLAG IS FLYING

MoD RANGE

MILITARY BUNKERS

KEEP TO TRACK ACROSS MOD LAND

DETOUR TO THE HEAD

IMPRESSIVE DEEP COVES

ST. GOVAN'S CHAPEL DON'T MISS IT!

ST. GOVAN'S HEAD

BROAD HAVEN

BROAD HAVEN

25 – 35 MINS

30 – 40 MINS

ST GOVAN'S HEAD

ST GOVAN'S HEAD

80 – 110 MINS TO CAR PARK, MAP 14

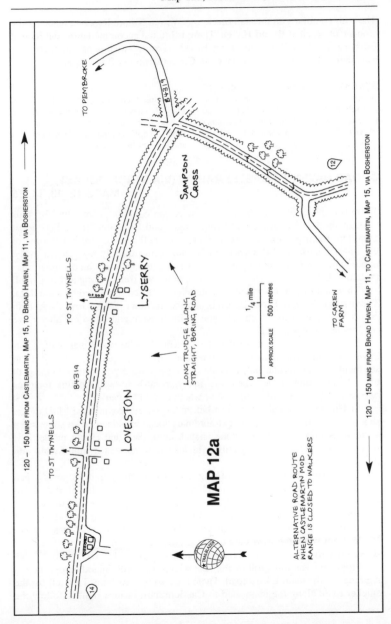

120 – 150 MINS FROM CASTLEMARTIN, MAP 15, TO BROAD HAVEN, MAP 11, VIA BOSHERSTON

120 – 150 MINS FROM BROAD HAVEN, MAP 11, TO CASTLEMARTIN, MAP 15, VIA BOSHERSTON

TO PEMBROKE

B4319

SAMPSON CROSS

TO ST TWYNELLS

LYSERRY

LONG TRUDGE ALONG STRAIGHT, BORING ROAD

TO ST TWYNELLS

B4314

LOVESTON

¼ mile

500 metres

0

0

APPROX SCALE

TO CAREW FARM

MAP 12a

ALTERNATIVE ROAD ROUTE WHEN CASTLEMARTIN MOD RANGE IS CLOSED TO WALKERS

TO ST TWYNELLS

TRAILBLAZER

(14)

(12)

The path continues on through Stackpole Warren Nature Reserve, reaching the wonderful beach at **Broad Haven**. There is limited accommodation and food at Bosherston (15 to 20 minutes from Broad Haven), which is on the alternative road detour route (see Broad Haven to Castlemartin via Bosherston).

STACKPOLE QUAY   MAP 10

At Stackpole Quay there is a **phone box** and **toilets**. More importantly there is also the National Trust's *Boathouse Tearooms* (☎ 01646-672058, 10.30am–3.30pm), the only eating hole for miles, with lobster creels and lifebuoys adorning the ceiling. They also have a display of the fossils that can be found in the area. The local crab salad is £6.95 and there are jacket potatoes and toasties from £3.95.

BROAD HAVEN TO CASTLEMARTIN (VIA STACK ROCKS)
MAPS 12, 13, 14, 15

There is a choice of route here. The route proper continues across the cliff tops through the Castlemartin MoD firing range, said to be one of NATO's most important training areas in Europe. Covering 5880 acres it also hides some of the finest limestone cliff scenery in Britain. Unfortunately it is closed to the public when firing is taking place. It is well worth checking the opening times (☎ 01646-662367) since the detour is a monotonous trudge along a boring road.

There are two points where the path may be closed (indicated by a red flag). The first is just above Broad Haven beach and the other is at St Govan's. At both points there are roads which take you to Bosherston and on to the alternative road route described later.

If the range is open it is **ten miles (16km, 3¼–4hrs)** to Castlemartin, following the jeep track along the flat limestone cliff tops. The cliffs, when you can see them, are spectacular but signs along the track warn you to stick to the path through the firing range. There are many rewards to walking this route as opposed to the road detour, the first of which is at St Govan's.

St Govan's Chapel, sitting just before the sentry box into the MoD range, should not be missed. It's in an extraordinary location hidden down some steep stone steps in a cleft. A tiny stone chapel, cold, dark and empty inside, it is squeezed between sheer rocky cliffs which seem to prevent it from falling into the heaving sea below.

On entering the Castlemartin firing range follow the jeep track across open grassland and scrubland with vertical limestone cliffs to your left all the way to the dead-end road at Stack Rocks. Just before the car park are **Elegug Stacks**, two impressive sea stacks sitting a short way offshore. A little further on, past the car park, is the natural arch known as the **Green Bridge of Wales**, a spectacular sight when the waves are crashing around it and the gulls are wheeling above the cliff tops. It's only a five-minute detour from the coast path.

From here you must follow the lane which takes you inland across the firing range to the main B4319 road. There are two options here. Turn left for the quicker route along the main road to **Castlemartin** or turn right to follow the

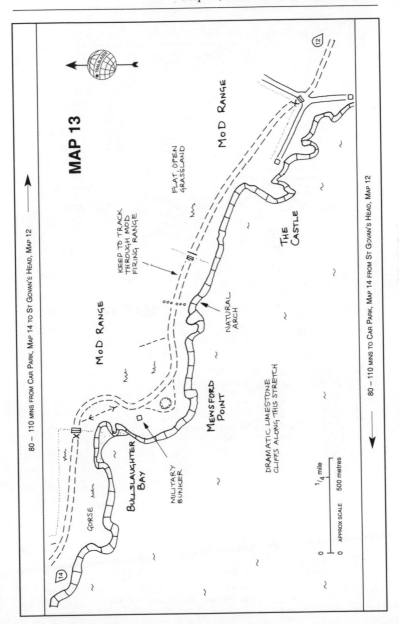

MAP 13

80 – 110 MINS FROM CAR PARK, MAP 14 TO ST GOVAN'S HEAD, MAP 12 →

MoD RANGE

MoD RANGE

KEEP TO TRACK
THROUGH MOD
FIRING RANGE

FLAT, OPEN
GRASSLAND

NATURAL ARCH

THE CASTLE

GORSE

BULLSLAUGHTER BAY

MILITARY BUNKER

MEWSFORD POINT

DRAMATIC LIMESTONE
CLIFFS ALONG THIS STRETCH

¼ mile

500 metres

APPROX SCALE

0

0

80 – 110 MINS TO CAR PARK, MAP 14 FROM ST GOVAN'S HEAD, MAP 12 →

12

14

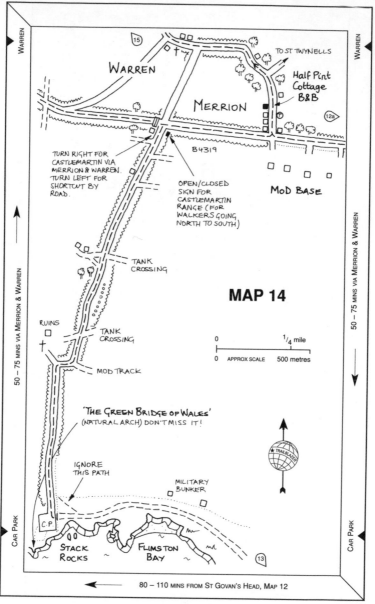

WARREN

WARREN

15

TO ST TWYNELLS

WARREN

Half Pint
Cottage
B&B

MERRION

12a

TURN RIGHT FOR
CASTLEMARTIN VIA
MERRION & WARREN.
TURN LEFT FOR
SHORTCUT BY
ROAD.

B4319

OPEN/CLOSED
SIGN FOR
CASTLEMARTIN
RANGE (FOR
WALKERS GOING
NORTH TO SOUTH)

MOD BASE

TANK
CROSSING

50 – 75 MINS VIA MERRION & WARREN

MAP 14

RUINS

TANK
CROSSING

MOD TRACK

0   1/4 mile
0   APPROX SCALE   500 metres

'THE GREEN BRIDGE OF WALES'
(NATURAL ARCH) DON'T MISS IT!

★ TRAILBLAZER

IGNORE
THIS PATH

MILITARY
BUNKER

C.P

13

STACK
ROCKS

FLIMSTON BAY

CAR PARK

80 – 110 MINS FROM ST GOVAN'S HEAD, MAP 12

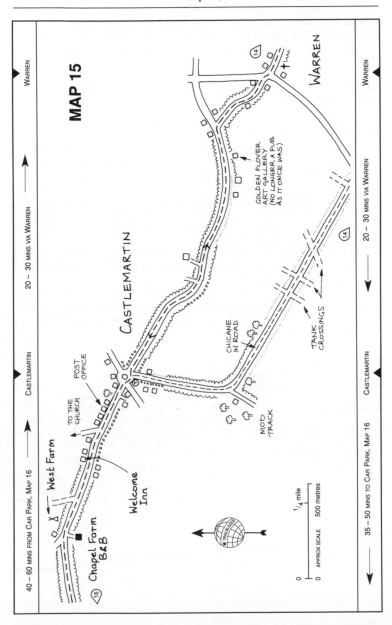

MAP 15

WARREN

CASTLEMARTIN

Golden Plover Art Gallery (no longer a pub as it once was)

CHICANE IN ROAD

MOD TRACK

TANK CROSSINGS

POST OFFICE

TO THE CHURCH

West Farm

Welcome Inn

Chapel Farm B&B

16

¼ mile

500 metres

0

0   APPROX SCALE

TRAILBLAZER

40 – 60 MINS FROM CAR PARK, MAP 16 ——→   ←—— 20 – 30 MINS VIA WARREN

◄ WARREN   ◄ CASTLEMARTIN

20 – 30 MINS VIA WARREN   →   35 – 50 MINS TO CAR PARK, MAP 16

WARREN ►   CASTLEMARTIN ►

14

country lanes through the villages of **Merrion** and **Warren**. These villages are pretty enough and country lanes are always preferable to main roads but the truth is you really won't miss much if you choose to take the quicker, main road route.

DETOUR ROUTE BROAD HAVEN TO CASTLEMARTIN
(VIA BOSHERSTON)   MAPS 12, 12a, 14, 15

If the Castlemartin firing range is closed you must follow the road north via Bosherston. The village of Bosherston and the lily ponds of the same name are the only real highlights if you are going this way. Otherwise these **six and a half miles (10km, 2–2¹/₂hrs)** comprise a rather tedious trudge along roads hemmed in by high hedges. If you have the time, it really is worth waiting for the trail through the firing range to reopen.

From Broad Haven, where the main path crosses the stone bridge at the southern tip of the lily ponds, you must follow the path inland up the east bank of the beautiful lake, crossing the three bridges over the arms of the lake and up the steep rocky track to Bosherston.

Here the road heads north through farmland to **Sampson Cross** and then along the very straight and boring B4319 road to the turn off for **Merrion** where you rejoin the main coast path.

At Merrion you can choose to continue along the B4319 road which is slightly quicker but slightly more tedious too. The better route follows the country lanes through Merrion and Warren – where there is a nice church, St Mary's – all the way to Castlemartin.

BOSHERSTON   MAP 12

If you are taking the road detour either from Broad Haven or St Govan's you will pass through the quaint little village of Bosherston with its photogenic church. Even if you are taking the cliff-top route through the military firing range it is worth making the short detour to the village.

This is partly because it is the only place with any accommodation along this stretch and also because it gives you the opportunity to explore the intricate creeks and woodland of **Bosherston** lily ponds. These peaceful lakes, reed beds and heavily wooded slopes contrast greatly with the crashing waves on the beach. It's a great place to spot wildlife. Otters can sometimes be seen at dusk if you are quiet and there is plenty of birdlife from coots and moorhens to herons and buzzards.

The village itself is small and compact with a tiny **shop** and **toilets** on the main

street. At the end of the main street is *St Govan's Inn* (☎ 01646-661311, food 7–9pm). They do B&B from £15 a night.

Opposite the church there is B&B at *Cornerstones* (☎ 01646-661660, 1T/1D) with en-suite rooms at £22 per person. Ask for James. If he has no space he can usually direct you to somewhere that does.

Lying above the dunes of Broad Haven Bay near the visitor kiosk is *Trefalen Farm* (☎ 01646-661643, ▤ trefalen@aol.com, 3D) with three double rooms. Prices from £18.50 person. There is a small single person's supplement. They also allow **camping**.

There are two places to eat; *St Govan's Inn* offers Sunday roasts for £5.95 while *Ye Olde Worlde Café* (☎ 01646-661216) has a wide variety of snacks which you can eat in their big front garden.

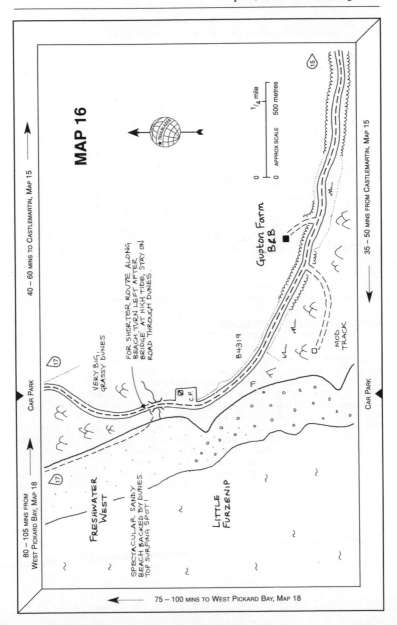

MAP 16

TRAILBLAZER

40 – 60 MINS TO CASTLEMARTIN, MAP 15

80 – 105 MINS FROM WEST PICKARD BAY, MAP 18

CAR PARK

35 – 50 MINS FROM CASTLEMARTIN, MAP 15

75 – 100 MINS TO WEST PICKARD BAY, MAP 18

CAR PARK

VERY BIG, GRASSY DUNES

FOR SHORTER ROUTE ALONG BEACH TURN LEFT AFTER BRIDGE. AT HIGH TIDE, STAY ON ROAD THROUGH DUNES.

B4319

Gupton Farm B&B

MOD TRACK

FRESHWATER WEST

SPECTACULAR SANDY BEACH BACKED BY DUNES. TOP SURFING SPOT!

LITTLE FURZENIP

APPROX SCALE

¼ mile

500 metres

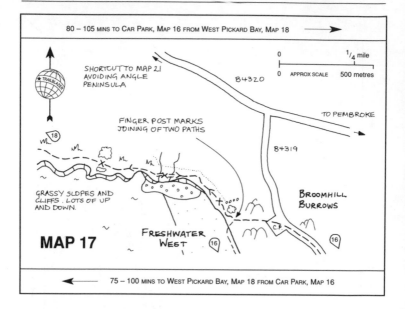

80 – 105 MINS TO CAR PARK, MAP 16 FROM WEST PICKARD BAY, MAP 18 ⟶

SHORTCUT TO MAP 21
AVOIDING ANGLE
PENINSULA

★ TRAILBLAZER

B4320

0   ¹/₄ mile

0   APPROX SCALE   500 metres

TO PEMBROKE

FINGER POST MARKS
JOINING OF TWO PATHS

18

B4319

GRASSY SLOPES AND
CLIFFS. LOTS OF UP
AND DOWN.

BROOMHILL
BURROWS

MAP 17

FRESHWATER
WEST   16

C.P.

16

⟵ 75 – 100 MINS TO WEST PICKARD BAY, MAP 18 FROM CAR PARK, MAP 16

MERRION, WARREN & CASTLEMARTIN (CASTELLMARTIN)   MAPS 14, 15

These three small villages sit along a hilly ridge. Milford Haven estuary is in the distance to the north while to the south is the MoD's vast Castlemartin firing range. Along the road between Warren and Castlemartin the MoD have kindly set aside a 'spectator area' from where you can safely watch the army shooting at things.

All of these villages have a laidback friendly feel to them but there is little on offer for the weary walker. There is a tiny **post office** at Castlemartin and also a **phone box** both there and at Merrion.

Accommodation can be found at *Half Pint Cottage* in Merrion (☎ 01646-661278 or ☎ 07979-535623, 1S/2D). It's run by the very welcoming Sue and is a great place to stay with clean, smart rooms and a cosy living-room for guests. It caters for a maximum of four at any one time. Rooms cost £18 per person.

Continuing down the road out of Castlemartin towards Freshwater West there is cheap camping for £3 per person at *West Farm* (☎ 01646-661227, Apr–Oct). *Chapel Farm* (☎ 01646-661312, 2D) is a smart place with six en-suite double rooms. Prices are £27 per room.

Closer to Freshwater West, just over a mile west of Castlemartin, is *Gupton Farm* (☎ 01646-661268, 1S,2D) with rooms at £17 per person.

There is only one place to eat, the *Welcome Inn* (☎ 01646-661752) at the western end of Castlemartin, a very cosy pub where the bar meals are filling and the locals friendly. Even the resident doberman is pretty relaxed. You can get a good curry for under £7. There is no fixed time for ordering food but they usually stop around nine o' clock.

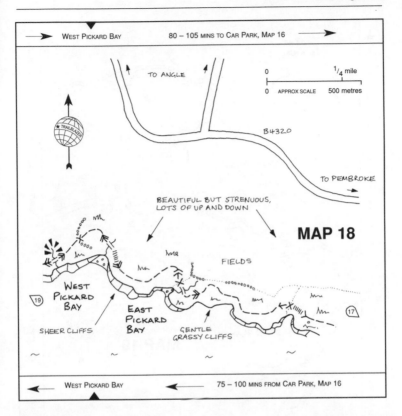

WEST PICKARD BAY   80 – 105 MINS TO CAR PARK, MAP 16

TO ANGLE

0   ¼ mile
0   APPROX SCALE   500 metres

★ TRAILBLAZER

B4320

TO PEMBROKE

BEAUTIFUL BUT STRENUOUS, LOTS OF UP AND DOWN

MAP 18

FIELDS

WEST PICKARD BAY

19

EAST PICKARD BAY

SHEER CLIFFS

GENTLE GRASSY CLIFFS

17

WEST PICKARD BAY   75 – 100 MINS FROM CAR PARK, MAP 16

CASTLEMARTIN TO ANGLE   MAPS 15–20

Some beautiful scenery can be found along these **ten and a half miles (17km, 4½–6hrs)** but you must work for it. After the relatively easy walking of the previous section the going once again gets tougher with plenty of ups and downs along the southern side of the Angle peninsula.

Remember to bring plenty of food and water as there is nowhere to find any along this stretch.

Things begin easily enough following the lane across farmland and through enormous grassy dunes to the magnificent beach at **Freshwater West**, renowned as being one of Pembrokeshire's finest sweeps of sand. The relentless crashing of the surf makes this a popular haunt for surfers but it is not a safe place for swimming.

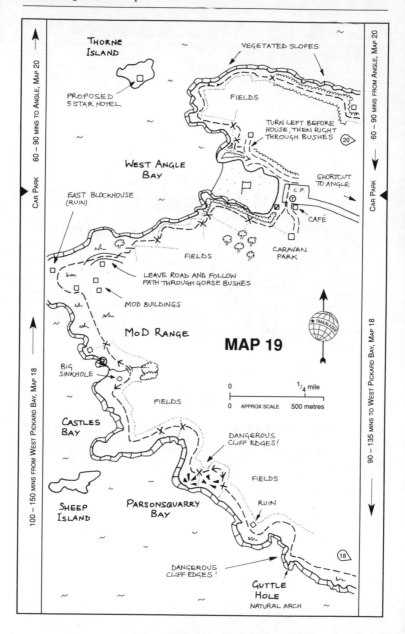

THORNE ISLAND

PROPOSED 5 STAR HOTEL

VEGETATED SLOPES

FIELDS

TURN LEFT BEFORE HOUSE, THEN RIGHT THROUGH BUSHES 20

WEST ANGLE BAY

SHORTCUT TO ANGLE

EAST BLOCKHOUSE (RUIN)

C.P.

CAFÉ

CARAVAN PARK

FIELDS

LEAVE ROAD AND FOLLOW PATH THROUGH GORSE BUSHES

MOD BUILDINGS

MoD RANGE

MAP 19

TRAILBLAZER

0   1/4 mile

0   500 metres
APPROX SCALE

BIG SINKHOLE

FIELDS

CASTLES BAY

DANGEROUS CLIFF EDGES!

FIELDS

RUIN

SHEEP ISLAND

PARSONSQUARRY BAY

DANGEROUS CLIFF EDGES!

GUTTLE HOLE

NATURAL ARCH

18

CAR PARK   60 – 90 MINS TO ANGLE, MAP 20

CAR PARK   60 – 90 MINS FROM ANGLE, MAP 20

100 – 150 MINS FROM WEST PICKARD BAY, MAP 18

90 – 135 MINS TO WEST PICKARD BAY, MAP 18

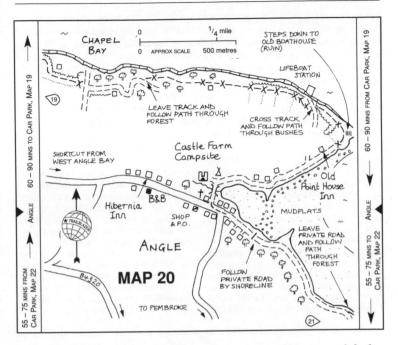

At the bridge just past the car park there are two options. You can turn left after the bridge and follow the wonderful beach north or continue along the road which winds its way through high sand dunes. At times the road almost seems to get swallowed up by the shifting sands.

Whichever way you choose the paths meet at the northern end of the beach and climb up above grassy, heathery slopes with wonderful views back across the sands. Although not as high or precipitous as other parts of the coastline this section is beautiful all the same. It is a wild and remote stretch of coast and is probably the least frequented. You would be foolish to miss it out but you can do exactly that by continuing along the main road north from Freshwater West, taking the first left and next right to bring you onto Angle Bay. Doing this means you have missed out the entire Angle peninsula which may be worth doing if you are behind schedule but is not really recommended.

For those still circumnavigating the Angle peninsula the cliffs become more and more spectacular as you head west, passing the natural arch of **Guttle Hole** and the grassy **Sheep Island**. Look out for the ruins of **East Blockhouse** constructed as a defence building during the reign of Henry VIII. At **West Angle Bay** there is the *Wavecrest Café*, **toilets** and a **phone box** but little else.

Once again there is the option of a shortcut since Angle village is agonizingly close, almost within touching distance along the road leading east. Diehards who want to 'do' the whole path must continue on around the northern half of the peninsula. The consolation is that the walking is less strenuous, passing above gentle slopes and on through some beautiful woodland on the steep water's edge. To the west, looking very much like Alcatraz, is Thorne Island and its 19th-century military defensive building which was once the venue for the World Hopscotch Championships. There are plans afoot to turn the forbidding fortress into a luxury five-star hotel accessible by cable car from the mainland. It is already being dubbed a hideaway for the rich and famous so expect the room rates to be a little higher than your average B&B. Tired legs will be pleased to reach the village of **Angle**.

ANGLE   MAP 20

Angle is nothing to get too excited about but it is pleasant enough with boats bobbing in the pretty little estuary and some old castle ruins by the stream. Fishing is the main industry and seaweed is also harvested here as it is used as a principal ingredient of the Welsh speciality, laver bread.

There is a **post office**, a well supplied **shop** on the main street opposite the school and some public **toilets** but little else. For blister sufferers there are **buses** to Pembroke. Campers will find *Castle Farm Campsite* (☎ 01646-641220, Apr–Oct) the

perfect spot to pitch at just £2 per person. It's situated in the field to the right just before you cross the bridge into the village. For a roof over your head there is bed and breakfast at *19 Angle* (☎ 01646-641212, 2T) with rooms from £20 per person. It's near the Hibernia Inn.

Where the coast path comes in from the north you will see *Old Point House* (food from 7pm), the first building you come to overlooking Angle Bay. Rustic and eccentric this is a fantastic, unpretentious pub with great pub grub and probably the

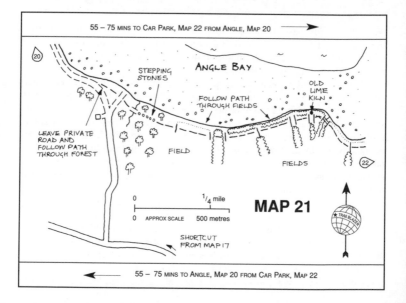

55 – 75 MINS TO CAR PARK, MAP 22 FROM ANGLE, MAP 20 →

ANGLE BAY

STEPPING STONES

FOLLOW PATH THROUGH FIELDS

OLD LIME KILN

LEAVE PRIVATE ROAD AND FOLLOW PATH THROUGH FOREST

FIELD

FIELDS

0   1/4 mile
0   APPROX SCALE   500 metres

MAP 21

TRAIL BLAZER

SHORTCUT FROM MAP 17

← 55 – 75 MINS TO ANGLE, MAP 20 FROM CAR PARK, MAP 22

best chips in Pembrokeshire. The gulls are pretty fond of them too so be on your guard if you are eating in the garden. Chicken and chips is £4.50. If this isn't your thing then there is always the more expensive and conventional *Hibernia Inn* (☎ 01646-641517, 12–2pm, 7–9.30pm) at the eastern end of the village.

ANGLE TO HUNDLETON
MAPS 20–25

The sad truth is that after such wonderful coastal scenery things really do go downhill from here until Sandy Haven, just under 30 miles (48km) away. Many people choose to catch the bus to Herbrandston, or even as far as Dale, to avoid the oil refineries, power station and urban sprawl that blights the Milford Haven estuary. No doubt it was once a beautiful harbour, described by Nelson as one of the world's finest, but sadly it has been very spoilt.

If you can happily skip this bit and still hold your head up high when you get home there are buses in both directions between Angle and Pembroke Dock. However, services are infrequent to say the least (see public transport map p37).

These **nine miles (14km, 3–4^1/$_2$hrs)** begin pleasantly following the shoreline of **Angle Bay** through some nice woodland and fields. However, on reaching Fort Popton on the other side of the bay the first of two oil refineries looms above you belching out acrid fumes. To be fair the path does its best to avoid any possible eye contact with this blot on the landscape passing through some beautiful old oak and beech woodland wherever it can, but at times it is impossible not to notice it. The stench of crude oil is certainly hard to miss. The path crosses farmland and then joins a small lane before passing the church at **Pwllcrochan**.

Having left the delights of the oil refinery you now have the power station to walk around. Again the path does well to hide in the woodland but even without the power station the scenery is nothing compared to what has gone before or is to come further ahead. Leaving the power station and its fizzing, crackling overhead power lines behind, the path continues across farmland passing the two creeks (locally known as 'pills') at Goldborough mudflats and joins the Goldborough Rd, a country lane that climbs steeply up to the village of **Hundleton**. The coast path actually heads down the farm track to Brownslate Farm a few hundred metres short of the village.

HUNDLETON
MAP 25

Hundleton has little to offer and it is probably better to carry on to Pembroke which isn't far away. The post office has disappeared but the **phone box** and **bus stop** can be found in the centre next to the green.

A cheap place to pitch your tent is at *Ash Ford Campsite* (Apr–Oct). It is slightly out of the way on the B4320 road south, near the recreation ground, but for only £2 per person it is worth it.

The only place to stay in the centre of the village is the *Highgate Inn Hotel* (☎ 01646-685904, 🖳 windy.gail@virgin.net,

5D). The beds are a rather pricey £45 for a single but only £27.50 per person if sharing a room.

Heading east along the B4320 road to Pembroke is *Bowett Farmhouse* (☎ 01646-683473, 1S/1T) with B&B accommodation from £23. It is easiest to reach it from Quoits Mill which is further along the coast path from Hundleton.

You can eat at the *Highgate Inn Hotel*. Meals are served from 11.30am to 2pm and from 6.30 to 11pm. Sunday lunch is £7.95.

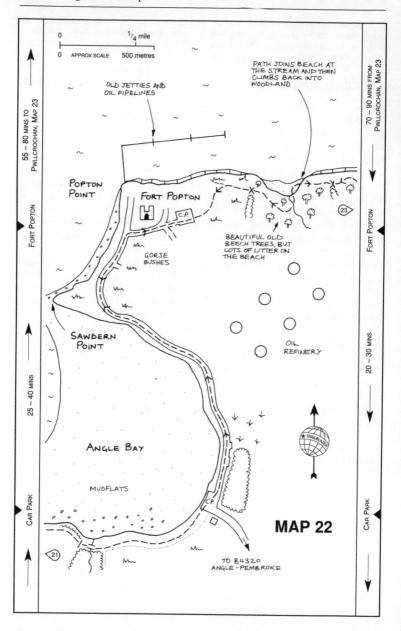

0   1/4 mile
0   APPROX SCALE   500 metres

PATH JOINS BEACH AT THE STREAM AND THEN CLIMBS BACK INTO WOODLAND

OLD JETTIES AND OIL PIPELINES

55 – 80 MINS TO PWLLCROCHAN, MAP 23

70 – 90 MINS FROM PWLLCROCHAN, MAP 23

FORT POPTON

POPTON POINT

FORT POPTON

C.P.

23

BEAUTIFUL OLD BEECH TREES, BUT LOTS OF LITTER ON THE BEACH

GORSE BUSHES

SAWDERN POINT

OIL REFINERY

25 – 40 MINS

20 – 30 MINS

ANGLE BAY

MUDFLATS

TRAILBLAZER

C.P.

MAP 22

CAR PARK

21

TO B4320 ANGLE - PEMBROKE

CAR PARK

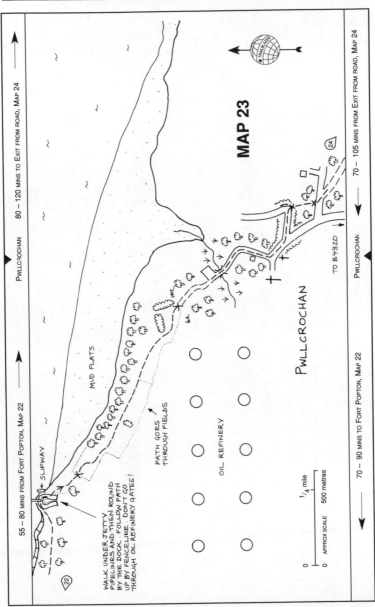

MAP 23

PWLLCROCHAN 80 – 120 MINS TO EXIT FROM ROAD, MAP 24

55 – 80 MINS FROM FORT POPTON, MAP 22

70 – 105 MINS FROM EXIT FROM ROAD, MAP 24

PWLLCROCHAN

70 – 90 MINS TO FORT POPTON, MAP 22

MUD FLATS

SLIPWAY

PATH GOES THROUGH FIELDS

OIL REFINERY

PWLLCROCHAN

TO B4320

WALK UNDER JETTY PIPELINES AND THEN ROUND BY THE DOCK. FOLLOW PATH UP BY FENCELINE. DON'T GO THROUGH OIL REFINERY GATES!

¼ mile

500 metres

0   APPROX SCALE

22

24

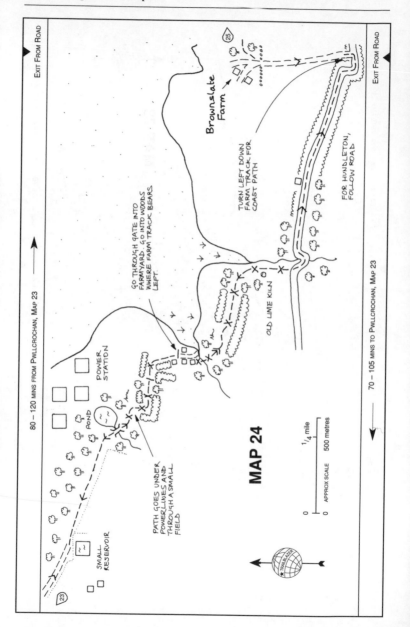

80 – 120 MINS FROM PWLLCROCHAN, MAP 23

EXIT FROM ROAD

EXIT FROM ROAD

25

Brownslate Farm

TURN LEFT DOWN FARM TRACK FOR COAST PATH

FOR HUNDLETON, FOLLOW ROAD

OLD LIME KILN

GO THROUGH GATE INTO FARMYARD. GO INTO WOODS WHERE FARM TRACK BEARS LEFT.

POWER STATION

POND

PATH GOES UNDER POWERLINES AND THROUGH A SMALL FIELD

SMALL RESERVOIR

23

MAP 24

APPROX SCALE

0   ¼ mile

0   500 metres

70 – 105 MINS TO PWLLCROCHAN, MAP 23

HUNDLETON TO HAZELBEACH

MAPS 25–29

If you survived the last section then you may as well keep going. It's **ten and a half miles (17km, 3½–4½hrs)** to Hazelbeach on the other side of the Milford Haven estuary. This may not be the most stimulating stretch of the coast path but there are some pleasant bits. From Brownslate Farm the path continues across fields to **Quoits Mill** before passing through the housing estate of Monkton. The road then drops down into Pembroke with the impressive and

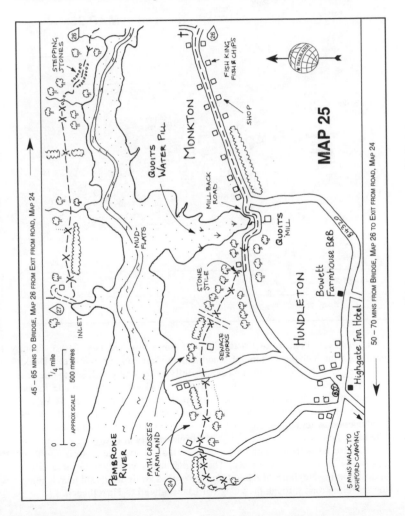

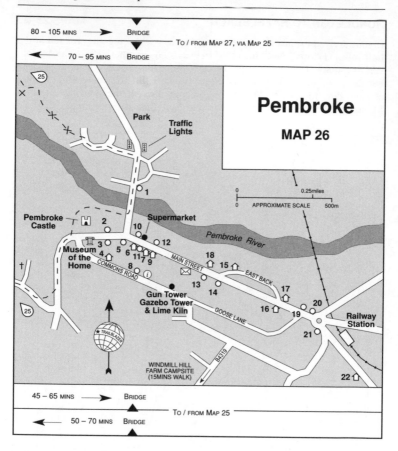

80 – 105 MINS → BRIDGE

To / FROM MAP 27, VIA MAP 25

← 70 – 95 MINS BRIDGE

Park

Traffic Lights

Pembroke

MAP 26

1

Pembroke Castle

Supermarket

2

10

Pembroke River

0   0.25miles
APPROXIMATE SCALE   500m

3   12

Museum of the Home   4   5   6   11   9

COMMONS ROAD   8   MAIN STREET   18   15

13   14   EAST BACK

★ TRAILBLAZER

17

Gun Tower Gazebo Tower & Lime Kiln   16   19   20

GOOSE LANE   21

Railway Station

25

WINDMILL HILL FARM CAMPSITE (15MINS WALK)   B4319

22

45 – 65 MINS → BRIDGE

To / FROM MAP 25

← 50 – 70 MINS BRIDGE

well preserved **Pembroke Castle** the first thing you see (see p108). From Pembroke the path passes through woodland and farmland to **Pembroke Dock**. Dropping steeply down Treowen Rd and Bellvue Terrace you'll see the **defensible barracks**, which were built to protect the dockyard from land attacks, on the top of the hill to the left. The coast path passes along **Front St** by the seafront where you can see the first terraced houses to be built when the dockyard opened. After negotiating the streets of Pembroke Dock you must cross the **Cleddau Toll Bridge**. Don't worry; environmentally friendly walkers go for free! It also takes them much longer to cross than it does the motorists so they can really savour the experience. The bridge takes you over to more urban sprawl and the **Neyland Marina**. From here it's a straightforward march along the shoreline road through the village of Llanstadwell to **Hazelbeach**.

KEY

Where to stay
4 Ushers Moat House
6 Lion Hotel
7 Old King's Arms Hotel
9 Middlegate Hotel
15 Merton Place House
16 Old Cross Saws Inn
17 Coach House Hotel
18 Beech House
22 High Noon

Where to eat
1 Golden Park Chinese
2 Richmond's Restaurant
3 Haven Christian Coffee Shop
5 Henry's Coffee Shop
8 Pembroke Carvery Chinese
10 Rowlies Takeaway
11 Renaissance
12 Jays Sandwich Shop
13 Brown's Restaurant
14 Left Bank
19 Top of the Town
20 Royal Oak
21 The Ship Inn

PEMBROKE (PENFRO)   MAP 26

Pembroke, birthplace of Henry VII, is steeped in history and comes as a pleasant surprise. Stretched out along one long street on top of a ridge by the river, there are plenty of pubs and places to stay. The 900-year-old Norman **castle** is the focal point of the town, standing guard over the river and well worth a visit (see p108).

Down on Commons Rd you can see the remains of **Gun Tower** and **Gazebo Tower**; mediaeval defensive towers which formed part of the old town wall. Next to them is a 200-year-old lime kiln, one of many scattered along the Pembrokeshire coast. Aside from these sights there is also the **Museum of the Home**; an odd little place full of household curiosities. It can be found opposite the castle at the far end of Main St.

Services

The **TIC** (☎ 01646-622388) is on Commons Rd near the Chinese takeaway. There are a number of **banks** as well as a **post office**, plenty of **shops** and a Somerfield **supermarket**. These are all on Main St.

Buses depart from outside the Somerfield supermarket and outside the castle on Main St. The **train station** is at the far end of the town past the roundabout on Station Rd. There are regular services to Pembroke Dock or back to Tenby, Kilgetty and Swansea for connections elsewhere.

Where to stay

There are plenty of places to spend the night. Campers will have to head up the steep B4319 road for about half a mile where you will find **Windmill Hill Farm Caravan and Campsite** (☎ 01646-682392, open all year) with prices starting from £3.

One of the cheapest places in town is **Usher's Moat House** (☎ 01646-684557, Commons Rd) near the TIC which has five chalets each sleeping four people. Each chalet costs £15 per person per night based on four sharing. At the other end of town, near the station, is the very comfortable and friendly **High Noon Guest House** (☎ 01646-683736, 🖵 www.highnoon.co.uk, Lower Lamphey Rd, 3S/1T/3D/2F), with beds from £18.50 per person.

There are lots of places on Main St such as **Beech House** (☎ 01646-683740, 78 Main St, 1S/2T/1D/1F) which has B&B at £15 per person catering for a maximum of six at any one time.

Just off Main St is **Merton Place House** (☎ 01646-684796, 3 East Back, 1S/3T) with B&B from £17.50. At the eastern end of Main St is the **Old Cross Saws Inn** (☎ 01646-682475) with B&B from £17.

A little further on, opposite the Texaco garage is the smart but expensive **Coach House Hotel** (☎ 01646-684602, 🖵 www. coachhouse-hotel.co.uk) with 15 en-suite rooms. Prices start from £50 for a single mid-week up to £75 at weekends. The **Old**

❏ **Pembroke Castle**

The mighty Pembroke Castle (☎ 01646-681510, open all year, admission £3), birthplace of Henry VII, is a picture-book, turreted castle overlooking the town and the river estuary. It is one of many Norman castles in Pembrokeshire built in the 11th century to keep the Welsh at bay and can proudly claim to be the only one that never fell to the Welsh.

It has been the scene of many a bloody battle; most famously in 1648 during the civil war. The local mayor John Poyer caused consternation in parliament when he switched his allegiances, deciding to support the king. A rather annoyed Oliver Cromwell marched over, blew up the town walls and took Poyer prisoner.

During the summer there are a number of organized events within the castle walls, including falconry and archery displays, battle re-enactments and Shakespeare plays.

King's Arms Hotel (☎ 01646-683611, Main St, 12S/4D) is a quite luxurious place with prices starting at £35 per person.

Close by are two more upmarket hotels: *Middlegate Hotel* (☎ 01646-622442, Main St) and the *Lion Hotel* (☎ 01646-684501, 2S/5T/5D/2F) with en-suite rooms from £25 for a single.

Where to eat

There is a wide variety of choice for food in Pembroke with most of the eating holes lining Main St. For a touch of class try the swanky French *Left Bank* (☎ 01646-622333, Wed–Sun 12–2pm, 7–9.30pm), a restaurant with an arty interior and quite a pricey menu, though at least they can guarantee their ingredients are locally produced.

Another good choice is the smart but slightly touristy *Richmond's Restaurant* (☎ 01646-685460, 6pm–late) next to the castle while *The Renaissance* (Mon–Thu 10am–5pm, Fri 10am–11pm, Sat 10am–late) is a smart new joint offering lamb shank for £9.95 and scampi for £4.95. They also have a late bar at weekends.

Many of the pubs and hotels do food. The *Old King's Arms Hotel* (7–9pm) has a good restaurant in a rustic, dimly lit room with a good choice including duck at £5.75 and steaks at £12.75. The *Middlegate Hotel* has some cheap food including chicken and chips for £3.95 and sandwiches from £2.65.

At the other end of Main St is the *Coach House Hotel* (7.30–9am, 12–2pm, 7–9.30pm) with an expensive à la carte menu in their award winning Griffins Bistro.

Along Main St you'll find *Brown's Restaurant* is a great greasy spoon place, while *Jay's Sandwich Shop* is a good spot to get a packed lunch for the day. Meanwhile there are a number of cafés and coffee shops, the best of which are *Henry's Coffee Shop* (☎ 01646-622293, 9am–5pm) which does everything from jacket potatoes to Welsh rabbit (£3.95) and the simple *Haven Christian Coffee Shop* (10am–3pm) opposite the castle. It's a no-frills place but they do great toasties for £2.20.

There are also a number of kebab, pizza and fish and chip shops along Main St and a fish and chip shop, *Fish King*, on the main road through the Monkton housing estate.

On Commons Rd is the *Pembroke Carvery and Chinese Takeaway*; a large restaurant with typical Chinese fare and English food to eat in or take away. *Golden Park Chinese* (☎ 01646-681315, Tue–Sun 5.30pm–12am), on the other side of the river on the main road, only does takeaway.

Good places for a pint include the *Royal Oak* and the *Ship Inn* both of which are at the far eastern end of Main St by the roundabout.

❏ THE DAUGLEDDAU AND THE LANDSKER BORDERLANDS

The one part of the national park that is completely by-passed by the coast path, thanks to the Cleddau Bridge, is the Daugleddau estuary. This is a shame because it is also one of the most beautiful and quietest parts. In stark contrast to the rest of the coastline there are no dramatic cliffs or crashing waves. Instead the intricate creeks and waterways are sheltered by heavily wooded banks, offering peaceful walks far from the rest of the crowds who flock to the coast.

This part of Pembrokeshire is known as the Landsker Borderlands. The invisible Landsker Line separates the Welsh speaking north of Pembrokeshire from the southern half where the Norman influence is predominant. Along this invisible line are a number of Norman castles and fortresses, one of which can be seen at Carew on the banks of the estuary east of Pembroke. To this day southern Pembrokeshire has a distinctly English feel to it earning itself the unofficial title of 'Little England Beyond Wales'.

Walks

Unfortunately, circumnavigating the entire estuary is a little complicated since the western side is distinctly lacking in rights of way. Most of it would have to be walked on roads, many of which are not even that close to the estuary. It is best to explore the eastern side by following part of the Landsker Borderlands Trail and starting your walk from Cresswell Quay.

Important! It is paramount that you check the tide tables for the following walks since the path at Garron Pill and the stepping stones at Cresswell Quay are submerged at high tide. Aim to reach Garron Pill as the tide is falling so that you have time to reach the crossing at Cresswell Quay before it comes back in.

A long walk via Landshipping If your feet are not too tired from the coast path you could try the long circular walk from Cresswell Quay, up the lane to Martletwy and on to Landshipping Quay. From here the Landsker Borderlands Trail can be followed back along the shoreline passing the pretty village of Lawrenny on the way. This walk is 13$\frac{1}{2}$ miles (22km) and takes about 6 hours.

A short walk via Garron Pill and Lawrenny (see map p110) A shorter **six-and-a-half-mile (10km, 2$\frac{1}{4}$–3$\frac{3}{4}$hrs)** walk is described here for coast path walkers who are looking for an easy day. (Note the times below are cumulative.).

From **Cresswell Quay** head north up the left-hand lane. After crossing Cresswell Bridge take the first left up a steep hill through woodland. Follow this lane bordered by hedges. Ignore the left turn and go straight over at the crossroads where there is a letterbox. The lane drops down through woodland to reach another set of crossroads. Turn left here to reach **Garron Pill** estuary (1–1$\frac{1}{4}$hrs).

At the grassy car park by the estuary walk directly onto the mudflats and after five minutes look out for the less than obvious path cutting up into the shore-side forest and over a stile. Follow the path through woodland, past a shed and south along the wooded shoreline of the main Daugleddau estuary, the heather and oak trees stunted by the prevailing wind. Across the water is the white tower of Benton Castle poking through the trees. The path then crosses a stile, passes a caravan park and comes out on a track which you follow through the boatyard and onto the road at **Lawrenny Quay** (1$\frac{1}{4}$–1$\frac{3}{4}$hrs). Between 1780 and 1860 Lawrenny Quay was an important shipbuilding site. *(Continued on p111)*

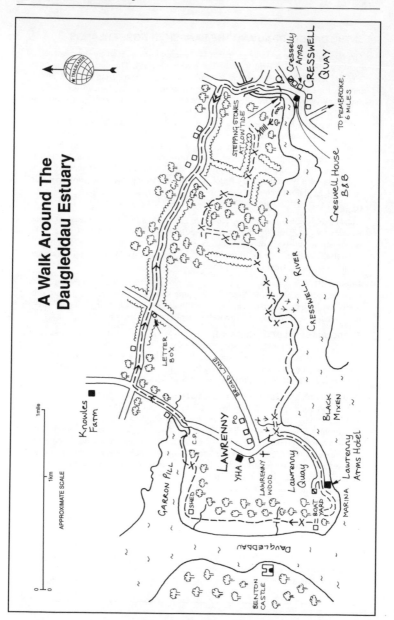

A Walk Around The Daugleddau Estuary

❑ THE DAUGLEDDAU AND THE LANDSKER BORDERLANDS

A short walk via Garron Pill and Lawrenny

(*Continued from p109*) Follow the lane past the Lawrenny Arms Hotel. After ten minutes the path leaves the road on the right-hand side just before reaching the village of **Lawrenny**. It's worth popping up to the village to see the pretty Norman church.

Back on the path, hop over the stone wall and cross the wooden boardwalk through the reed bed. The path follows the edge of the field, passes a marshy inlet and then continues through more fields, crossing a number of stiles before reaching a farm track next to woodland. Go up the farm track and turn right following the hedgerow before crossing a stile into the woods. Another stile takes you back into another field. Follow the edge of the woodland and then bear left following another hedgerow. Cross through a small field to reach a farm track. Leave the track at the sharp left hand bend and follow the steps down through some beautiful woodland to reach the stepping stones across the Cresswell River and back to **Cresswell Quay** ($2^{3}/_{4}$–$3^{1}/_{4}$hrs). By now you deserve some liquid refreshment in the wonderfully traditional *Cresselly Arms* where you can also get bar meals.

● **Transport** There's a daily bus to Cresswell Quay from either Kilgetty, Tenby (Upper Park Rd) or Pembroke Dock (Albion Sq); see public transport map p37. Cresswell Quay is about six miles (10km) from Pembroke so you could get a taxi if you have a bit of spare cash. To return to the coast path there are two or three afternoon buses back to Kilgetty, Tenby and Pembroke Dock.

● **Accommodation** Rather than catching a bus back to the coast path the same day you could spend the night locally. In Cresswell Quay *Cresswell House* (☎ 01646-651435, 🖳 www.cresswellhouse.co.uk, 3D en suite) has rooms from £22.50. In the village of Lawrenny there is the *Lawrenny Youth Hostel* (☎ 01646-651270, 23S, open all year). Beds are £8.50 per night per member. For a little more luxury there are en-suite rooms from £20 at *Knowles Farm* (☎ 01834-891221, 🖳 www.lawrenny.org.uk, 3D) while the *Lawrenny Arms Hotel* (☎ 01646-651367, 🖳 www.lawrenny-quay.co.uk) has 12 en-suite rooms from £25 per person.

PEMBROKE DOCK (DOC PENFRO)
MAP 27

Pembroke Dock won't win any beauty contests but if you look closer you will find it is a place with a short but interesting history. The town sprung up quite suddenly in the early 1800s when the Royal Navy came to the tiny hamlet of Paterchurch. They had a dockyard built and started constructing ships. In 1814 **Front St** was the first terraced row built to house the workers. The coast path runs along the road. A number of defensive fortifications sprang up to protect the town. One of the two **Martello Towers** can be seen off Front St and now houses the tourist information centre. These days the oil industry provides most of the employment and the Irish ferry terminal keeps a steady flow of visitors going through the town.

Services

The **TIC** is at the Martello Tower off Front St (☎ 01646-622246, 11am–3pm). As you would expect there are plenty of **shops** with all the high-street names. There are three **banks** and a **post office**. They can all be found in Dimond St which can be reached by leaving the coast path on Pembroke St; take the second right after the Dolphin Hotel into Queen St; head down here for Dimond St and all the shops and best places to eat. There are two big **superstores**; Co-op is across the road after leaving Front St while Tesco can be found off London Rd near the Llanion roundabout.

In Water St, near Co-op, there is a **health centre**. There are three **bus stops**, one outside Tesco, one in Laws St and the

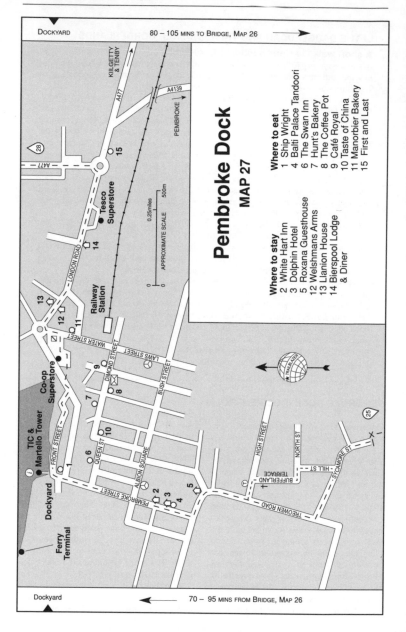

Pembroke Dock
MAP 27

Where to stay
2 White Hart Inn
3 Dolphin Hotel
5 Roxana Guesthouse
12 Welshmans Arms
13 Llanion House
14 Bierspool Lodge & Diner

Where to eat
1 Ship Wright
4 Balti Palace Tandoori
6 The Swan Inn
7 Hunt's Bakery
8 The Coffee Pot
9 Café Royal
10 Taste of China
11 Manorbier Bakery
15 First and Last

APPROXIMATE SCALE
0   0.25miles
0   500m

other in Albion Sq, which is not square at all but decidedly road-shaped. For the **train station** walk to the far eastern end of Dimond St. This is a terminus so there are no trains heading north but there are regular services to Tenby, Kilgetty and Swansea for connections elsewhere.

Adventurous types might want to take a day trip to Rosslare in Ireland. Passenger-only day returns are £9 and 24hr returns are £16. Phone **Irish Ferries** for details and bookings (☎ 08705-134252).

Where to stay

The first place you come to is the *Roxana Guest House* (☎ 01646-683116, Victoria Rd, 12T) just off Treowen Rd. Prices start from £20 per person in a twin room. At the bottom of the hill is the *Dolphin Hotel* (☎ 01646-685581, Pembroke St). It's not in the nicest part of town but it has en-suite rooms at £20 per person. Almost next door is the *White Hart* (☎ 01646-681687, Pembroke St). The three sheets of A4 paper on the door which list nearly 100 people who have been barred from drinking there is not the best advertisement for the place.

On London Rd, following the coast path through West Llanion, there are a number of places. The *Welshman's Arms* (☎ 01646-685643, 23 London Rd) has B&B from £12.50. Opposite, *Llanion House* (☎ 01646-685481, 26 London Rd) has rooms from £20 to £25 per person. Further along, next to Tesco, *Bierspool Lodge & Diner* (☎ 01646-621318, London Rd) is a motel open 24 hours with rooms from £15 per person.

The luxurious option is the *Cleddau Bridge Hotel* (☎ 01646-685961, Essex Rd, see map p114) with single en-suite rooms at £55 or double rooms for £69.50. Take the left turn at the roundabout just before the toll booth on the bridge and be sure to wipe your feet on entering.

Where to eat

For an Indian head for the *Balti Palace Tandoori Restaurant* (☎ 01646-683358, 6.30–11pm, 9 Pembroke St), next to Dolphin Hotel and for Chinese try *Taste of China* (☎ 01646-686132, Tue–Sun 5–11pm, 28 Queen St). An ideal place for a takeaway lunch or late breakfast is *Hunt's Bakery* (10am–4pm, Queen St) where all the food is guaranteed to be of Pembrokeshire origin. They have tasty jam doughnuts for 35p and cream buns for 40p along with sausage rolls, pies and other savoury bits and bobs. Another bakers, *Manorbier Bakery*, can be found in Water St.

In Dimond St there is a good café, *The Coffee Pot* (☎ 01646-622314) with great toasties from £2.95. Along the same road you will find the *Café Royal* (8am–late) which is not as regal as it might sound but they have some cheap, tasty food such as chicken korma for £5.95. Of a similar ilk is the *Swan Inn* (☎ 01646-686964, 23 Queen St, 12–2pm, 7–9.30pm) which has cheap pub grub and also does takeaway pizzas.

On the corner of Front St, right on the official coast path, the *Ship Wright* (☎ 01646-682090, 7–9pm) has traditional pub grub. Front St used to be home to a number of old taverns that served as drinking dens for the dockyard workers back in the early 1800s. The Ship Wright is the only survivor.

Heading out of Pembroke Dock is *Bierspool Lodge and Diner* (see Where to stay) which is a bit like a motorway service station. Chips and jacket potatoes both start at £1, and they also do all-day breakfasts from £2.30.

Keep going for the *First and Last* next to the roundabout where the road heads north to the Cleddau Bridge. It is the first and last pub on this side of Milford Haven harbour. It's open all day for £1 toasties and has some great real ales.

NEYLAND & HAZELBEACH MAPS 28, 29

Having crossed the Cleddau toll bridge and left the delights of Pembroke Dock behind you, Neyland is nothing to get excited about, being only marginally less ugly than Pembroke Dock and certainly less interesting. The modern marina is the only attractive part of the town. From the big car park at the end of the marina village you can follow the main street up the hill for five minutes to reach the **post office** and a **small supermarket**. If you are looking for a bed you are probably better off back in Pembroke Dock as there is little choice here. North of Neyland in Great Honeyborough is *Y Ffynnon* (☎ 01646-601369, 45 Honeyborough Rd, 1S/1T/1D) with beds from £16 per person.

The *Ferry House Inn* (☎ 01646-600 270, 🖳 ferryhouseinn@freenetname.co.uk,

3T/3F) in Hazelbeach has B&B for £30–35 and is also the best place to get food (12–2pm & 7–11pm). It has a nice conservatory with harbour views, albeit including the refinery and power station. Despite this, Hazelbeach is a lot prettier than Neyland.

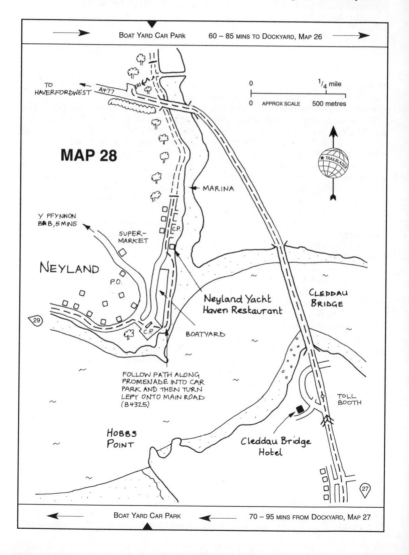

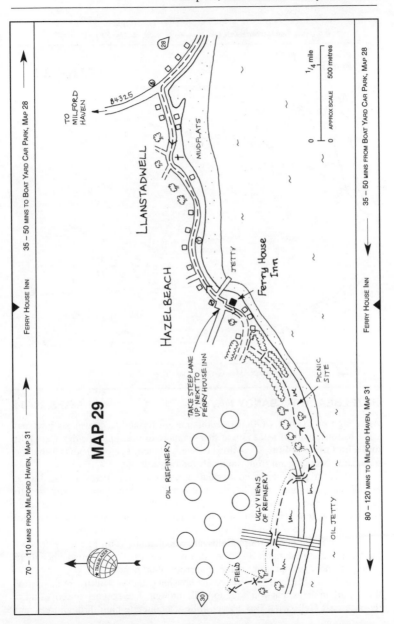

MAP 29

70 – 110 MINS FROM MILFORD HAVEN, MAP 31

FERRY HOUSE INN

35 – 50 MINS TO BOAT YARD CAR PARK, MAP 28

35 – 50 MINS FROM BOAT YARD CAR PARK, MAP 28

FERRY HOUSE INN

80 – 120 MINS TO MILFORD HAVEN, MAP 31

OIL REFINERY

UGLY VIEWS OF REFINERY

FIELD

OIL JETTY

TAKE STEEP LANE UP NEXT TO FERRY HOUSE INN

HAZELBEACH

LLANSTADWELL

Ferry House Inn

JETTY

PICNIC SITE

MUDFLATS

B4325

TO MILFORD HAVEN

¼ mile

500 metres

0

0

APPROX SCALE

TRAILBLAZER

28

30

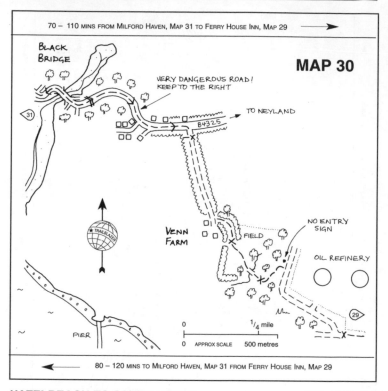

BLACK
BRIDGE

MAP 30

VERY DANGEROUS ROAD!
KEEP TO THE RIGHT

TO NEYLAND

B4325

31

VENN
FARM

FIELD

NO ENTRY
SIGN

OIL REFINERY

29

PIER

0   ¼ mile

0   APPROX SCALE   500 metres

HAZELBEACH TO SANDY HAVEN   MAPS 29–34

After nigh on 20 miles (30km) negotiating oil refineries, power stations and conurbations, the bad news is that there is more of the same for the next **eight and a half miles (14km, 2-¾–4hrs)** to Sandy Haven. The good news is that the good stuff begins again from Sandy Haven onwards.

The coast path heads up a small lane beside the Ferry House Inn at Hazelbeach, passing through fields and woodland. You may be surprised to realize that there is a second vast oil refinery to the right. Once again the vegetation does well to keep the eyesore from view, that is until you come to an ugly red bridge over the oil pipelines when it becomes all too obvious.

The path continues through fields and woodland to **Venn Farm** and follows the farm track to the main B4325 road. Take great care on the road since there is no pavement and there are some dangerous blind bends.

Thankfully **Milford Haven** and the housing estate of **Hakin** are the last of the big urban areas that you have to walk through. The scenery improves a little once past **Gelliswick Bay** as you follow a concrete path through trees and scrubland and on around the perimeter of an abandoned oil refinery. The land here has been well restored and apart from the ugly oil pipelines and disused jetty there is little evidence of the site at all from the path. The pretty beach of **Sandy Haven** is a very welcome sight. Ahead you can see the harbour opening out with the Angle peninsula on the left and the Dale peninsula on the right.

MILFORD HAVEN (ABERDAUGLED-DAU)   MAP 31

The town of Milford Haven, named after the harbour on which it lies, is a relatively modern place. It dates back to 1790 when it was settled by a group of American whalers who provided whale oil for the London street lamps. The town later became an important fishing port and although fishing is still of importance here, it is now tourism and oil that bring in most of the money.

For a greater insight into the town's history there's the small **Milford Haven Museum** (☎ 01646-694496, Easter–Oct, daily, admission £1.20) by the dockyard.

The enormous harbour, lauded by both Nelson and Defoe, is one of the natural wonders of the British Isles but has sadly been exploited by the oil giants as anyone who has walked from Angle can testify. Only two of the original four terminals remain in operation but the jetties and pipelines still scar the coastline.

Services

Milford Haven is the last of the big towns around the harbour. From here there is little chance of getting any provisions until Broad Haven, about 30 miles (48km) away, although there is a small shop at Dale. The next cash machine is also at Broad Haven with another at St David's, a further 17 miles (27km) on from Broad Haven.

Charles St is where you'll find most of the shops and services including the TIC (☎ 01646-690866, 94 Charles St, 10am–5pm). The main **post office** is a little further down the same road. This is also where you will find the Gareth James **pharmacy** (47 Charles St), the **laundrette** (17 Charles St) and a Somerfield **supermarket**. There's also a big Tesco **superstore** in the retail park by the docks and opposite is the **train station** with services to Haverfordwest and Clarbeston Rd for connections to Fishguard.

There are also trains to Swansea and London. Most **buses** leave from Hamilton Terrace. The **Puffin Shuttle bus**, however, departs from Robert St for services along the coast as far as St David's (see p38).

Where to stay

Where the coast path enters the town along the seafront there's bed and breakfast for £15 per person at *1 Pier Rd* (☎ 01646-694531, 1S/1T/1D) just off The Rath; it's strictly non-smokers only.

On the official route of the coast path, along the seafront road, is the *Belhaven House Hotel* (☎ 01646-695983, 29 Hamilton Terrace) which has eleven rooms from £25 to £38 per person. Also on Hamilton Terrace is the *Lord Nelson Hotel* (☎ 01646-695341) with 31 en-suite rooms from £38 per person and the *Starboard Hotel* (☎ 01646-692439, 21 Hamilton Terrace) with rooms at £17 per person.

If you don't mind the smell of curry wafting up through the floorboards the *Momtaj Balti Restaurant* (☎ 01646-690880, Charles St) offers bed but no breakfast for only £13 per person.

After passing the dockyard into Hakin you'll find the *Cleddau Villa Guesthouse* (☎ 01646-690313, 21 St Annes Rd; see Map 32) with good value beds at £14 per person.

Where to eat

For Indian food head to *Momtaj Balti* at the eastern end of Charles St. Alternatively, opposite the Torch Theatre is *Motirraj Tandoori Restaurant* (☎ 01646-698333, 11 Charles St, Wed–Mon 6–11.30pm) with more of the same.

For something from even further east there is the *Mandarin Chinese* (☎ 01646-693336, 20 Hamilton Terrace, 5–11.30pm) for chicken fried rice and the like.

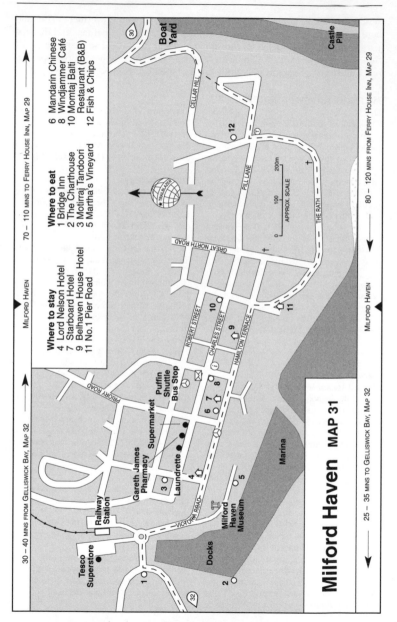

Milford Haven MAP 31

Where to stay
4 Lord Nelson Hotel
7 Starboard Hotel
9 Belhaven House Hotel
11 No.1 Pier Road

Where to eat
1 Bridge Inn
2 The Charthouse
3 Motiraj Tandoori
5 Martha's Vineyard
6 Mandarin Chinese
8 Windjammer Café
10 Momtaj Balti Restaurant (B&B)
12 Fish & Chips

30 – 40 MINS FROM GELLISWICK BAY, MAP 32

70 – 110 MINS TO FERRY HOUSE INN, MAP 29

MILFORD HAVEN

80 – 120 MINS FROM FERRY HOUSE INN, MAP 29

25 – 35 MINS TO GELLISWICK BAY, MAP 32

MILFORD HAVEN

Tesco Superstore
Railway Station
Gareth James Pharmacy
Supermarket
Puffin Shuttle Bus Stop
Laundrette
PRIORY ROAD
ROBERT STREET
CHARLES STREET
HAMILTON TERRACE
VICTORIA ROAD
GREAT NORTH ROAD
CELLAR HILL
PILL LANE
THE RATH
Milford Haven Museum
Docks
Marina
Boat Yard
Castle Pill

APPROX. SCALE
0   100   200m

Milford Haven – Where to eat *(cont'd)*
For something different look out for the little *Windjammer Café* (☎ 01646-693999, 11 Priory St, Mon 10am–3pm, Wed–Thu 10am–8pm, Tue, Fri–Sun 10am– 4pm) between Hamilton Terrace and Charles St; look for the green sign. They specialize in Italian, Mediterranean (best paella in Milford Haven, £4.55) and local seafood dishes like lobster for £5.95. Highly recommended is their organic Welsh rib eye steak at £4.45. The *Lord Nelson* (see p117) does food for non-residents and also has a nightclub open till 2am (Fri & Sat). There's fish & chips at the *Hake Inn* on St Anne's Rd in Hakin. *(Cont'd on p121).*

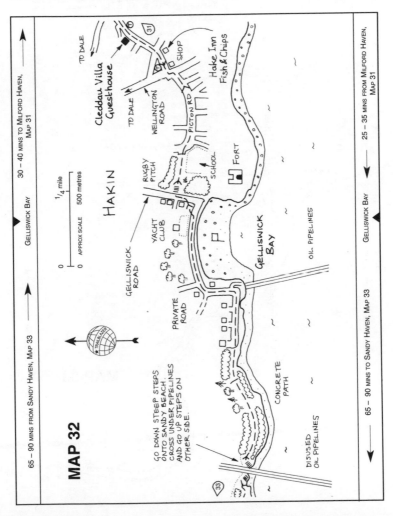

MAP 32

GELLISWICK BAY

30 – 40 MINS TO MILFORD HAVEN, MAP 31

65 – 90 MINS FROM SANDY HAVEN, MAP 33

GELLISWICK BAY

25 – 35 MINS FROM MILFORD HAVEN, MAP 31

65 – 90 MINS TO SANDY HAVEN, MAP 33

HAKIN

Cleddau Villa Guesthouse

TO DALE

TO DALE

WELLINGTON ROAD

PICTON RD

SHOP

Hake Inn Fish & Chips

RUGBY PITCH

SCHOOL

FORT

YACHT CLUB

GELLISWICK ROAD

PRIVATE ROAD

GELLISWICK BAY

OIL PIPELINES

CONCRETE PATH

DISUSED OIL PIPELINES

GO DOWN STEEP STEPS ONTO SANDY BEACH. CROSS UNDER PIPELINES AND GO UP STEPS ON OTHER SIDE.

0   1/4 mile
0   APPROX SCALE   500 metres

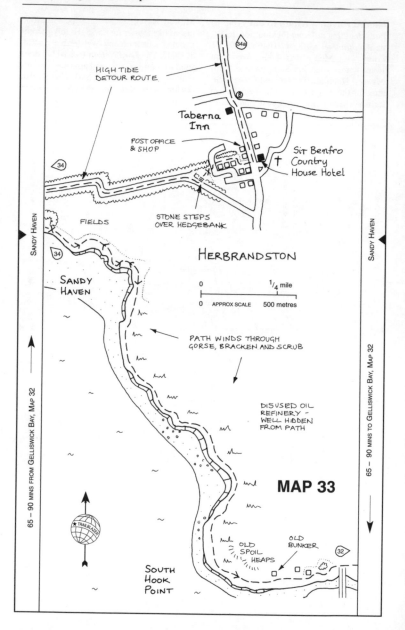

HIGH TIDE
DETOUR ROUTE

34a

Taberna
Inn

POST OFFICE
& SHOP

Sir Benfro
Country
House Hotel

34

STONE STEPS
OVER HEDGEBANK

SANDY HAVEN

SANDY HAVEN

FIELDS

34

HERBRANDSTON

SANDY
HAVEN

0   1/4 mile

0   APPROX SCALE   500 metres

PATH WINDS THROUGH
GORSE, BRACKEN AND SCRUB

DISUSED OIL
REFINERY –
WELL HIDDEN
FROM PATH

MAP 33

★ TRAILBLAZER

OLD SPOIL
HEAPS

OLD
BUNKER

32

SOUTH
HOOK
POINT

65 – 90 MINS FROM GELLISWICK BAY, MAP 32

65 – 90 MINS TO GELLISWICK BAY, MAP 32

Milford Haven – Where to eat (*cont'd*)
Down by the dockyard is the swish *Martha's Vineyard* (☎ 01646-697083, daily 12–2.15pm, 6.30–9.30pm) with a smart upstairs bar and restaurant where all food is guaranteed to be of local origin. They specialize in deep-sea fish dishes; the tuna steak is £8.95. It's popular with locals

so book in advance. They also have satellite TV. The *Charthouse Restaurant* (☎ 01646 690098, 🖥 www. thecharthouse.co.uk) by the docks near Tesco specializes in local dishes with the cawl (lamb broth) at £3.75.

For a drink before you leave town head for the *Bridge Inn* near the end of St Anne's Rd above the docks.

EAST BANK OF SANDY HAVEN AND HERBRANDSTON   MAPS 33, 34

Sandy Haven is a beautiful spot with a sandy beach and a long creek, or 'pill', stretching inland. Herbrandston lies on the high-tide detour route and is only a short distance from the main coast path at Sandy Haven. This quiet little village can be reached by following the lane up from the campsite. It has a **post office**, incorporating a small **shop**, found in the centre of the village by the church hall, and a couple of good pubs.

    Buses run to Milford Haven, Pembroke, Dale and Marloes. There is also the very useful **Puffin Shuttle bus** (see p38) which serves all the coastal villages as far as St David's. Don't make the mistake of waiting for the bus in the centre of the village. Most of the buses stop only on the main road opposite the Taberna Inn.

Right next to Sandy Haven on the coast path is the *Sandy Haven Caravan and Campsite* (☎ 01646 698844, Apr–Oct) with pitches from £4 per person.

    In the village there are two places to stay and eat. The cheaper of the two is the *Taberna Inn* (☎ 01646-693498, daily 12–3pm, 6–9.30pm), a good pub with B&B at £19 per person. They have an interesting menu which is largely seafood based but there is something for everyone. Jacket potatoes start at £1.50, or try the Sws-y-Ddraig (Welsh dragon curry) for a reasonable £5.95.

    The more expensive choice is the *Sir Benfro Country Hotel* (☎ 01646-694242, 🖥 sirbenfro@ic24.net, 12T) with en-suite rooms from £35 per person and great food. It even has an outdoor swimming pool.

SANDY HAVEN TO DALE   MAPS 34–37

These **five and a half miles (9km, 2–3hrs)** are quite easy going and, although not spectacular, the scenery is a vast improvement on the industrial landscape around Pembroke Dock and Milford Haven.

❑ **High Tide Obstacles**
It is worth giving advance warning here of two significant obstacles on the next section. The inlet at Sandy Haven and the estuary at The Gann near Dale, four miles (6km) further west, can both be crossed at low tide but at high tide the crossing points are completely submerged necessitating lengthy detours along roads. The trick is to cross the stepping stones at Sandy Haven as the tide is going out. In this way you have time to reach the next crossing near Dale before the tide has had time to come back in. For example if low tide is at 2pm you should be able to cross at 1pm. The tide won't have cut off the next crossing near Dale until about 6pm giving you plenty of time to reach it. Tide times are posted all over the place, in shops, on noticeboards and in the national park's annual newspaper *Coast to Coast*.

The cliffs at the beginning of this section are quite low compared to the rest of the coastline so there is nothing too strenuous. If you have timed it right you will be able to cross the stepping stones across **Sandy Haven Pill** at low tide (see p121). If, however, you find yourself faced with a barrier of water at high tide you will have to take the long road detour described at the end of this section.

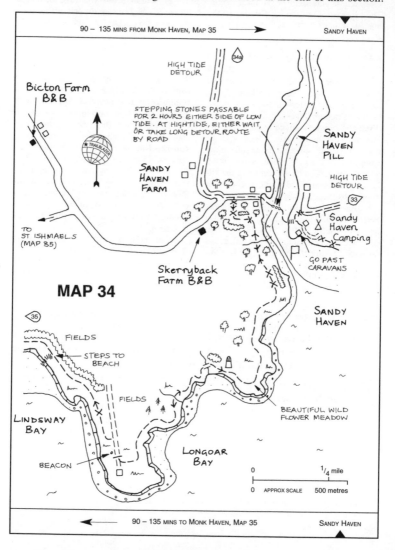

HIGH TIDE DETOUR

Bicton Farm B&B

STEPPING STONES PASSABLE FOR 2 HOURS EITHER SIDE OF LOW TIDE. AT HIGHTIDE, EITHER WAIT, OR TAKE LONG DETOUR ROUTE BY ROAD

TRAILBLAZER

SANDY HAVEN FARM

SANDY HAVEN PILL

HIGH TIDE DETOUR

33

TO ST ISHMAEL.S (MAP 35)

Sandy Haven Camping

Skerryback Farm B&B

GO PAST CARAVANS

MAP 34

SANDY HAVEN

35

FIELDS

STEPS TO BEACH

FIELDS

LINDSWAY BAY

BEACON

LONGOAR BAY

BEAUTIFUL WILD FLOWER MEADOW

0   ¼ mile

0   APPROX SCALE   500 metres

Once across the stepping stones the path takes you into some waterside woodland. It continues along the edge of a number of fields above low cliffs passing the ugly beacon above **Butts Bay**. The scenery becomes more spectacular around **Lindsway Bay**, a lovely sandy beach protected by steep cliffs on all sides. Here a path leading to **St Ishmael's** leaves the coast path next to a bench.

At **Watch House Point** there are old military bunkers and lookout buildings which can provide very welcome shelter in wet weather. The coast path carries on, past the remains of a curious Victorian watchtower, to **Monk Haven**, a pretty little wooded valley with an impressive castle-like wall guarding the bay. It also provides another access point to the village of St Ishmael's.

The path now follows gentle slopes overgrown with gorse, hawthorn and bracken to the farm buildings at Musselwick. From the small raised pond in the farmyard the path cuts down through shady trees to the stony beach. On very rare occasions, when there are exceptionally high tides, the beach route is impassable and you will have to follow the short detour up the farm track from the raised pond following the fence line round to The Gann.

Whichever way you come, the next obstacle is the plank crossing of the creek at **The Gann**. As with Sandy Haven you will need to have checked the tide times as the crossing is only possible at low tide (see p121). At high tide you must take the detour route by the road (described at the end of this section). Once over the other side the path takes you across the shingle beach to the road and down to the village of **Dale**.

HIGH TIDE DETOUR AT SANDY HAVEN (VIA RICKESTON BRIDGE)
MAPS 33, 34a & 34

This detour will add an extra **four miles (6km, 1¹/₂hrs)** to your day. From the campsite at Sandy Haven follow the lane up the hill. Just after the second right-

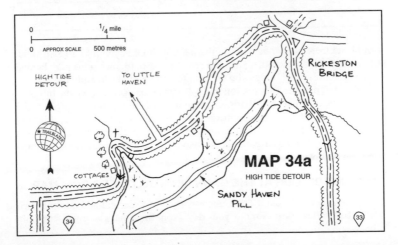

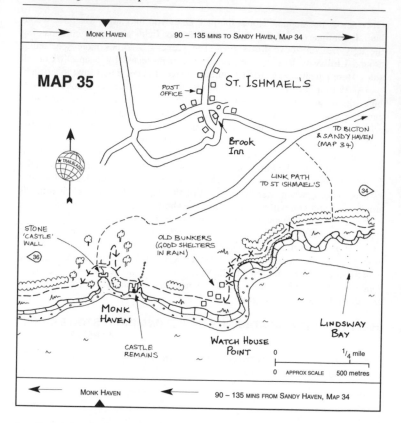

MONK HAVEN   90 – 135 MINS TO SANDY HAVEN, MAP 34

MAP 35

POST OFFICE

ST. ISHMAEL'S

Brook Inn

TO BICTON & SANDY HAVEN (MAP 34)

LINK PATH TO ST ISHMAEL'S

34

STONE 'CASTLE' WALL

36

OLD BUNKERS (GOOD SHELTERS IN RAIN)

MONK HAVEN

CASTLE REMAINS

WATCH HOUSE POINT

LINDSWAY BAY

0   1/4 mile

0   APPROX SCALE   500 metres

MONK HAVEN   90 – 135 MINS FROM SANDY HAVEN, MAP 34

hand bend there is a stone stile on the left which takes you into a small field. Cross the field, over another stile and cross the road, following the path behind a line of houses. This brings you out into the centre of **Herbrandston**.

Turn left past the Taberna Inn and follow the road north down the hill over Clay Bridge to **Rickeston Bridge**. Ignore turn-offs to the right and follow the road round to the left to the **cottages** at Sandyhill. Climb the steep hill and take the next left. Just after passing Sandy Haven Farm turn left towards Sandy Haven. The coast path proper leaves the road on your right up some steps through woodland.

HIGH TIDE DETOUR AT THE GANN (VIA MULLOCK BRIDGE) MAP 36

This second detour, around The Gann estuary near Dale, will add a further **two and a half miles (4km, 1hr)** to your day. From the point where you normally

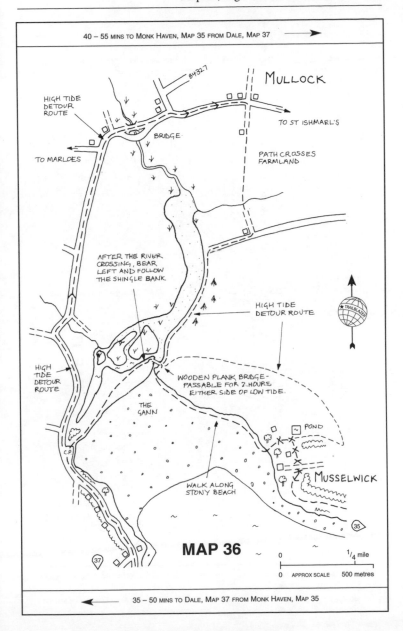

40 – 55 MINS TO MONK HAVEN, MAP 35 FROM DALE, MAP 37 →

B4327

MULLOCK

HIGH TIDE
DETOUR
ROUTE

BRIDGE

TO MARLOES ←

TO ST ISHMAEL'S

PATH CROSSES
FARMLAND

AFTER THE RIVER
CROSSING, BEAR
LEFT AND FOLLOW
THE SHINGLE BANK.

HIGH TIDE
DETOUR ROUTE

TRAILBLAZER

HIGH TIDE
DETOUR
ROUTE

WOODEN PLANK BRIDGE-
PASSABLE FOR 2 HOURS
EITHER SIDE OF LOW TIDE.

THE
GANN

POND

C.P.

MUSSELWICK

WALK ALONG
STONY BEACH

35

MAP 36

37

0   1/4 mile

0   APPROX SCALE   500 metres

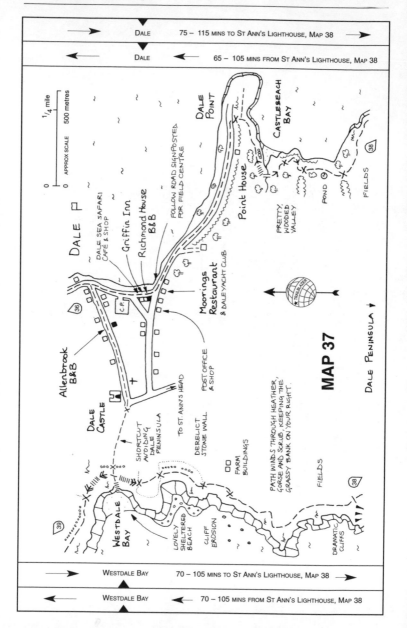

¼ mile   500 metres

APPROX SCALE

0   0

DALE POINT

CASTLEBEACH BAY

38

DALE

DALE SEA SAFARI CAFÉ & SHOP

Griffin Inn

Richmond House B&B

FOLLOW ROAD SIGNPOSTED FOR FIELD CENTRE

Point House

PRETTY WOODED VALLEY

POND

FIELDS

36

C.P.

Moorings Restaurant & DALE YACHT CLUB

Allenbrook B&B

TRAILBLAZER

MAP 37

DALE PENINSULA ↓

Dale Castle

SHORTCUT AVOIDING DALE PENINSULA

To ST ANN'S HEAD

POST OFFICE & SHOP

DERELICT STONE WALL

FARM BUILDINGS

PATH WINDS THROUGH HEATHER, GORSE AND SCRUB, KEEPING THE GRASSY BANK ON YOUR RIGHT

FIELDS

38

39

WESTDALE BAY

LOVELY SHELTERED BEACH

CLIFF EROSION

DRAMATIC CLIFFS

cross at low tide head north along the bank of the creek. Follow the narrow lane up the hill a short way and turn left at Whiteholme's Farm. Cross the farmland to the road at **Mullock Farm**. From here walk down the lane joining the B4327 road just before **Mullock Bridge**. After the bridge simply follow the road all the way to Dale, rejoining the coast path proper at the car park by the estuary.

WEST BANK OF SANDY HAVEN & ST ISHMAEL'S (LLANISMEL) MAP 35

St Ishmael's is a pretty village with a friendly pub. Again it requires a small detour from the coast path. The quickest way is to follow the public footpath from Lindsway Bay (look out for a bench by the coast path marking the trail to the village).

The route from Monk Haven is slightly longer. The **post office** is up the hill in the northern end of the village. There are no B&Bs in the village itself but two nearby farms offer accommodation. Just up the lane from Sandy Haven, *Skerryback Farmhouse*

(☎ 01646-636598, 🖳 www.pfh.co.uk/sker ryback, 2T) has B&B from £20. Further from the trail, *Bicton Farm* (☎ 01646-636 215, 1S/6T) at Bicton has B&B from £18. Rumour has it that they have been known to give residents a lift to and from the *Brook Inn* (☎ 01646-636277, 11am–11pm) in the village. This friendly little pub is the only place to eat. They have quite an extensive menu which includes ploughman's for £3.95. They also have a good choice of real ales including their own Brook Inn Ale.

DALE   MAP 37

Dale is a small village but it's alive with tourists in the summer months. Sitting on the neck of the Dale peninsula, it overlooks a sheltered bay popular with water-sports enthusiasts. If you want to have a go yourself then you can try everything from surfing and sailing to canoeing and coasteering (see p82) at **Dale Sea Safari** (☎ 01646-636642, 🖳 www.surfdale.co.uk). They offer tuition for beginners as well as equipment hire.

There is a small **shop** at the **post office** which can be found just around the corner from The Griffin Inn. It's open only in the morning from 9am to 12pm and is closed on Sundays. Another **shop** can be found at Dale Boat House.

There are few places to stay so booking in advance is recommended. *Richmond House B&B* (☎ 07974 925009, 7S/2D/1T) has bunkhouse accommodation for £15 or £18 with breakfast or en-suite double and

twin rooms for £23 per person with a £5 single-person supplement. On the northern side of the village, along the road towards Dale Castle, is *Allenbrook* (☎ 01646-636 254, 🖳 allenbrook@talk21.com, 1S/2T/1D) which charges from £25.

The *Griffin Inn* (☎ 01646-636227) is the only pub. They do food all day in the summer months. You can't miss it, sitting at the southern end of the village overlooking the water. As with many of the pubs along the coast the menu is very much influenced by the sea. The mussels in white wine are £5.50 and a half pint of prawns is £2.95. There are also jacket potatoes from £2.50 and sirloin steak for £7.50.

Close by is the *Moorings Restaurant* (☎ 01646-636362, Thu–Sat 7pm–late) situated in Dale Yacht Club, once again specializing in locally caught seafood. There are also snacks available at *Planet Dale Café* which is open in the summer only.

DALE TO MUSSELWICK SANDS (FOR MARLOES)   MAPS 37–41

The length of this beautiful section is **12 miles (19km, 5–6hrs)** and yet there is the temptation to shorten it by missing out the Dale peninsula. If you follow the official path around the peninsula it is five and a half miles (9km, 2¼hrs) to

Westdale Bay. If you take the shortcut it is less than a mile (1km, 15mins). Purists will want to do the whole thing and will be well rewarded since there is some beautiful scenery to enjoy. The peninsula protects Milford Haven harbour from the worst the Atlantic can throw at it. The eastern side is a mixture of gentle cliffs, small wooded valleys and pretty bays while the wind battered western side is characterized by high, rugged cliffs.

From Dale Yacht Club at the southern end of the village the route follows the lane to Point House and then on across farmland before dropping down to a pretty little bay surrounded by woodland.

Just past **Watwick Point** and its ugly beacon is the lovely Watwick Bay, then more farmland and low cliffs. At Mill Bay there is a stone on the field's edge commemorating the landing of Henry Tudor and his 55 ships and 4000 men from France on 7 August 1485 after 14 years in exile. From Mill Bay Henry marched east where he got the better of Richard III in the Battle of Bosworth on 22 August 1485. He then became Henry VII, founder of the Tudor dynasty.

St Ann's lighthouse, which is now a set of holiday homes, marks the northern lip of the Milford Haven harbour. North from here the cliffs are precipitous and in places are crumbling into the sea so take great care. The path passes through scrubland and heathland along the level cliff top, eventually dropping steeply to pretty **Westdale Bay**. People do swim here but it is not the safest place for a dip since there are strong undercurrents as the big warning sign indicates.

The path skirts an old disused aerodrome, rapidly becoming overrun with gorse and bracken, before arriving high above the great sweep of **Marloes Sands**, one of the finest beaches in Pembrokeshire. The islands of Gateholm, Grassholm and Skomer can all be seen on the western horizon.

Hostellers should look out for a path above **Raggle Rocks** which leads to the youth hostel (5mins from the coast path). The coast path continues on an easy course above some spectacular cliffs with twisted, folded rock dropping into the heaving sea below. This part of the coast is a marine nature reserve and with the proximity of some important breeding islands is a great place to spot seabirds. At **Martin's Haven** there is a National Trust visitor centre with information about the wildlife of the area. From here you can also take a boat trip to Skomer, where you have an even greater chance of spotting wildlife, particularly puffins (see p132).

The path then follows the fairly level cliff top to **Musselwick Sands**, another wonderful sandy beach with sheer cliffs all around. At the southern end of the bay next to a picnic bench there is a path leading down to the beach and another one heading inland to the village of Marloes.

(Opposite): Popular with surfers, Freshwater West (see p97) is one of the best beaches in Pembrokeshire.

(Overleaf, top and bottom): On the coast path near St Brides Haven (see p135).

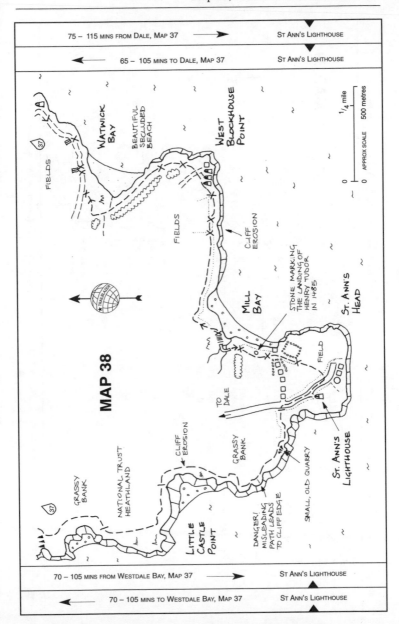

75 – 115 MINS FROM DALE, MAP 37 ➤ ST ANN'S LIGHTHOUSE

65 – 105 MINS TO DALE, MAP 37 ST ANN'S LIGHTHOUSE

WATWICK BAY

BEAUTIFUL SECLUDED BEACH

WEST BLOCKHOUSE POINT

FIELDS

FIELDS

CLIFF EROSION

1/4 mile

500 metres

APPROX SCALE

MAP 38

MILL BAY

STONE MARKING THE LANDING OF HENRY TUDOR IN 1485

ST. ANN'S HEAD

FIELD

TO DALE

NATIONAL TRUST HEATHLAND

CLIFF EROSION

GRASSY BANK

ST. ANN'S LIGHTHOUSE

SMALL, OLD QUARRY

GRASSY BANK

LITTLE CASTLE POINT

DANGER! MISLEADING PATH LEADS TO CLIFF EDGE

70 – 105 MINS FROM WESTDALE BAY, MAP 37 ➤ ST ANN'S LIGHTHOUSE

70 – 105 MINS TO WESTDALE BAY, MAP 37 ST ANN'S LIGHTHOUSE

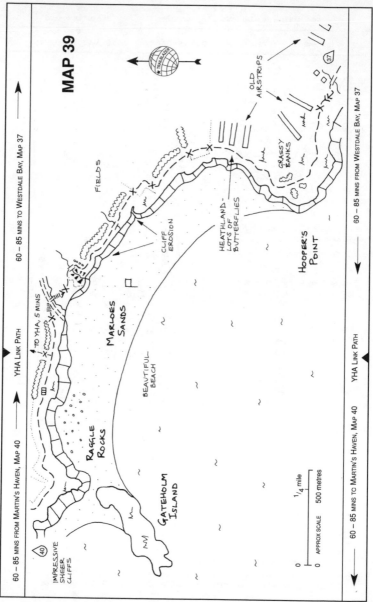

MAP 39

60 – 85 MINS TO WESTDALE BAY, MAP 37

60 – 85 MINS FROM WESTDALE BAY, MAP 37

60 – 85 MINS FROM MARTIN'S HAVEN, MAP 40

60 – 85 MINS TO MARTIN'S HAVEN, MAP 40

YHA LINK PATH

YHA LINK PATH

OLD AIRSTRIPS

GRASSY BANKS

FIELDS

CLIFF EROSION

HEATHLAND – LOTS OF BUTTERFLIES

HOOPER'S POINT

TO YHA, 5 MINS

MARLOES SANDS

BEAUTIFUL BEACH

RAGGLE ROCKS

GATEHOLM ISLAND

IMPRESSIVE SHEER CLIFFS

37

40

1/4 mile

APPROX SCALE

500 metres

0

0

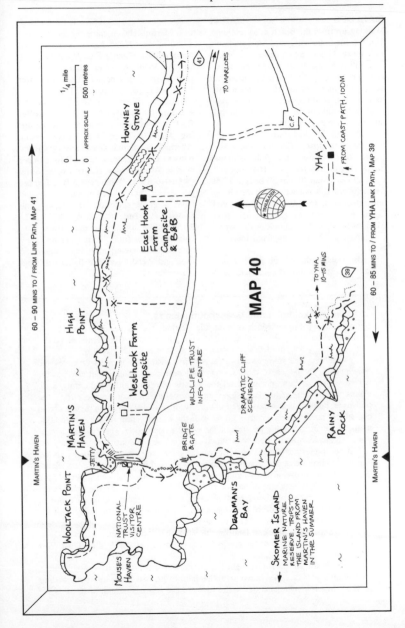

MARTIN'S HAVEN

60 – 90 MINS TO / FROM LINK PATH, MAP 41

WOOLTACK POINT

MOUSE'S HAVEN

MARTIN'S HAVEN

HIGH POINT

NATIONAL TRUST VISITOR CENTRE

JETTY

BRIDGE & GATE

Westhook Farm Campsite

WILDLIFE TRUST INFO CENTRE

HOWNEY STONE

¼ mile

500 metres

APPROX SCALE

East Hook Farm Campsite & B&B

41

TO MARLOES

C.P.

YHA

FROM COAST PATH, 100M

MAP 40

TO YHA, 10–15 MINS

39

DRAMATIC CLIFF SCENERY

DEADMAN'S BAY

RAINY ROCK

SKOMER ISLAND
MARINE NATURE RESERVE. BOAT TRIPS TO THE ISLAND FROM MARTIN'S HAVEN IN THE SUMMER.

MARTIN'S HAVEN

60 – 85 MINS TO / FROM YHA LINK PATH, MAP 39

MARLOES   MAP 41

Walking up from the beach at Musselwick you'll come to the village of Marloes half a mile away. This is not an especially attractive village although the strange clocktower is quite interesting, looking as though it needs to be on top of something like a town hall rather than sitting solemnly in a small field by the side of the road. The church is also very pretty and worth a look.

Close to the clocktower is where you will find the **post office** and there is a **phone box** opposite the pub. *Marloes Sands Youth Hostel* (☎ 01646-636667, open all year, Map 40) has 30 beds at £7.50 for members. It is not actually in the village and rather than coming from Musselwick Sands it is much easier to reach from Marloes Sands (a five-minute walk) where a signpost points the way from the coast path.

Also outside the village itself, a mile and a half (2km) before Musselwick Sands

near Martin's Haven, there is camping from £1.50 at *West Hook Farm* (Apr–Oct) and again at the adjoining *East Hook Farm* (☎ 01646-636291, Apr–Oct, Map 40) where a pitch costs £2 per person. They also offer B&B at £19 per person (2S/1T/2D).

In the village on Glebe Lane there's *Foxdale* (☎ 01646-636243 3T) who offer B&B accommodation from £20 and **camping** (Mar–Oct) from £1 to £3 per person. Alternatively there is *Greenacre* (☎ 01646-636400, Glebe Lane) with B&B for £14 per person. At the *Clock House Coffee Shop* (☎ 01646-636527) there is B&B at £20 per person or £25 en suite (Apr–Oct). They also have a good selection of snacks. The *Lobster Pot Inn* (☎ 01646-636233, 12–2.15pm, 7–8.30pm) also does B&B with en-suite rooms from £25 per person. They have a good menu, including vegetarian food and Welsh beer. The fisherman's pie is £4.95.

❏ Skomer, Skokholm and Grassholm Islands

Lying to the west of the Marloes peninsula are three barren islands brought to life by the thousands of sea birds which breed on the sheer cliffs. All of them can be visited quite easily with guided walks available on Skomer and Skokholm.

Skomer, a national nature reserve, with its coastline peppered with caves and blowholes, is the largest of the three and is closest to the mainland. It also has the widest variety of bird species of all the islands with razorbills, guillemots, kittiwakes, storm petrels, fulmars, shags and cormorants festooning the cliffs. The puffins and manx shearwaters breed in burrows on the cliff tops with pictures from one of the burrows relayed to a monitor in the island centre. There are 160,000 manx shearwaters making up 40% of the world's population. There are also peregrine falcons and short-eared owls which can often be seen during the daytime.

If you prefer the odd mammal or two there are grey seals on the rocky shoreline while porpoises and dolphins can often be spotted from the boat to the island. There are also plenty of rabbits and some other small mammals, most notably the Skomer vole, a sub-species of bank vole, unique to the island. For the botanist the island is carpeted in bluebells, heather, thrift and sea campion, creating a riot of colour in the spring. **Skokholm**, to the south, is smaller but no less noisy with the relentless chatter of seabirds. There are about 35,000 pairs of manx shearwater that breed on Skokholm. You can land on the island but can't wander around as you please. You must join one of the guided walks organized by the Wildlife Trust West Wales who manage the island.

Grassholm, an RSPB reserve, is a rocky outcrop 4 miles (7km) west of Skomer. It's Britain's only gannetry, home to 30,000 pairs of gannets in the summer breeding season when it can be hard to see the rock for the gannets. *(Continued on p134)*

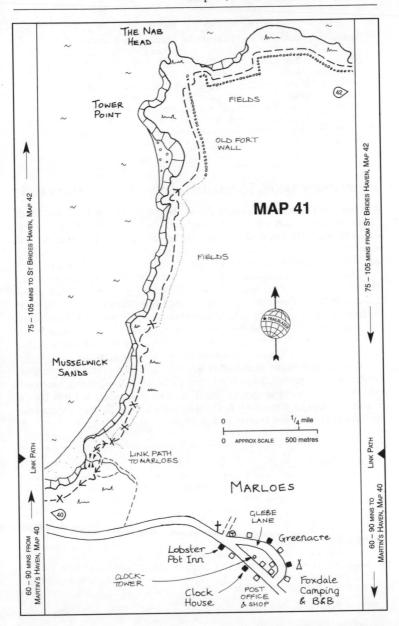

❏ **Skomer, Skokholm and Grassholm Islands (continued)**

(*Continued from p132*). Although you can't land on the island you can take a boat trip around it. **Dale Sailing** (☎ 01646-601636, 🖳 www.dale-sailing.co.uk) sail to Skomer from Martin's Haven on the *Dale Princess*. It costs £6 per person for the boat trip and an additional £6 to land (Tue–Sun 10am, 11am, 12pm, Easter–Oct). No bookings are necessary. From mid-June they also sail to Skokholm from Martin's Haven (Mon 10am). Bookings must be made through the Wildlife Trust West Wales (☎ 01437-765462). The cost is £6.50 for the boat ride and £9 for landing and the guided walk. They also offer a 3-hour trip around Grassholm (Mon 10am, Fri 12pm) for which bookings must be made through Dale Sailing.

MUSSELWICK SANDS TO BROAD HAVEN   MAPS 41–45

It is **eight and a half miles (14km, 3¹/₂–4¹/₂hrs)** from the link path for Marloes village to Broad Haven following the easy path above the cliffs. The next port of call is **St Brides Haven (Sainffraid)** a sheltered little bay where you will find toilets, a church and a cluster of houses but little else. The extravagant looking castle across the fields is actually the stately home of the St Brides estate.

The next stretch continues along easy-to-follow cliff tops. Once past **Mill Haven** things get a little tougher. The cliffs grow higher and the path roller-coasters its way up and down, passing **Brandy Bay**, a tiny little cove sheltered by frighteningly sheer cliffs. Take care here as the path is very close to the edge. Eventually the path settles down above high, vegetated cliffs at **Ticklas Point**. You can now see the immense sweep of St Brides Bay with Ramsey Island in the far distance, still a good two- to three-days' walking away.

Once past the mighty **Borough Head** with its 75-metre (246ft) slopes dropping steeply into the sea, the path enters some beautiful forest of oak, beech and pine which cling to the steep cliff side. The pretty little village of **Little Haven** is a little further on down the hill. From here it's a steep climb up the road out over the hill into **Broad Haven**, its bigger sister village.

❏ **Surfing**
Some of the best surfing in Britain can be found at places like Broad Haven and Newgale as the uninterrupted swell from the Atlantic comes rolling in. Even if you have never caught a wave before there are a number of patient instructors who will try to get you standing up on that board in the space of a day. **Newsurf** (☎ 01437-721398, 🖳 www.newsurf.co.uk) at Newgale filling station specializes in surfing tuition and surfboard and wetsuit hire. **West Wales Wind Surf and Sailing** (☎ 01646-636642, 🖳 www.surfdale.co.uk) at Dale offers half-day courses in surfing, windsurfing, canoeing and sailing with equipment hire too. Finally, based in St David's and Tenby is **TYF** (☎ 01437-721611, 🖳 www.tyf.com). They also have equipment for hire and offer safe tuition in windsurfing, canoeing, sailing and coasteering.

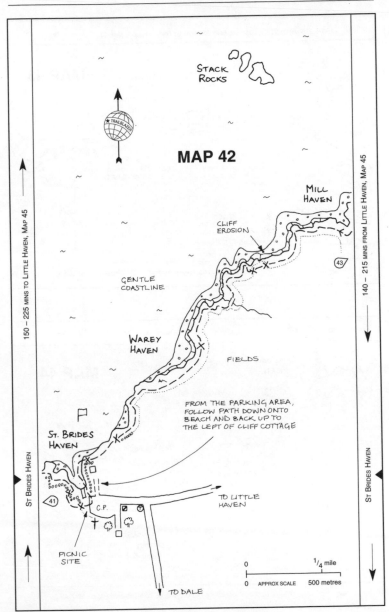

STACK ROCKS

★ TRAILBLAZER

MAP 42

MILL HAVEN

CLIFF EROSION

43

GENTLE COASTLINE

WAREY HAVEN

FIELDS

FROM THE PARKING AREA, FOLLOW PATH DOWN ONTO BEACH AND BACK UP TO THE LEFT OF CLIFF COTTAGE

St. BRIDES HAVEN

41

C.P.

TO LITTLE HAVEN

PICNIC SITE

150 – 225 MINS TO LITTLE HAVEN, MAP 45

140 – 215 MINS FROM LITTLE HAVEN, MAP 45

St BRIDES HAVEN

St BRIDES HAVEN

TO DALE

0   ¼ mile

0   APPROX SCALE   500 metres

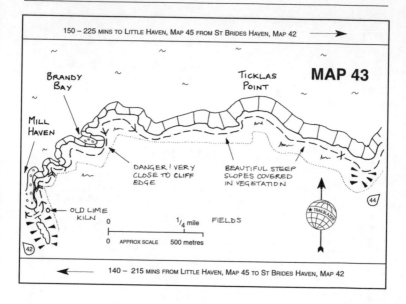

150 – 225 MINS TO LITTLE HAVEN, MAP 45 FROM ST BRIDES HAVEN, MAP 42 ➜

BRANDY BAY

TICKLAS POINT

MAP 43

MILL HAVEN

DANGER! VERY CLOSE TO CLIFF EDGE

BEAUTIFUL STEEP SLOPES COVERED IN VEGETATION

44

OLD LIME KILN

0 ¼ mile

0 APPROX SCALE 500 metres

FIELDS

★ TRAILBLAZER

42

◀ 140 – 215 MINS FROM LITTLE HAVEN, MAP 45 TO ST BRIDES HAVEN, MAP 42

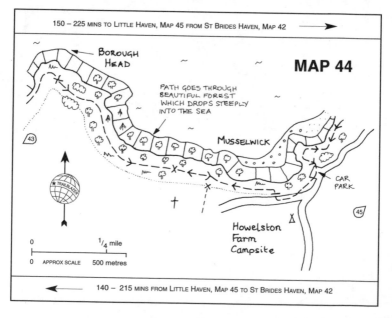

150 – 225 MINS TO LITTLE HAVEN, MAP 45 FROM ST BRIDES HAVEN, MAP 42 ➜

BOROUGH HEAD

MAP 44

PATH GOES THROUGH BEAUTIFUL FOREST WHICH DROPS STEEPLY INTO THE SEA

MUSSELWICK

43

★ TRAILBLAZER

CAR PARK

45

Howelston Farm Campsite

0 ¼ mile

0 APPROX SCALE 500 metres

◀ 140 – 215 MINS FROM LITTLE HAVEN, MAP 45 TO ST BRIDES HAVEN, MAP 42

LITTLE HAVEN (ABER BACH) MAP 45

Squeezed between two steep hillsides around a tiny cove, Little Haven is a lovely little place. It may be smaller than Broad Haven over the hill but it is far more appealing and has a good number of pubs to distract the exhausted walker.

Services

By turning right as you come into the village from the south you will find the **post office** and a small **shop**. For anything else of importance you will be better off carrying on to Broad Haven which is only ten minutes away over the hill.

Where to stay

For camping try *Howelston Farm* (☎ 01437 -781818, Apr–Oct) where a pitch costs around £6 for a small tent. It can be found close to where the coast path joins the lane above the village. Continue onwards and take the first right.

Down in the centre of the village, near the post office is *St Brides Inn* (☎ 01437-781266, ✉ georgemoody@tinyworld.com, 1D/1F) with rooms from £13. The *Castle Hotel* (☎ 01437-781445, ✉ castlehotel@ lineone.net) has rooms from £35.

On Settlands Hill, the lane leading to Broad Haven, *Whitegates* (☎ 01437-781 552, ✉ welshhaven@aol.com, 1S/1D/1F) has en-suite rooms from £18 per person.

BROAD HAVEN (ABER LLYDAN) MAP 45

The wonderful beach is the highlight here. The village itself would not win any beauty contests but it has a nice air about it all the same. Popular with holidaymakers who come for the endless expanse of sand, you may well be tempted to take a dip yourself to soothe those aching feet.

Services

The small **supermarket** on the seafront is probably the only place you will need since it also incorporates the **post office** and has a Link **cash machine** too. There is also an array of first aid bits and bobs which may be useful for anyone suffering from blisters. The next cash machine, chemist and shop is not until St David's, 17 miles (27km) away,

Further up Settlands Hill is the *Haven Fort Hotel* (☎ 01437-781401, Apr–Oct) with 15 en-suite rooms at £35 per person. Further still along this road and actually closer to Broad Haven is *Atlantic View* (☎ 01437-781589, ✉ www.atlantic-view.co.uk, 5T en suite) with prices from £20. It also has a small **campsite**; pitches from £4 per person.

Where to eat

St Brides Inn has good food on offer from 6.30pm until late with the menu changing regularly and barbecues in the summer. The post office on St Bride's Road has a small *tearoom* (☎ 01437-781233) where everything on the menu carries the Pembrokeshire Produce Mark guaranteeing locally produced ingredients. They sell everything from sandwiches to hot meals and claim to have the largest cappuccinos in the area.

The *Swan Inn* (☎ 01437-781256, 12–2pm, 7–9pm) sits overlooking the small bay and is the first pub you see as you come in from the coast path. For a local speciality try the crab bake for £5.25. In the centre of the village is the *Castle Hotel* with an extensive menu and a nice beer garden where you can watch the waves crashing on the small beach. Away from the beach is the *Nest Bistro* (☎ 01437-781728, 5.30pm– late), a quality fish restaurant. Booking is advised. They don't take credit cards.

although there is a small shop at Solva. There is an expensive **internet** terminal at Broad Haven Youth Hostel; it will set you back £5 for an hour.

Where to stay

Broad Haven Youth Hostel (☎ 01437-781688, email broadhaven@yha.org.uk, Apr–Oct) has space for 75. The price for members is £11 per person. It can be found by following the road along the seafront. Just before Haroldston Bridge there is a concrete path by the stream which leads into a big car park. The youth hostel is at the other end of the car park.

The *Anchor Guest House* (☎ 01437-781051, ✉ www.anchor-guesthouse.co.uk,

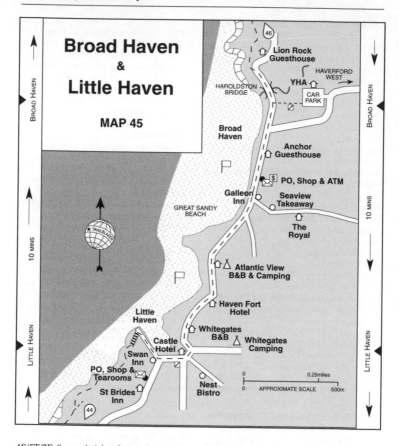

Broad Haven
&
Little Haven

MAP 45

4S/5T/2F, 8 en suite) is a large place on the seafront. Prices are from £22 to £30 for a single and £19 per person for a double. The *Royal* (☎ 01437-781249, 1S/2F) has accommodation from £20; turn right up the road next to The Galleon Inn, it's the big blue building on the right. Further out of the village to the north, *Lion Rock Guest House* (☎ 01437-781645, ☐ www.stayatlionrock. co.uk, 4S/3T en suite) is up Haroldston Hill, with beds from £25 per person.

Where to eat

The *Galleon Inn* (☎ 01437-781467, 12–2.30pm, 7–9pm) is the most popular spot with an extensive menu, a particular slant on eastern dishes and is a good spot for real ales. It's the big, yellow pub as you drop down into the village. The *Royal* (12–2pm, 5–9pm) has snacks and meals from £3.95. For cheaper, quicker fare look behind The Galleon Inn for the *Seaview Takeaway* where you can find fish and chips.

BROAD HAVEN TO NEWGALE

MAPS 45–49

This short stretch of **seven miles (11km, 2¹/₂–3¹/₄hrs)** follows easy ground over low cliffs, passing a number of intimate little coves before arriving at the wonderful Newgale Sands, two miles (3km) of uninterrupted sand battered by Atlantic rollers.

From Broad Haven the cliffs get steadily higher as you head north with the easy-to-follow path running through scrubland. Just past the rocky outcrops known as **Haroldston Chins** the old route turns inland to join the road but a new alternative continues straight ahead along the cliff top into a field and around Druidstone Villa, a big hotel and restaurant. Just past the villa look out for **The Roundhouse**. Tours of this 'eco-friendly' little building are by arrangement only (☎ 01437-781221, price £2).

There is a lovely beach at **Druidstone Haven** which tends to stay reasonably quiet since most people head for the beaches either side at Broad Haven and Newgale. From Druidstone Haven the path climbs over the top of an enormous grassy sand dune and then continues along the cliff top. Much of this section is

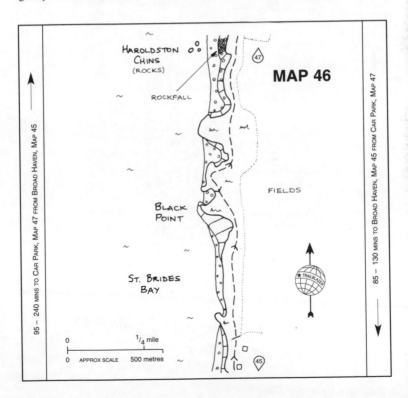

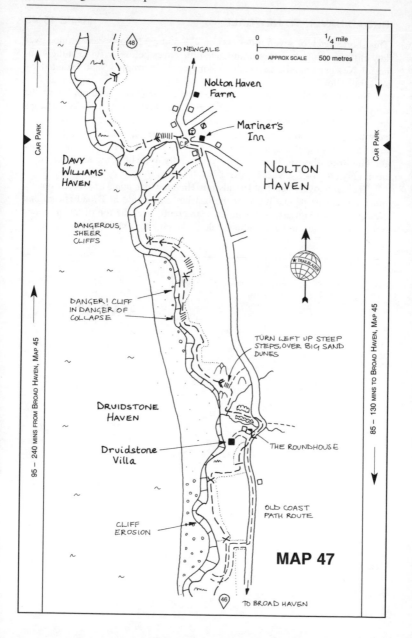

0 _____ 1/4 mile
0 _____ APPROX SCALE 500 metres

TO NEWGALE

Nolton Haven Farm

Mariner's Inn

NOLTON HAVEN

DAVY WILLIAMS' HAVEN

DANGEROUS, SHEER CLIFFS

DANGER! CLIFF IN DANGER OF COLLAPSE

TURN LEFT UP STEEP STEPS, OVER BIG SAND DUNES

DRUIDSTONE HAVEN

Druidstone Villa

THE ROUNDHOUSE

CLIFF EROSION

OLD COAST PATH ROUTE

MAP 47

TO BROAD HAVEN

CAR PARK

CAR PARK

95 – 240 MINS FROM BROAD HAVEN, MAP 45

85 – 130 MINS TO BROAD HAVEN, MAP 45

★ TRAILBLAZER

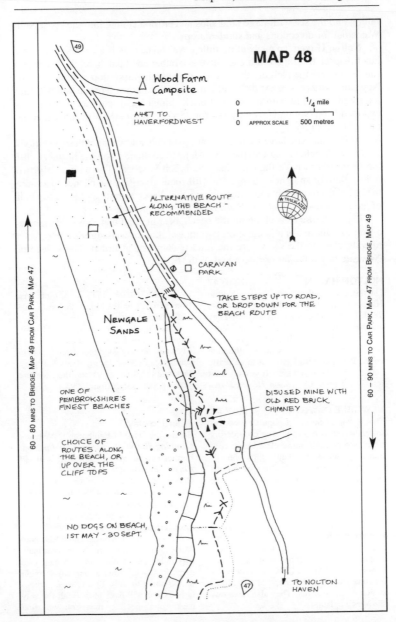

MAP 48

Wood Farm Campsite

A487 TO HAVERFORDWEST

0 — 1/4 mile
0 — 500 metres
APPROX SCALE

ALTERNATIVE ROUTE ALONG THE BEACH - RECOMMENDED

CARAVAN PARK

TAKE STEPS UP TO ROAD, OR DROP DOWN FOR THE BEACH ROUTE

NEWGALE SANDS

ONE OF PEMBROKSHIRE'S FINEST BEACHES

DISUSED MINE WITH OLD RED BRICK CHIMNEY

CHOICE OF ROUTES. ALONG THE BEACH, OR UP OVER THE CLIFF TOPS

NO DOGS ON BEACH, 1ST MAY - 30 SEPT.

TO NOLTON HAVEN

60 – 80 MINS TO BRIDGE, MAP 49 FROM CAR PARK, MAP 47

60 – 90 MINS TO CAR PARK, MAP 47 FROM BRIDGE, MAP 49

falling into the sea with large land slips and erosion cutting into the coast path. Watch out for diversions and sudden drops.

Nolton Haven, an enchanting little cove and hamlet, is a good spot to have lunch, especially if it's raining as there is a rather good pub here, the Mariner's Inn. From here the path climbs steeply above high grassy slopes with views of **Newgale Sands** ahead. At the southern end of this immense beach you will find a disused mine still with the old red-brick chimney and spoil heaps. Coal was exported from Nolton Haven by sea for 25 years before the mine closed at the turn of the century.

At the mine you have a choice. You can clamber down the rather precarious path to the beach, or head up the steep slope to continue along the heathery cliff top. Both routes have their merits. The beach is spectacular with nearly two miles (3km) of straight walking. The cliff route gives you the chance to admire the beach from up high and you still have the chance to walk along the top half of the beach once you climb down from the high ground.

If you choose to walk along the beach, bear in mind that loose, dry sand is a pain to walk in. As it is close on two miles (3km) of walking it's a good idea to walk close to the sea where the sand is damper and firmer. The village of **Newgale** lies at the far northern end of the beach.

NOLTON HAVEN   MAP 47
On the coast path a mile before Nolton Haven is *Druidstone Villa* (☎ 01437-781221). It has rooms from £33.50. They also have a restaurant open to non-residents.

Nolton Haven itself is a tiny place hidden in another of the coast's attractive coves. It is a beautiful spot but there really isn't much to keep you here. If you do want to stay the night try *Nolton Haven Farm*

(☎ 01437-710263, 15T) which charges from £16. It's up the hill on the north side of the village.

Mariner's Inn (☎ 01437-710469, 1S/6T/1F) does B&B from £19 per person. They also do very good food from Indian to seafood (12.30–2.15pm, 6.30–8.30pm). Fish and chips are £4.95 and the excellent jacket potatoes start from £2.95.

NEWGALE (NÎWGWL)   MAP 48
This is one of the most popular spots for surfers which is not surprising considering it has two miles of immaculate beach continually pounded by Atlantic surf. The village itself is just a collection of houses stretched along the northern end of the beach and up the hill.

Services
There is a **phone box** next to the Duke of Edinburgh pub on the seafront. If you want to try your hand at surfing, tuition is available as well as wetsuit and board hire from **Newsurf** (☎ 01437-721398, 🖳 www.newsurf.co.uk) who can be found at the filling station on the seafront. They also have **hot showers** available.

Where to stay
Behind the Duke of Edinburgh is *Newgale Camping Site* which charges £3 per person. Further behind up the main road is *Wood Farm Campsite* (☎ 01437-710253, Apr–Oct) which costs £2 per person. Or there is *Wyndhurst* B&B (☎ 01437-720162, 7S/2T/1F) just up the hill from the beach; there are signs to lead you in the right direction. Prices are from £15.

There is a youth hostel and B&B about 45 minutes to an hour from the coast path, two miles (3km) north of Newgale (see maps 49 & 49a). After a long day it might be too much to walk all this way, particularly as you will have to walk all the way back again the next day. You will find

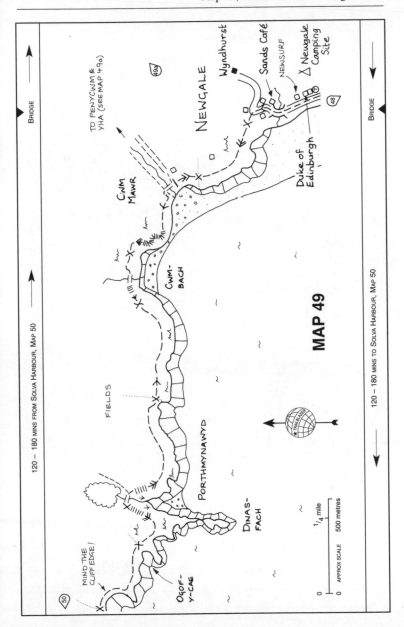

120 – 180 MINS FROM SOLVA HARBOUR, MAP 50

BRIDGE

TO PENYCWM & YHA (SEE MAP 49a)

NEWGALE

Wyndhurst

Sands Café

NEWSURF

Newgale Camping Site

CWM MAWR

CWM-BACH

Duke of Edinburgh

FIELDS

PORTHMYNAWYD

MAP 49

DINAS-FACH

MIND THE CLIFF EDGE!

OGOF-Y-CAE

BRIDGE

120 – 180 MINS TO SOLVA HARBOUR, MAP 50

TRAIL BLAZER

¼ mile

0   APPROX SCALE

0   500 metres

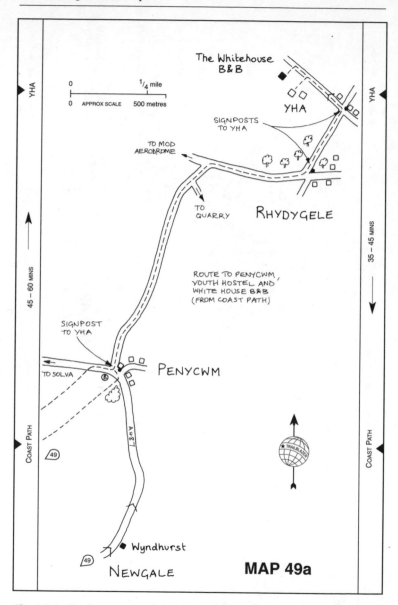

The Whitehouse
B & B

YHA

SIGNPOSTS
TO YHA

TO MOD
AERODROME

TO
QUARRY

RHYDYGELE

ROUTE TO PENYCWM,
YOUTH HOSTEL AND
WHITE HOUSE B&B
(FROM COAST PATH)

SIGNPOST
TO YHA

TO SOLVA

PENYCWM

0   1/4 mile
0   APPROX SCALE   500 metres

YHA

YHA

45 – 60 MINS

35 – 45 MINS

COAST PATH

COAST PATH

★ TRAILBLAZER

A487

49

Wyndhurst

49

NEWGALE

MAP 49a

(Opposite): Heading north from Newgale Sands (see p143).

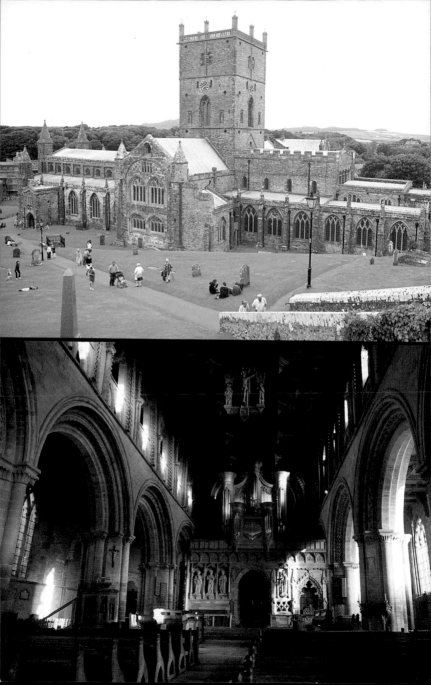

Penycwm Youth Hostel (☎ 01437-721940, 📧 penycwm@ yha.org.uk, open all year) by continuing along the coast path from Newgale to the small but deep valley of Cwm Mawr. Here you need to leave the coast path by following the public footpath up to the main A487 road at Penycwm. Cross the road and follow the lane to Rhydygele (signposted for the YHA). Turn left at Rhydygele and after 200 yards turn left again to reach the hostel. It has 26 beds at £11 for members (see p11). Next to it is the guesthouse, *Whitehouse* (☎ 01437-720 959, 📧 b+b@whitehouse.prestel.co.uk, 5T). Prices start at £22.

Where to eat

For a substantial meal try the *Duke of Edinburgh* (☎ 01437-720586, 12–3pm, 6–9.00pm), the pub on the front. It is just south of the village on the beach road.

For food, head to *Sands Café* which has a variety of snacks and sandwiches. It's the blue building on the corner across the bridge.

NEWGALE TO CAERFAI BAY (FOR ST DAVID'S)   MAPS 49–52

These **nine miles (14km, 3¹/₂–4¹/₂hrs)** begin with some very strenuous terrain just north of Newgale but become somewhat less arduous once past Solva.

From Newgale the path climbs up a very steep hillside and then drops all the way down the other side into **Cwm Mawr**, a small, deep valley. If you are heading for Penycwm Youth Hostel or Whitehouse Guesthouse (see above) it is here that you should follow the public path up the valley to the road (see Map 49a).

Those sticking to the coast path continue over some more tough cliffs, the path eventually settling down somewhat following a high cliff top before dropping into another small valley and passing the rocky promontory of **Dinas-Fach**.

The scenery is quite magnificent along this stretch and at **Dinas-Fawr** you can take the short detour to the end of the headland for great views along the coast. Ahead you can see the southern tip of Ramsey Island while back the way you came are the high cliffs that you have just come over and the sweeping sands at Newgale. Add 15 to 20 minutes to your time if you choose to explore the Dinas-Fawr headland. Follow the line of the cliffs all the way to Solva Harbour and the beautiful village of **Solva**. The village is well worth spending some time in but the coast path continues along the north bank of the harbour before climbing up the steep hillside to **Upper Solva**. The rest of the route is quite straightforward following the obvious path along the cliff edge. The cliffs become less high but no less spectacular as you approach **Caerbwdy Bay** passing through slopes of bracken, around a low headland to **Caerfai Bay**. Take care of the low but precipitous cliffs immediately to the left.

SOLVA (SOLFACH)   MAP 50

Solva is probably the prettiest village on the coast path. It is worth keeping a couple of hours spare to stop for lunch here or, even better, to spend the night.

The lower village is a line of painted houses tucked below the steep hillside that leads to the little harbour. The claustrophobic nature of this part is due to its situation. It sits in an old glacial meltwater channel formed some 10,000 years ago at the end of the last ice age. Melting ice sent torrents of water towards the sea carving out deep

---

(Opposite): St David's Cathedral (see p152), the most important cathedral in Wales, is one of the high points of the walk and should not be missed.

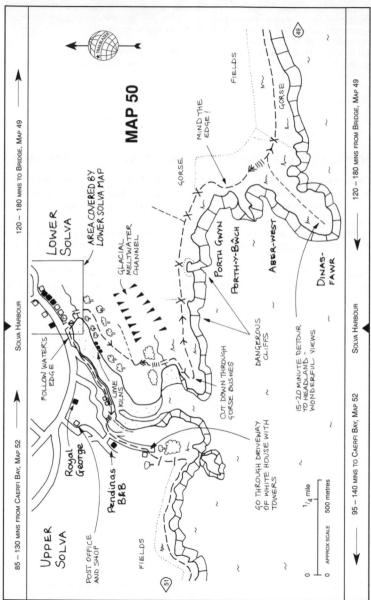

MAP 50

85 – 130 MINS FROM CAERFI BAY, MAP 52

120 – 180 MINS TO BRIDGE, MAP 49

SOLVA HARBOUR

120 – 180 MINS FROM BRIDGE, MAP 49

SOLVA HARBOUR

95 – 140 MINS TO CAERFI BAY, MAP 52

LOWER SOLVA

AREA COVERED BY LOWER SOLVA MAP

FOLLOW WATER'S EDGE

GLACIAL MELTWATER CHANNEL

GORSE

MIND THE EDGE!

FIELDS

GORSE

PORTH GWYN

PORTH-Y-BWCH

ABER-WEST

DINAS-FAWR

DANGEROUS CLIFFS

15-20 MINUTE DETOUR TO HEADLANDS WITH WONDERFUL VIEWS

CUT DOWN THROUGH GORSE BUSHES

LIME KILNS

UPPER SOLVA

POST OFFICE AND SHOP

Royal George

Pendinas B&B

GO THROUGH DRIVEWAY OF WHITE HOUSE WITH TOWERS

FIELDS

¼ mile

500 metres

APPROX SCALE

gorges. There are many examples of this in Pembrokeshire, often with a small bay or cove at the end, but the one at Solva is one of the finest examples. In fact there are two here: the second, the southern one, is crossed on the way to the village along the main coast path.

Next to the harbour there are some well preserved **lime kilns** which can be seen at many of the coves and inlets along the coast.

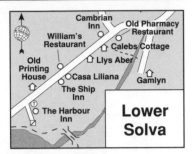

Services

The prettiest part of the village is Lower Solva which has most of the eating places. There is also a **phone box** by the harbour car park and some public **toilets.**

Upper Solva, meanwhile, has the **post office** and a small **shop** all in one.

Where to stay

Campers should continue past the village along the coast path for another mile where there is cheap camping at *Naw Ffynnon Campsite* (☎ 01437-721809). It is set back from the coast so there is a short detour to reach it from the coast path.

In Lower Solva there is B&B at *Gamlyn* (☎ 01437-721542, 1T,1D) which is just off Main St by the river. Beds are from £20 per person but unfortunately there are no single rooms.

Alternatively there is *Calebs Cottage* (☎ 01437-721737, 7 Main St, 1S/2D) with beds at £24 per person during the week, or £30 at weekends. The *Old Printing House* (☎ 01437-721603, 20 Main St, 1S/2T/1D) is a comfortable and friendly B&B with rooms from £20 per person. Also on Main St is *Llys Aber* (☎ 01437-721657) which charges from £20.

In Upper Solva there is the *Royal George* (☎ 01437-720002, 13 High St, 1T/2D) offering en-suite B&B at £50 for two people sharing.

Pendinas (☎ 01437-721283, ✉ pendinas@solva.net, St Brides View, 3T) has rooms from £20. It can be found by leaving the path where it joins the track above the harbour. It is near the end of the small lane, St Brides View.

Where to eat

The *Harbour Inn* (☎ 01437-720013, Main St, 12–3pm, 6–9pm, take away 6–11pm) is where its name suggests it is. It's a lovely spot with tables out by the river and good food. They have jacket potatoes from £2.80, curries from £6.95 and beef and stout pie for £7.50. Look out for popular bingo nights on Tuesdays and quiz nights on Sundays.

The *Old Printing House* (see Where to stay) has a smart restaurant in the 'olde worlde' vein. Open from April to October only they do good home cooked food and are very proud of their herbal teas. All the food is guaranteed to be of local origin.

Opposite this, the *Ship Inn* (☎ 01437-721247, 12–2pm, 6pm–late, Mon–Sat, Main St) has more tasty pub grub while next door is *Casa Liliana* (☎ 01437-720149, ✉ liliana47@btinternet.com, 11 Main St) a colourful place which specializes in Polish cuisine using local fish and game. A little further along the street is the *Old Pharmacy* (☎ 01437-720005, 5 Main St, 6pm–late) specializing in local seafood and vegetarian dishes. *William's Restaurant* (☎ 01437-720802, 12 Main St) is quite a smart place with a wide variety of high quality food. The pork and leek sausage dish is £5.50.

Up by the bridge is the *Cambrian Inn* (☎ 01437-721210, 6.30–9pm) with good food but at a price. It's often very popular so it's worth booking in advance. Steak dishes start at £11.75. In Upper Solva is cheaper food at the *Royal George* (see Map 50).

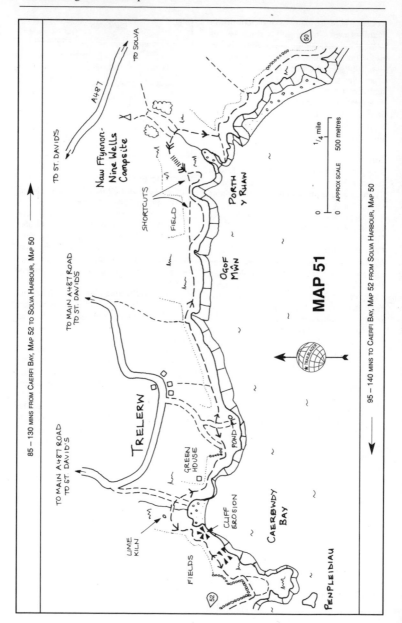

85 – 130 MINS FROM CAERFI BAY, MAP 52 TO SOLVA HARBOUR, MAP 50

TO ST DAVIDS

A487

TO SOLVA

Naw Ffynnon-
Nine Wells Campsite

SHORTCUTS

FIELD

PORTH
Y RUAN

OGOF
MWN

MAP 51

50

¼ mile

0

APPROX SCALE

0   500 metres

TO MAIN A487 ROAD
TO ST DAVIDS

TO MAIN A487 ROAD
TO ST DAVIDS

TRELERW

GREEN
HOUSE

POND

TRAILBLAZER

TO MAIN A487 ROAD
TO ST DAVIDS

LIME
KILN

FIELDS

CLIFF
EROSION

CAERBWDY
BAY

52

PENPLEIDIAU

95 – 140 MINS TO CAERFI BAY, MAP 52 FROM SOLVA HARBOUR, MAP 50

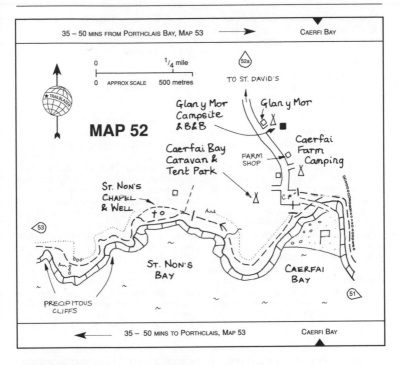

0   1/4 mile
0   APPROX SCALE   500 metres

★ TRAILBLAZER

MAP 52

52a
TO ST. DAVID'S

Glan y Mor Campsite & B&B

Glan y Mor

Caerfai Bay Caravan & Tent Park

FARM SHOP

Caerfai Farm Camping

ST. NON'S CHAPEL & WELL

53

ST. NON'S BAY

CAERFAI BAY

PRECIPITOUS CLIFFS

51

CAERFAI BAY   MAP 52

This is the best access point for St David's, only a mile from the coast path and one of the highlights of the walk.

At Caerfai Bay itself there is a small **farm shop** with a limited stock at the organic Caerfai Farm. If you need money, more food or new socks your last chance before Fishguard, 40 miles (64km) away, is in St David's.

Campers will find themselves spoilt for choice here. The biggest of the three campsites is the *Caerfai Bay Caravan and Tent Park* (☎ 01437-720274, Apr–Oct). It has a camping ground with showers and a

laundrette. Prices start at £3. On the other side of the lane and a little further up the hill is *Caerfai Farm* (☎ 01437-720548, Apr–Oct) with prices starting at £4.

A little further still on the right hand side is *Glan y Mor Guesthouse & Campsite* (☎ 01437-721788, 🖳 Clive@divewales. com, 9T) with rooms from £20. The camping pitches are £4 per person and they are open from Easter to October. They also have a **bar restaurant** open for breakfast (8.15–9.30am) lunch (11.30am–3.30pm) and dinner (6–9.30pm). As if all this wasn't enough they also run **scuba diving** courses.

ST DAVID'S (TYDDEWI)   MAP 52a

St David's is the smallest city in Britain, qualifying for this grand status thanks to its wonderful cathedral. To call it a city seems to paint an unfair picture of the place. It is

really somewhere between a big village and a small town with a definite lazy air pervading the sleepy lanes. In the quieter months the croaking of the ravens in the trees in

Cross Sq can sometimes be the only sign of life. Summer is a different matter as hundreds come to this remote pilgrimage site.

Services

As mentioned before, once past St David's you won't find another shop or bank until Fishguard (40 miles, 64km away) so think carefully about what you will need for the next few days.

The **TIC** (☎ 01437-720392) is also the new **National Park Information Centre**. If you are coming up the lane from Caerfai Bay you will see the TIC on the left where the lane joins the main road entering St David's. There are also public **toilets** and **phone boxes** here.

Cross Sq is the hub of the city. A number of roads radiate outwards where you will find plenty of B&Bs, coffee shops and restaurants. There are a number of **banks** around Cross Sq and a **chemist** for any blister problems. The **post office** and main **supermarket**, meanwhile, are on New St.

Just off Cross Sq, a good place to replace any holey socks or buy any camping equipment is **TYF Outdoor** (☎ 01437-721611, 🖳 www.tyf.com, 1 High St). This is also the place to go for an adrenaline rush since they run sessions in a variety of outdoor activities from surfing and canoeing to climbing and coasteering (see p82). Next door you can book a boat trip around the RSPB reserve of Ramsey Island or take a trip to see whales and dolphins with Voyages of Discovery or, on the other side of Cross Sq, there is Thousand Islands Expeditions, who actually land on the

island. For more information on Ramsey Island and boat trips see p153.

Where to stay

Thanks to the city's fame as a popular tourist and pilgrimage site St David's is full of places to stay. For the coast-path walker the most convenient places are on or near Caerfai Rd, the lane leading from Caerfai Bay. *Golwg y Mor* (☎ 01437-721862, 15 Caerfai Rd, 2T) is a terraced house with beds from £20 per person. At the top of Caerfai Rd, just off the main road to Solva, is *The Waterings* (☎ 01437-720876, waterings@supanet.com, 1T/1D/1F) which has en-suite rooms from £30 per person.

For a place with more character there is the friendly little *Pen Albro* (☎ 01437-721865, 18 Goat St, 1S/1T/1D) which offers very comfortable beds for just £14.50 per person and a hearty breakfast to boot. It's also just a short stagger away from the best pub in town.

Along High St leading to Cross Sq from the tourist information centre are another couple of cheap options; *Bryn Awel* (☎ 01437-720082, 1D/1T) which has en-suite rooms from £19.50 per person and the smart *Coach House* (☎ 01437-720632, 15 High St, 2S/2T/5D/1F) with rooms from £20 per person. More cheap beds can be found along Nun St: *Y-Glennydd Hotel* (☎ 01437-720576, 51 Nun St, 2S/8D) has affordable rooms from £15.50 per person and *Y-Gorlan* (☎ 01437-720837, 77 Nun St, 1S/3T/1F en suite) with rooms from £24.

Also on Nun St are a number of guesthouses which are a bit pricier but offer a

---

KEY – Where to stay

1 Ty'r Wennol
2 Ty Olaf
3 Y-Gorlan
4 Y Glennydd Hotel
5 Alandale
9 Glendower
10 Old Cross Hotel
15 Pen Albro
16 Ramsey House
17 Warpool Court Hotel

18 Swn-y-Don
22 The Coach House
24 Bryn Awel
25 The Waterings
26 Golwg y Mor

Other

11 Supermarket
12 Thousand Island Expeditions
19 Chemist
21 TYF & Voyages of Discovery

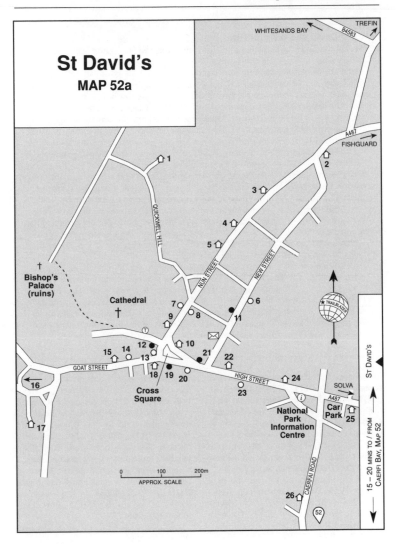

Where to eat

6 City Inn
7 The Sampler Coffee Shop
8 Morgan's Brasserie
13 Cartref Restaurant

14 Farmers Arms
20 Dyfed Fish & Chips
23 Cox's Restaurant

❏ St David and the cathedral

St David was one of a number of Celtic saints from the 6th century and is now the patron saint of Wales. He was born at St Non's (a village named after his mother), where the chapel and the holy well can be seen just off the coast path to the south of the city. As a missionary his influence was such that the city which now bears his name became an important pilgrimage site and still is to this day.

The cathedral was built on the site of St David's monastery and you can still see a casket in the Holy Trinity Chapel which is purported to contain the bones of St Justinian and St David himself. The cathedral has had a turbulent history. During the 10th and 11th centuries the Vikings regularly raided it and even killed two of the serving bishops in 999 and again in 1080. The present-day cathedral came into being in 1181 but was all but destroyed by parliamentary soldiers in 1648. Over the years it has been restored to more than its former glory with the 12th-century nave the oldest part of the building. The fantastic 16th-century Irish oak ceiling is testament to the earthquake of 1247 which caused the western wall of the nave to lean outwards.

While one of the original mediaeval bells can still be seen on the nave floor, the current bells of the cathedral, which were hung in the 1930s, are surprisingly not in the cathedral. They were hung in the Porth y Twr, the 14th-century gateway which sits at the top of the steps above the cathedral, because it was feared the cathedral tower could collapse with the weight.

It is well worth trying to catch the atmospheric sound of the bells ringing out across the dell. The local bell ringers practise their pealing on Wednesdays between 7.45 and 9pm. For something even more moving try getting a ticket for the Cathedral Festival of Classical Music which is held over a ten-day period at the end of May and beginning of June each year. The acoustics of the building make for an unforgettable concert. To miss out on St David's Cathedral is like going to Paris and not seeing the Eiffel Tower. **Guided tours** (☎ 01437-720199) are available.

little more comfort and luxury. *Glendower Guesthouse* (☎ 01437-721650, 7 Nun St, 2S/3T) has B&B from £35 per person while further down the road is the *Alandale Guesthouse* (☎ 01437-720404, 🖳 www.stdavids.co.uk/guesthouse/alandale.htm, 43 Nun St, 1S/8T/3F) which has en-suite rooms from £25. Also worth a try is the new *Swn y Don B&B* on Cross Square.

If everything is booked up you may have to try somewhere further afield. At the far end of Nun St is *Ty Olaf* (☎ 01437-720885, Mount Gdns, 1S/1T/2D) with B&B from £18.

Ty'r Wennol (☎ 01437-720406, Quickwell Hill, 4T) is in a similarly off-the-beaten-track location to the north of the city with B&B from £19 per person. Closer to the coast path is *Ramsey House* (☎ 01437-720321, 🖳 www.ramseyhouse.co.uk, Lower Moor, 6S/1T en suite), sitting all on its own in a quiet location south-west of the city on the lane to Porthclais, where beds start from £31 per person. Or if money is no obstacle and you fancy the height of luxury then head for the *Warpool Court Hotel* (☎ 01437-720300) which has nearly 60 beds. The cheapest single room will set you back around £88. For a touch of class at a more affordable price go to Cross Sq where you will see the grand *Old Cross Hotel* (☎ 01437-720387, 🖳 www.oldcrosshotel.co.uk, Cross Sq, 2S/13T/2F) with en-suite rooms from £30.

Where to eat

There are all sorts of places to eat in St David's, although many of them can be a bit on the expensive side. On Cross Sq is one of the cheaper places, *Cartref Restaurant* (☎ 01437-720422, 11–2pm, 6–8.30pm), an old yellow and green cottage

❏ **Ramsey Island**

Ramsey Island is the most northerly of the Pembrokeshire Islands and is another important wildlife reserve managed by the RSPB. It is a vital seal breeding area. The fluffy, white and grey seal pups can be seen in late summer and autumn on the rocky beaches around the island. Like the other islands further south there are thousands of seabirds breeding on the cliffs including puffins and manx shearwaters. In Ramsey Sound you can take a boat ride over 'The Bitches', an unusual phenomenon where the confluence of two currents creates churning rapids in the middle of the sea.

Thousand Islands Expeditions (☎ 01437-721686, 🖳 www.tiex.co.uk, Ocean Base, Cross Sq, St David's) offer a number of trips from exploration of the sea caves to whitewater rafting on 'The Bitches'. They also land on the island and run wildlife excursions including a sunset manx shearwater watch and a puffin watch. Prices start from £10.

Voyages of Discovery (☎ 01437-721911, 🖳 www.ramseyisland.co.uk, High St, St David's) offer trips around the island for £10. Alternatively you can bounce around on their powerful inflatables, exploring the caves and gorges for £14. They also run a popular whale and dolphin watch. Departures are from St Justinian's (see Map 54).

with a low-slung ceiling. Try their shepherdess pie, a vegetarian slant on the more familiar dish for £5.80, or Welsh cheese and leek sausages for £5.40.

Also on Cross Square are cheap cakes and sandwiches in the café at the *Swn y Don B&B* (see p152).

For good pub grub head down Goat St to one of the best pubs in town, the *Farmers Arms* (☎ 01437-720328). Another good port of call is the *City Inn* (☎ 01437-720829, New St) which has a separate restaurant and also does takeaways.

A lovely little coffee shop is *The Sampler* (☎ 01437-720757, 17 Nun St, Mar–Oct, Thu–Tue from 10am) with friendly service and an open fire. Welsh cakes are only 55p or there are filling jacket potatoes from £3.25, toasties from £2.95 and pizza from £3.25. In the same street is

Morgan's Brasserie (☎ 01437-720508, 7–9pm, 20 Nun St) where the menu changes from season to season. It's good food but a little pricey.

On High St is the *Coach House* (see p150) with jacket potatoes from £2.20 and toasties from £2.85 while the *Old Cross Hotel* (see p152, 12–2pm, 7–8.30pm) in Cross Sq has Welsh lamb for £11. *Cox's Restaurant* (☎ 01437-720491, 7pm–late) is a smart little place on High St that does elaborate dishes with curries from £11.50 and steaks from £15.50.

Fish and chips to take away can be found at the *Dyfed Café*, itself tucked away just off Cross Sq on High St, opposite the TYF outdoor shop.

There is also a good **takeaway café** selling hot snacks a short way up Nun St on the right.

CAERFAI BAY TO WHITESANDS BAY   MAPS 52–55

This is a wonderful part of the coast. It is **eight and a half miles (14km, 3–4hrs)**, all of them beautiful, to yet another of Pembrokeshire's fantastic sandy beaches at Whitesands Bay. As the path ventures further west the scenery gets progressively wilder with a real sense of isolation out on the windswept headlands by Ramsey Sound. From Caerfai Bay the path follows steep vegetated

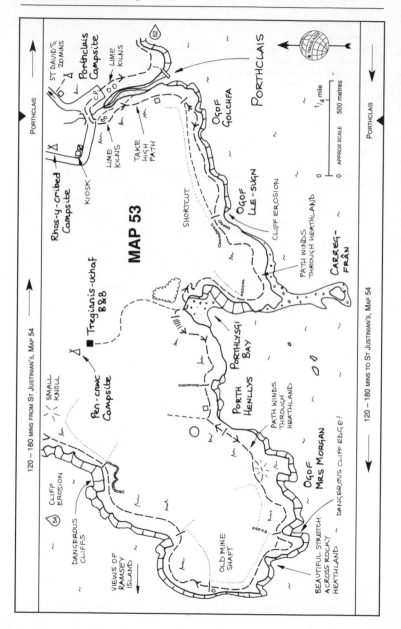

120 – 180 MINS FROM ST JUSTINIAN'S, MAP 54

MAP 53

Rhos-y-cribed Campsite

KIOSK

St David's, 20 MINS

Porthclais Campsite

LIME KILNS

C.P.

LIME KILNS

TAKE HIGH PATH

SHORTCUT

OGOF GOLCHFA

OGOF LLE-SUN

CLIFF EROSION

PATH WINDS THROUGH HEATHLAND

CARREG-FRÂN

PORTHCLAIS

Treginnis-uchaf B&B

Pen-cnwc Campsite

SMALL KNOLL

Porthlysgi Bay

PORTH HENLLYS

PATH WINDS THROUGH HEATHLAND

OGOF MRS MORGAN

OLD MINE SHAFT

BEAUTIFUL STRETCH ACROSS ROCKY HEATHLAND

DANGEROUS CLIFF EDGE!

CLIFF EROSION

DANGEROUS CLIFFS

VIEWS OF RAMSEY ISLAND

54

52

0   APPROX SCALE   500 metres
0   1/4 mile

120 – 180 MINS TO ST JUSTINIAN'S, MAP 54

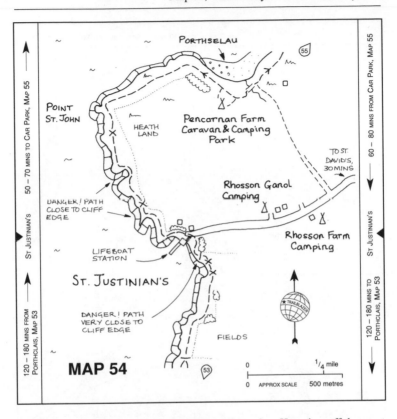

PORTHSELAU

55

POINT ST. JOHN

HEATH LAND

Pencarnan Farm Caravan & Camping Park

TO ST. DAVID'S, 30 MINS

Rhosson Ganol Camping

DANGER / PATH CLOSE TO CLIFF EDGE

LIFEBOAT STATION

Rhosson Farm Camping

ST. JUSTINIAN'S

DANGER / PATH VERY CLOSE TO CLIFF EDGE

FIELDS

★ TRAILBLAZER

MAP 54

53

0   1/4 mile

0   APPROX SCALE   500 metres

50 – 70 MINS TO CAR PARK, MAP 55

ST JUSTINIAN'S

120 – 180 MINS FROM PORTHCLAIS, MAP 53

60 – 80 MINS FROM CAR PARK, MAP 55

ST JUSTINIAN'S

120 – 180 MINS TO PORTHCLAIS, MAP 53

slopes to St Non's Bay, named after St David's mother. Here, just off the coast path, you can see the remains of **St Non's Chapel**, the birthplace of the patron saint and the **Holy Healing Well**. More low cliffs lead to the beautiful little harbour of **Porthclais** where you can see more fine examples of some lime kilns. At the wild and lonely **Porthlysgi Bay** a footpath heads north to the guesthouse at Treginnis-uchaf and the campsite at Pen-cnwc.

Staying on the coast path the terrain becomes progressively more barren and wild. Rocky knolls decorate the headland around the tiny cove of **Ogof Mrs Morgan** and low but precipitous cliffs form a twisting savage coastline. Above Ramsey Sound there are fine views over to Ramsey Island. Keep an eye out for seals on the shoreline and schools of dolphins and porpoises further out.

Once past the lifeboat station at **St Justinian's** take extra care along the level cliff top as the narrow path brushes the edge without warning on a number of occasions. Moving on around the headland the sands of **Whitesands Bay** come into view with the small rocky hills of Carn Llidi and Carn Perfedd behind.

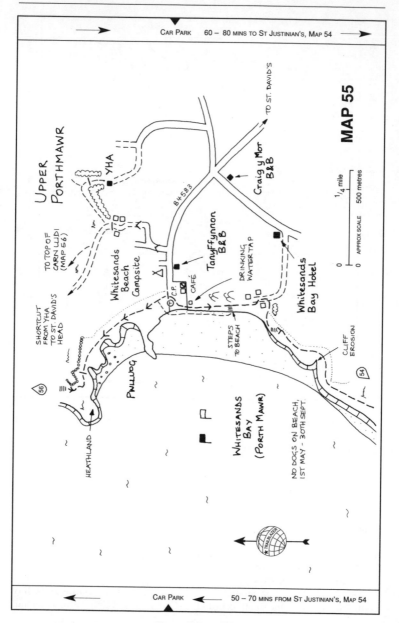

MAP 55

UPPER PORTHMAWR

YHA

TO ST. DAVID'S

B4583

Craig y Mor B&B

TO TOP OF CARN LLIDI (MAP 56)

Whitesands Beach Campsite

TanyFfynnon B&B

DRINKING WATER TAP

CAFÉ

C.P.

SHORTCUT FROM YHA TO ST. DAVID'S HEAD

Whitesands Bay Hotel

CLIFF EROSION

54

STEPS TO BEACH

PWLLDDG

56

HEATHLAND

WHITESANDS BAY (PORTH MAWR)

NO DOGS ON BEACH, 1ST MAY - 30TH SEPT

¼ mile

APPROX SCALE

0   500 metres

TRAIL & SON

PORTHCLAIS, ST JUSTINIAN'S AND WHITESANDS BAY (PORTH MAWR)

This lonely stretch of wild coast is dotted with a number of coves and small bays with little in the way of accommodation. However, there are a few farms that offer camping and one or two B&Bs.

At **Porthclais** there is a National Trust **kiosk** and **toilets** and a **campsite** at *Porthclais Farm* just up the road, heading east from the inlet. Heading the other way, up the road from the inlet, is *Rhos-y-cribed* offering cheap **camping** from £2 per person from Easter to October.

At **Porthlysgi Bay** you can leave the coast path and reach *Treginnis Uchaf Farmhouse* (☎ 01437-720234, 🖳 treginnis @hotmail.com, 6T) by heading north for half a mile on the public footpath. It has rooms from £20. Next door is the *Pencnwc Campsite* (☎ 01437-720523, Apr–Oct) with prices at £2.75 per person.

At **St Justinian's** there is a summer ferry to Ramsey Island (see p153) and inland there are two spots for camping along the lane which heads towards St David's. The first is *Rhosson Ganol* (Apr–Oct) and the other is a little further on at *Rhosson Farm* (Apr–Oct).

At the southern end of Whitesands Bay at **Porthselau Beach** there is a large caravan and **campsite** at *Pencarnan Farm* (☎ 01437-720324, 🖳 pencarnan@aol. com, open all year) in a wonderful location overlooking the bay. At the car park by **Whitesands Bay** there is a **phone box**, public **toilets** and a **drinking-water tap** but little else. Those staying at the youth hostel will find a small **shop** at the reception desk. Despite the name *St David's Youth Hostel* (☎ 01437-720345, Apr–Oct) is not in St David's. It is here above Whitesands Bay! It's in a great spot below the craggy hill called Carn Llidi in an old farmhouse with 40 beds at £8.50 per member (see p11). To reach it follow the lane up from the car park, turn left by the campsite, bear right then left to Upper Porthmawr and follow the footpath around the hillside.

The *Whitesands Beach Campsite* (Apr–Oct) is on the left as you walk up from the car park. Prices are from £3 to £7 depending on the size of your tent. Opposite the campsite is B&B at *Tan y Ffynnon* (☎ 01437-720076) with beds at £18.50 per person. *Craig-y-Mor* is a lonely looking house with basic accommodation. *Whitesands Bay Hotel* (☎ 01437-720403, 2S/ 10T/1F) has en-suite rooms from £38 per person for a single or £76 for a double. There is a short cut from the coast path to the hotel, avoiding the longer way by road.

The only places to get food are in the rather basic *café* in Whitesands Bay car park, or at the other extreme there is the *Whitesands Bay Hotel* which has a very upmarket and consequently pricey restaurant. They specialize in seafood and game dishes and also have an extensive range of whiskeys including Welsh whiskey if that rocks your boat.

WHITESANDS BAY TO TREFIN

Once again the rugged coastline of the St David's peninsula makes this a wonderful but tough **eleven miles (18km, 5–6hrs)**. From the car park the path climbs up above cliffs and back down to the sandy bay at **Porthmelgan**. For people staying at the youth hostel there is a more direct route from the hostel that avoids having to return to the car park (see Maps 55 & 60).

From Porthmelgan the path crosses beautiful slopes of heather to the craggy **St David's Head** jutting into the Atlantic. The path can be rather indistinct in places, crossing rocky heathland to some old fields enclosed by stone walls.

The route takes a sharp right at **Penllechwen Head** and skirts the pretty coves and bays that make up the coastline until it reaches **Carn Penberry** hill.

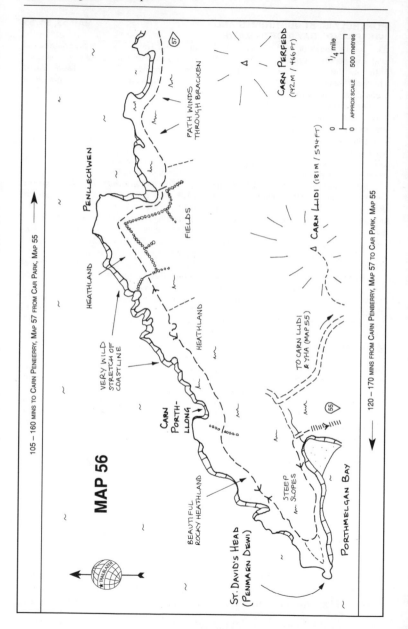

105 – 160 MINS TO CARN PENBERRY, MAP 57 FROM CAR PARK, MAP 55 →

120 – 170 MINS FROM CARN PENBERRY, MAP 57 TO CAR PARK, MAP 55

MAP 56

ST. DAVID'S HEAD (PENMAEN DEWI)

BEAUTIFUL ROCKY HEATHLAND

CARN PORTH-LLONG

VERY WILD STRETCH OF COASTLINE

HEATHLAND

PENLLECHWEN

HEATHLAND

PATH WINDS THROUGH BRACKEN

FIELDS

CARN PERFEDD (142M / 466FT)

△ CARN LLIDI (181M / 594FT)

STEEP SLOPES

TO CARN LLIDI & YHA (MAP 55)

PORTHMELGAN BAY

0   ¼ mile
APPROX SCALE
0   500 metres

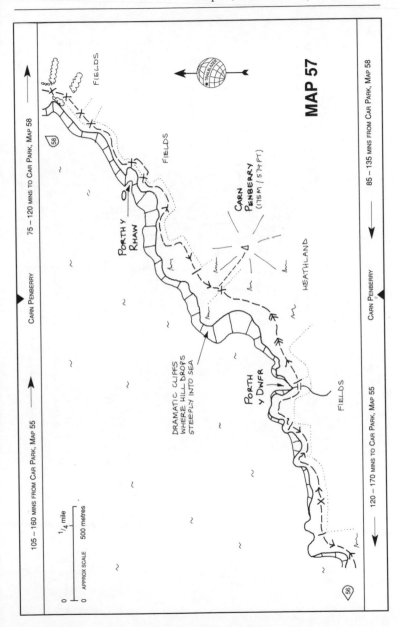

MAP 57

105 – 160 MINS FROM CAR PARK, MAP 55

75 – 120 MINS TO CAR PARK, MAP 58

CARN PENBERRY

85 – 135 MINS FROM CAR PARK, MAP 58

CARN PENBERRY

120 – 170 MINS TO CAR PARK, MAP 55

FIELDS

FIELDS

FIELDS

PORTH Y RHAW

CARN PENBERRY (175M / 574FT)

HEATHLAND

DRAMATIC CLIFFS WHERE HILL DROPS STEEPLY INTO SEA

PORTH Y DWFR

FIELDS

¼ mile

500 metres

0 APPROX SCALE

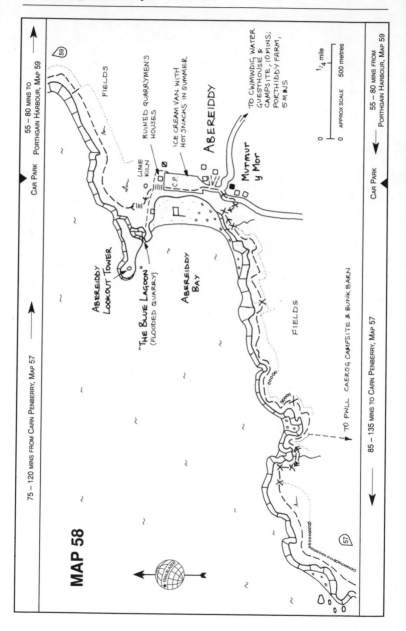

MAP 58

75 – 120 MINS FROM CARN PENBERRY, MAP 57

CAR PARK PORTHGAIN HARBOUR, MAP 59

55 – 80 MINS TO PORTHGAIN HARBOUR, MAP 59

55 – 80 MINS FROM PORTHGAIN HARBOUR, MAP 59

CAR PARK

85 – 135 MINS TO CARN PENBERRY, MAP 57

FIELDS

RUINED QUARRYMEN'S HOUSES

ICE CREAM VAN WITH HOT SNACKS IN SUMMER

ABEREIDDY

TO CWMWDIG WATER GUESTHOUSE & CAMPSITE, 10 MINS; PORTHIDDY FARM, 5 MINS

LIME KILN

C.P.

Murmur y Mor

ABEREIDDY LOOKOUT TOWER

"THE BLUE LAGOON" (FLOODED QUARRY)

ABEREIDDY BAY

FIELDS

TO PWLL CAEROG CAMPSITE & BUNK BARN

0   1/4 mile

APPROX SCALE

0   500 metres

TRAILBLAZER

This small hill crashes dramatically into the sea, a mess of twisted rock at its wave-battered foot. Unfortunately, for the walker the only way past this obstacle is over it, rather than around.

About two miles (3km) from Carn Penberry the path drops down into a small gorge the other side of which there is a sign and footpath leading to Pwll Caerog Campsite & Bunk Barn (500 metres from the coast path, see Abereiddy, below). At the beach of **Abereiddy** you can see the remains of the old quarrymen's houses, destroyed by floods in the 1920s (see p163). As you climb up above the bay you will see **The Blue Lagoon**, a flooded quarry, to the left.

The path follows a nice level cliff top around the beautiful beach of **Traeth-Llwyn** and past a few coves to arrive at some old quarry buildings, slate slag heaps and evidence of the old mine tramway on the cliffs above the village of **Porthgain**. From Porthgain the path follows gentle cliffs to the little bay of **Aber Draw**. This is the first of the access routes to Trefin, climbing up the steep road ahead, but a better idea is to continue along the coast path until you see the signpost for the youth hostel. This is the path that takes you into **Trefin**.

ABEREIDDY   MAP 58

Don't expect to find much at this hamlet and the nearby village of Cyffredin. In the summer there is usually an ice cream van in the beach car park selling **drinks and hot snacks**, as well as ice creams. At the far end of the car park is a public **toilet**.

Pwll Caerog Campsite and Bunk Barn (☎ 01348-831682, Apr–Oct), one mile back along the coast path, is a possible place to stay. A sign indicates the point where you have to leave the coast path to reach it. Beds in the barn, where there are showers, cost £8 per person while the campsite pitches are from £5 for a small tent.

Open in the summer only, *Murmur y Mor Guest House* (☎ 01348-831670, 4T) has beds from £18 per person.

A mile up the hill from the bay is the *Cwmwdig Water Guesthouse* (☎ 01348-

831434, 🖳 andrewcwmwdig@aol.com, 10T) which has B&B from £30 per person. Some of the rooms are en suite. They also have a good restaurant which is open to non-residents; booking is essential. Next door the *Cwmwdig Campsite* (☎ 01348-831376 before 8pm) is run by the Camping and Caravanning Club of Great Britain. Each one of the 40 pitches costs from £4.30 for non-members.

To get to Cwmwdig from the coast path climb up the lane (see Map 58) for 200 yards. Just past Porthiddy Farm take the public footpath on the right. This takes you up to the guesthouse, a big peach coloured building by the road junction and the campsite.

PORTHGAIN   MAP 59

This is an unusual little place with a great pub, a modern café and an explosion of art galleries. Up on the hill is an old, disused stone quarry that hints at the once thriving stone industry of the 19th century. The tiny harbour was used to export stone for building projects elsewhere. Nowadays the village is home to artists and tourists.

The *Sloop Inn* (☎ 01348-831449, 🖳 www. sloop.co.uk) is one of the best pubs

on the whole trail. Easily spotted on the far side as you drop down into the village, it usually has a trail of smoke coming from the chimney. It is a lovely rustic old inn dating from 1743. In the past it was, no doubt, a popular haunt for the quarrymen but is now a regular stop-off for coast-path walkers. It does good food (12–2.30pm, 6–9.30pm) including smoked mackerel for £8.95, or a simple crab sandwich for £3.90. In the sum-

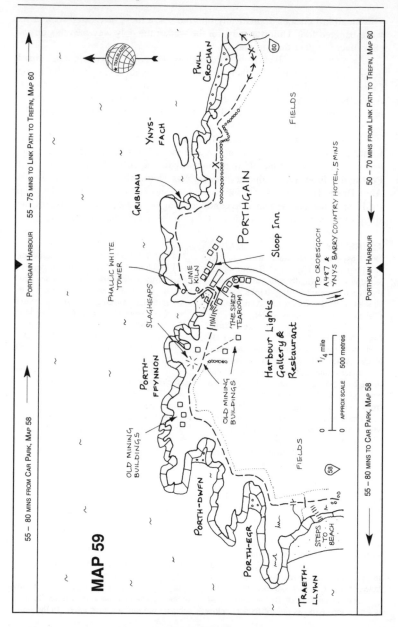

MAP 59

TRAETH-LLYWN

PORTH-EGR

PORTH-DWFN

FIELDS

OLD MINING BUILDINGS

PORTH-FFYNNON

SLAGHEAPS

PHALLIC WHITE TOWER

GRIBINAU

YNYS-FACH

PWLL CROCHAN

TRAIL BLAZER

OLD MINING BUILDINGS

THE SHED TEAROOM

LIME KILN

MINE

PORTHGAIN

Sloop Inn

FIELDS

Harbour Lights Gallery & Restaurant

TO CROESGOCH
A487 &
YNYS BARRY COUNTRY HOTEL, 5MINS

STEPS TO BEACH

¼ mile

500 metres

0

0

APPROX SCALE

58

60

mer you can get breakfast at The Sloop from 9.30–11.30am seven days a week.

Opposite the Sloop is the slightly newer *Harbour Lights Restaurant* (☎ 01348-831549) which incorporates a small art gallery and sells some interesting books about local history and myths. The award-winning menu concentrates on seafood but they do some other vegetarian dishes and there is a good selection of home-made cakes. Booking is advised. By the small harbour is *The Shed Tearoom* (☎ 01348 831518, 10am–5.30pm, bistro open from 7.30pm Thu–Sat, booking essential) where, aside from the usual variety of cakes and snacks, you can arrange a boat trip.

Places to stay are thin on the ground. The *Ynys Barry Country Hotel* (☎ 01348-831180) is only a short distance from the coast path up the lane. Hotel rooms are £23 per person while their more basic lodge rooms are £19 per person. In the summer months they charge a single-person's supplement.

❏ A lost industry

A number of ruins can be seen around Abereiddy and Porthgain, evidence of a once thriving industry. From around 1840 until the 1930s slate, brick and stone were quarried on the cliff tops between the two villages where the old slag-heaps and evidence of the tramway, which carried the slate from the quarry at Abereiddy to the harbour at Porthgain, can still be seen. At Porthgain you can also see the restored brickworks by the tiny harbour.

Look out too for the flooded slate quarry known as 'The Blue Lagoon' as you climb up onto the cliffs above Abereiddy and the ruins of the quarrymen's houses by Abereiddy Bay. The sad remains of these houses which were built in the 1840s are testament to the great storm of January 14, 1938, when the swell of the sea severely damaged five of the homes. The storm damage and an ensuing typhoid epidemic effectively brought the local slate quarry industry to an end.

Yet even to this day the product of the quarry can be seen in Porthgain. One of the boats carrying slate from Porthgain sank in Ramsey Sound. About 100 years later the boat was found on the seabed and the slate was recovered to re-roof the houses of Porthgain.

TREFIN   MAP 60

Trefin (pronounced 'Tre-feen', like 'ravine') is a quiet little village sitting on top of a windswept hill. It feels like you have stepped back in time when you first set foot in the place and is worth visiting either for a quick pint or an overnight stop.

The best way to get to the village from the coast path is by the footpath from the cliffs at Trwyn Llwyd. Alternatively you can come straight up the steep road from the bay at Aber Draw.

Services

The **post office**, which has rather irregular opening times, is not very obvious. It's the small pebble-dashed bungalow on the left as you enter the village by the steep road from the coast. Be warned that there is no shop in the village.

Buses leave outside the Glan-y-mor Gallery Tearooms. There are buses roughly every two hours to St David's, Haverfordwest and Fishguard.

Where to stay

Turn right down the hill in the centre of the village for *Trefin Youth Hostel* (☎ 01348-831414, 11 Ffordd-y-Avon, open all year) which used to be the old village schoolhouse. It has 26 beds and costs £8.50 for members. Just down the lane from the hostel is where you will find the *Prendergast Holiday Park* (☎ 01348-831368, open all year) which has a **campsite**. Prices start at £3.

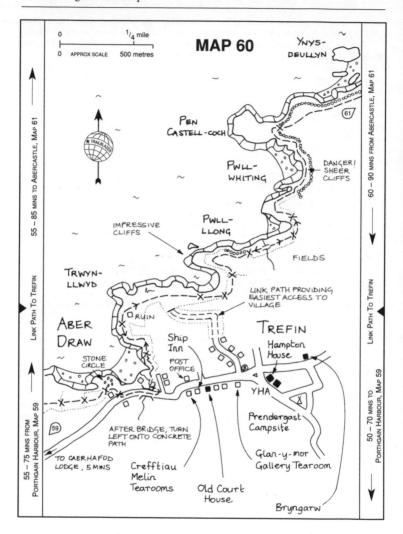

There is a bunkhouse near the village of Llanrhian, which is about half a mile from the coast path; *Caerhafod Lodge* (☎ 01348-837859, 🖳 www.carehafod.co.uk, open all year) is a wonderful, friendly place with five en-suite dormitories and a self catering kitchen. It has a capacity for 26 people at a price of £10.75 per person. From the point where the coast path joins the road before Trefin, follow the road uphill in the St David's direction; the bunkhouse is about half a mile up the road on the left.

The Old Court House (☎ 01348-837292, 🖳 www.pembrokeshire-online.co.uk/courthouse, 1S/2T) is next to the Ship Inn and offers en-suite rooms for £22.50 per person. Carnivores should be aware that the breakfasts are strictly vegetarian. Guests are also welcome for dinner and can even enrol on a course in vegetarian cooking and bread making, an enterprise the proprietor set up in 1998. All the ingredients at the guesthouse qualify for the Pembrokeshire Produce Mark which guarantees locally produced food.

In the centre of the village there is B&B at *Hampton House* (☎ 01348-837701, 1S/4T) with rooms from £19 per person. *Bryngarw Guest House* (☎ 01348-831211, 🖳 a.r.johnson@dial.pipex.com, Abercastle Rd, 2S/3T/3F en suite) is a little way out of the village. It has rooms starting at £27 per person, with a £5 surcharge for people on their own.

Where to eat

The pink building on your right coming up the road from the coast is the *Crefftiau Melin Hand Weaving Centre and Tearooms* where you can have Welsh cakes for 65p, toasties from £1.75, or a slice of pizza for £1.65. Even if you are not hungry it is worth taking a look at the incredible 300-year-old working hand-looms.

For something more substantial go to the *Ship Inn* (☎ 01348-831445, food until 9.30pm) where you can get your last pint before Goodwick 19 miles (30km) away, or indulge in their nut cutlets or local trout, both £6.95, or a curry for £5.50. Further up the road in the centre of the village is the *Glan-y-mor Gallery Tearooms* (☎ 01348-837843, 10.30am–5pm Mon–Fri, 2–5pm Sun) in the living room of the artist's home with paintings on display all over the walls. It's a very friendly place with good home-made food. Ham and salad baguettes are £2.95 and cheese rolls only £1.50. On Wednesdays it's Welsh night, concentrating on Welsh food and Welsh music when a local harpist comes to play. Booking for this is essential since it's not a big living room!

TREFIN TO PWLL DERI   MAPS 60–63

These **nine and a half miles (15km, 3^1/$_2$–4^1/$_2$hrs)** begin by following a beautiful line of snaking cliffs to the hamlet of **Abercastle** sitting at the end of yet another pretty cove. There are no facilities for the walker here.

Just before Abercastle you should keep an eye out for the stones of **Carreg Sampson** marking the site of a neolithic burial chamber, or cromlech, dating back 5000 years. It is only a short detour from the coast path. Look out for the signpost just before the coast path drops down the steps to the cove.

From Abercastle the path climbs up through cliff-top fields and past the bay at **Pwllstrodur**. If you want to stop for a dip in the sea the beaches at Abermawr and Aber-Bach are nice enough but it's much better to wait until you get to **Pwllcrochan**. This is a fantastic location for a swim; well sheltered with a backdrop of sheer cliffs. It's all the more interesting because the only way to get to it is by climbing down a rope hanging over a short section of cliff. It's not quite as dangerous as it sounds but you should be careful as you climb down. Since climbing over cliffs isn't everybody's cup of tea the beach is usually pretty quiet. Look out for the path leading to the rope at the southern end of the bay.

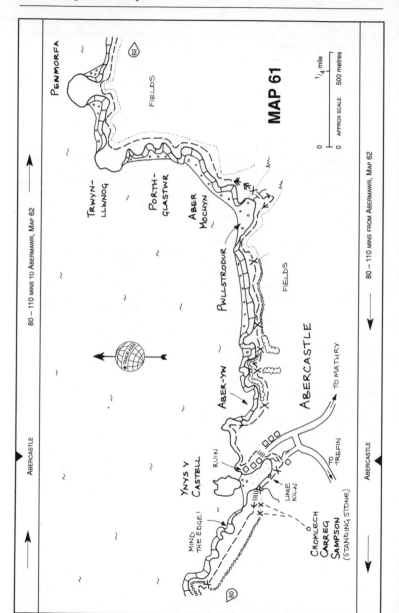

MAP 61

APPROX SCALE

0 ———————— ¼ mile

0 ———————— 500 metres

PENMORFA

62

FIELDS

TRWYN-LLWNOG

PORTH-GLASTWR

ABER MOCHYN

PWLLSTRODUR

FIELDS

ABER-YW

ABERCASTLE

TO MATHRY

YNYS Y CASTELL

RUIN

TO TREFIN

LIME KILN

MIND THE EDGE

CROMLECH CARREG SAMPSON
(STANDING STONE)

60

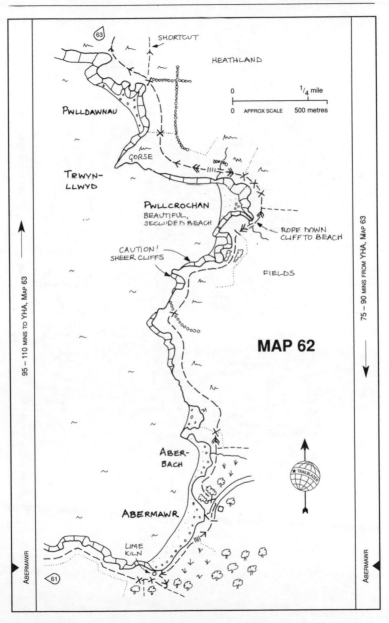

MAP 62

SHORTCUT

HEATHLAND

0   1/4 mile

0   APPROX SCALE   500 metres

PWLLDAWNAU

GORSE

TRWYN-
LLWYD

PWLLCROCHAN
BEAUTIFUL,
SECLUDED BEACH

ROPE DOWN
CLIFF TO BEACH

CAUTION!
SHEER CLIFFS

FIELDS

ABER-
BACH

ABERMAWR

LIME
KILN

TRAILBLAZER

95 – 110 MINS TO YHA, MAP 63

75 – 90 MINS FROM YHA, MAP 63

ABERMAWR

ABERMAWR

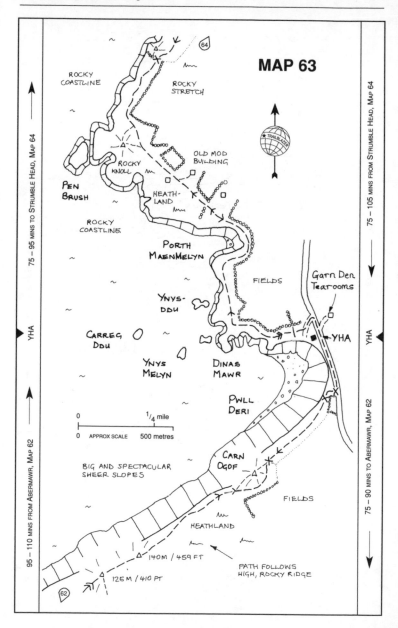

MAP 63

★ TRAILBLAZER

ROCKY COASTLINE

ROCKY STRETCH

OLD MOD BUILDING

PEN BRUSH

ROCKY KNOLL

HEATHLAND

ROCKY COASTLINE

PORTH MAENMELYN

FIELDS

Garn Den Tearooms

YNYS-DDU

YHA

CARREG DDU

YNYS MELYN

DINAS MAWR

PWLL DERI

0   1/4 mile
0   APPROX SCALE   500 metres

BIG AND SPECTACULAR SHEER SLOPES

CARN OGOF

HEATHLAND

FIELDS

140M / 459 FT

125 M / 410 FT

PATH FOLLOWS HIGH, ROCKY RIDGE

75 – 95 MINS TO STRUMBLE HEAD, MAP 64

YHA

95 – 110 MINS FROM ABERMAWR, MAP 62

75 – 105 MINS FROM STRUMBLE HEAD, MAP 64

YHA

75 – 90 MINS TO ABERMAWR, MAP 62

After a swim it's back to the hard grind. The path climbs relentlessly uphill to gain the long ridge leading to Pwll Deri. This rugged ridge of heather and rocky bluffs provides great views of the Pembrokeshire countryside to the east but even more outstanding are the 100-metre (300ft) cliffs, covered in bracken and scrub, which plunge down into the sea. It all culminates in the wonderful circle of cliffs around **Pwll Deri**. It's worth sitting down on top of the ridge to take in the view.

PWLL DERI AND STRUMBLE HEAD
MAP 63, 64

Directly above the cliffs at Pwll Deri is *Pwll Deri Youth Hostel* (☎ 01348-891385, Apr–Oct). It is surely one of the most impressive locations for a youth hostel, sitting precariously 125 metres (410ft) above the sea below. It can be found just off the lane that skirts the cliff tops. After a hard day's walk, sitting in the conservatory with your dinner admiring the sun setting over the sea is a great way to chill out. On a clear day you can see southern Ireland. There are 30 beds at £8.50 each for members (see p11). In the summer months you can get a

light lunch across the lane from the youth hostel at the informal *Garn Den Tearooms*.

Three miles (5km) further north along the coast path, past Strumble Head, there is **camping** for £1 on the road inland at *Fferm Tresinwen* (☎ 01348-891238, Apr–Oct). It can be found by either following the road inland from Strumble Head for about half a mile or following the coast path east from Strumble Head as far as Porthsychan Bay where a footpath leads from the coast path to the campsite (see Map 64).

PWLL DERI TO FISHGUARD   MAPS 63–68

The coast along these **ten and a half miles** (17km, 4–5hrs) is wild and in places rough going. The cliffs are less sheer and sometimes relatively low but they are rugged and hide countless rocky coves and bays.

The path begins by crossing through wild country of rocky hillocks, grass and heather, passing a barren headland with fine views all around. Parts of the trail here can be boggy when the weather is bad.

Just past a narrow cleft in the cliffs the path comes to the car park at **Strumble Head** where the white lighthouse can be seen on the island just off the headland. The path continues through heathland and bracken to **Porthsychan Bay** where a footpath heads inland for the **campsite** at *Fferm Tresinwen* (see Pwll Deri and Strumble Head, above). At **Carreg Wastad Point** make sure you take the quick detour to the top of the heathery hill to see the stone commemorating the last invasion of Britain, when a French fleet landed at this point on 22 February 1797. Around the bay of **Aber-Felin** the path passes through some pretty woodland before winding its way up and over rough hillocks with the cliffs becoming less severe, eventually tapering to gentle heathery slopes at **Penanglas**. Here the path swings southwards through a number of old fields before joining the residential road (New Hill) down into the centre of **Goodwick**. Once past the seafront filling stations the coast path follows the tarmac path known as **Marine Walk**. This effectively bypasses much of the residential part of **Fishguard**. At the end of Marine Walk there are a number of signposted routes which will quickly take you into the town centre.

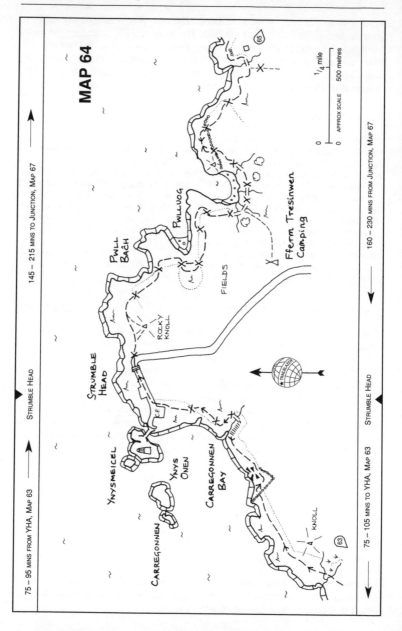

MAP 64

75 – 95 MINS FROM YHA, MAP 63 ——▶ ——▶ STRUMBLE HEAD ——▶ ——▶ 145 – 215 MINS TO JUNCTION, MAP 67 ——▶

◀—— 75 – 105 MINS TO YHA, MAP 63 ◀ STRUMBLE HEAD ◀ 160 – 230 MINS FROM JUNCTION, MAP 67 ——▶

YNYSMEICEL

Ynys Onen

CARREGONNEN

CARREGONNEN BAY

STRUMBLE HEAD

ROCKY KNOLL

PWLL BACH

PWLLUOG

FIELDS

Fferm Tresinwen Camping

KNOLL

63

65

TRAIL BLAZER

0 ¼ mile
APPROX SCALE
0 500 metres

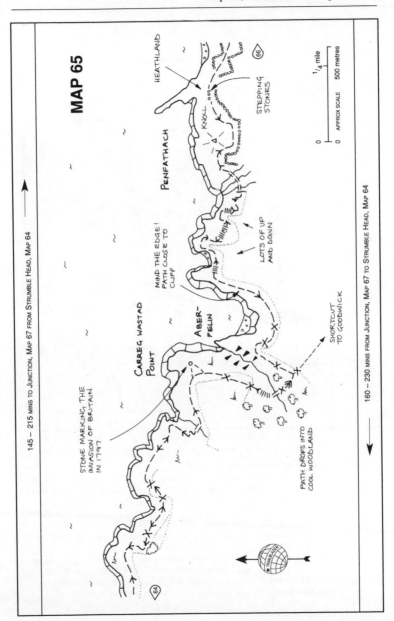

MAP 65

HEATHLAND

PENFATHACH

KNOLL

STEPPING
STONES

66

0   ¼ mile
0   APPROX SCALE   500 metres

MIND THE EDGE!
PATH CLOSE TO
CLIFF

LOTS OF UP
AND DOWN

CARREG WASTAD
POINT

ABER-
FELIN

SHORTCUT
TO GOODWICK

STONE MARKING THE
INVASION OF BRITAIN
IN 1797

PATH DROPS INTO
COOL WOODLAND

64

TRAILBLAZER

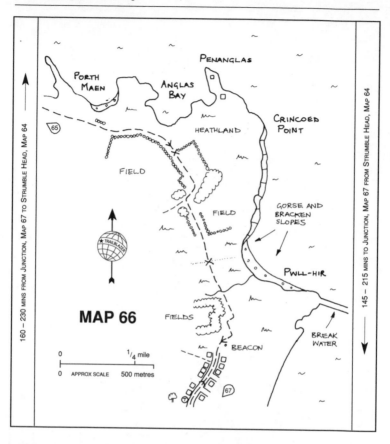

PORTH MAEN

PENANGLAS

ANGLAS BAY

HEATHLAND

CRINCOED POINT

65

FIELD

FIELD

★ TRAILBLAZER

GORSE AND BRACKEN SLOPES

PWLL-HIR

MAP 66

FIELDS

0 .... 1/4 mile

0 .... 500 metres
APPROX SCALE

BEACON

BREAK WATER

67

145 – 215 MINS TO JUNCTION, MAP 67 FROM STRUMBLE HEAD, MAP 64

❏ The Last Invasion of Britain

On 22 February 1797 four French sailing vessels, led by the American Colonel Tate, anchored off Carreg Wastad Head, west of Fishguard. This was the beginning of the last invasion of Britain, a somewhat half-hearted and short lived affair. The 1400 or so Frenchmen occupied the stretch of coast around Strumble Head for a grand total of two days. The story goes that they got so drunk on stolen beer that the locals soon overpowered them, finally surrendering on the sands of Goodwick on 24 February 1797.

The hero of the whole affair was one Jemima Nicholas who, to this day, is something of a local folk hero. Armed with her pitchfork she single-handedly rounded up 12 Frenchmen and is now honoured by having a local ale named after her. A memorial stone to the last invasion stands at Carreg Wastad Point.

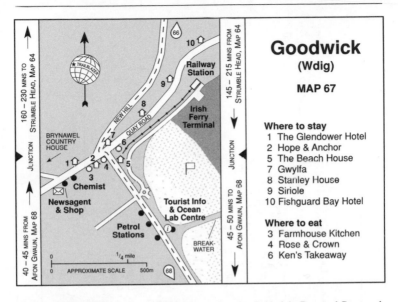

Goodwick
(Wdig)

MAP 67

Where to stay
1 The Glendower Hotel
2 Hope & Anchor
5 The Beach House
7 Gwylfa
8 Stanley House
9 Siriole
10 Fishguard Bay Hotel

Where to eat
3 Farmhouse Kitchen
4 Rose & Crown
6 Ken's Takeaway

GOODWICK (WDIG)   MAP 67

Goodwick is often considered to be an extension of Fishguard but it's really a separate town. Its main claim to fame is its role as a ferry port, shipping holidaymakers to and from Ireland. It may be somewhat overshadowed by its bigger twin but it does have plenty of eating places and accommodation, most notably the very grand Fishguard Bay Hotel, originally built for passengers when the ferry route to Ireland opened in 1906. Since then it has been used to house the film crew of *Moby Dick*, which was filmed in Lower Fishguard, and, later, the men who constructed one of the Milford Haven oil refineries.

Services

The **TIC** (☎ 01348-872037/874737) is in the **Ocean Lab Centre** on Fishguard Rd, opposite the filling stations. There is also an **internet café** here and a **Deep Sea Adventure** display created by 'muppet man' Jim Henson.

As you come down New Hill into the town centre you will see a small **shop and newsagent** on the other side of the road and

a **chemist**. Behind the Rose and Crown pub you will find the **post office**.

Fishguard **train station** is actually here in Goodwick on the road up to the ferry terminal. There are services to Clarbeston Rd, for connections to Milford Haven, and to Swansea and London. There are regular **buses** into Fishguard town centre for connections elsewhere. Look for the 410 town service.

Goodwick is where the **ferry** leaves for Ireland. Adventurous sorts could take a daytrip over to sample the Guinness. The catamaran takes less than two hours to Rosslare while the slower ferry takes under four hours. Passenger-only fares start from £9 on the ferry and £16 on the catamaran. A 24hr return fare starts at £14. Contact Stenaline Ferries (☎ 08705-421107) for bookings.

Where to stay

On Quay Rd is *Stanley House* (☎ 01348-873024, ✉ stanleyhouse@btinternet.com, 6T) which has rooms (some of them en suite) at £17.50 per night or £16.50 if you can go without breakfast. Also on Quay Rd, *Siriole* (☎ 01348-872375, 2D/3F) has big

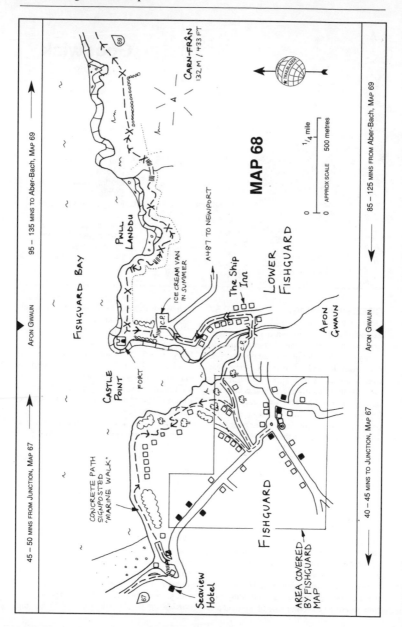

AFON GWAUN

45 – 50 MINS FROM JUNCTION, MAP 67

95 – 135 MINS TO ABER-BACH, MAP 69

FISHGUARD BAY

CARN-FRÂN
132 M / 433 FT

PWLL LANDDU

69

CASTLE POINT

FORT

ICE CREAM VAN IN SUMMER

C.P.

A487 TO NEWPORT

The Ship Inn

LOWER FISHGUARD

AFON GWAUN

C.P.

CONCRETE PATH SIGNPOSTED "MARINE WALK"

FISHGUARD

AREA COVERED BY FISHGUARD MAP

Seaview Hotel

67

MAP 68

0 .... ¼ mile
0 APPROX SCALE 500 metres

40 – 45 MINS TO JUNCTION, MAP 67

AFON GWAUN

85 – 125 MINS FROM ABER-BACH, MAP 69

rooms from £19, or £17 without breakfast.

In the centre of town is *Glendower Hotel* (☎ 01348-872873, 🖳 glendowerhotel @hotmail.com) where some of the rooms are en suite. A single costs £31.50. *Gwylfa* (☎ 01348-873730, Goodwick Sq, 4T) has rooms from £16 per night while the wonderful *Beach House* (☎ 01348-872085, 9D) has en-suite rooms from £13 to £15. Also by The Square is the *Hope & Anchor* (☎ 01348-872314) with en-suite rooms at £25 per person.

On top of the hill, about half a mile from town, is the very welcoming *Brynawel Country House* (☎ 01348-874155, 🖳 bry nawel@amserve.net, 1T/2D/2F). They provide free transport for coast-path walkers. Phone to confirm a booking and to arrange a lift from Goodwick when you arrive. They will even pick you up and drop you off anywhere between St David's and Cardigan meaning you can base yourself here for several days while tackling the entire northern section of the coast path. If you are coming by car they will happily keep your car in a safe place for the duration of your stay. The price is £18 per person for bed and breakfast which includes your own lounge and self-catering kitchen. There is no surcharge for lone travellers using the double rooms.

FISHGUARD (ABERGWAUN) MAP 68

Fishguard is a surprisingly amenable place. It is big enough to provide everything you need and small enough to maintain a quiet charm. This is the capital of 'Last Invasion Country' (see p172). You can see an embroidered tapestry commemorating this event at St Mary's Church Hall (☎ 01348-874997,10am–5pm Mon–Sat, adults £1.50) just off Market Sq. The main town of Fishguard sits on high ground above Fishguard Harbour but down the hill to the north of the town, where the Afon Gwaun drains the Cwm Gwaun valley and the Preseli Hills, is **Lower Fishguard**. This pretty quayside village comes as a pleasant surprise. It was the setting for Dylan Thomas' *Under Milk Wood* and was also used in the 1956 film *Moby Dick*.

For complete pampered luxury (though at a price), *Fishguard Bay Hotel* (☎ 01348-873571, 🖳 mhar177485@aol.com, 59 en suite) is a grandiose building set in woodland at the end of Quay Rd. Built a century ago when a room would set you back five shillings, these days an en-suite room starts at £45 for a single or £35 per person if you are sharing. Make sure you wipe your hiking boots before you enter.

Where to eat

In The Square, the *Rose & Crown* (☎ 01348-874449) does pub grub such as sausage, egg and chips for £3.25 and chicken Kiev for £5.95 until 9pm. On the corner of The Square is the *Hope and Anchor* (11.30am –3.30pm, 6–11pm) with the likes of chicken curry for £3.50 and beef stew for £2.95.

Next door is the *Farmhouse Kitchen* (☎ 01348-873907, 6–10pm Tue–Sat; 12– 2.30pm, Sun 7–9pm) where the menu is constantly changing. They do a good three-course menu for £9.95.

For something fast there is *Ken's Takeaway* near the Hope and Anchor, with fish and chips and burgers. At the other end of the spectrum is the restaurant at the *Fishguard Bay Hotel* (see above) which is open to non-residents.

Services

Market Sq is the hub of the town where you will find plenty of high street **shops** and a chemist, as well as the **TIC** (☎ 01348-873484) in the old town hall building. The **post office** is in West St and there is a big **superstore** on High St (up from Market Sq). If you're searching for supplies on a Saturday the fortnightly **farmers' market** is well worth visiting; it's held in the Kwiksave car park on Main St (9am–2pm).

Buses leave from Market Sq. The regular 410 town service goes to Goodwick and there are also buses to Cardigan (for St Dogmaels), Trefin, St David's, Newgale and Haverfordwest. Fishguard **train station** is not actually in Fishguard but in Goodwick.

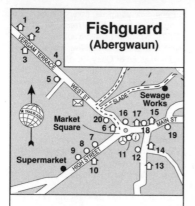

Fishguard
(Abergwaun)

KEY

Where to stay
1 Tara Hotel
2 Camelot
3 Inglewood
6 Abergwaun Hotel
10 Cartref Hotel
13 Cri'r Wylan
14 Hamilton Backpackers
15 Manor Town House Hotel
17 Three Main Street

Where to eat
4 The China Chef
5 Jean's Diner
7 Old Coach House
8 Ship & Anchor
9 Taj Mahal
11 Fish & Chips
12 Dragon House Chinese
16 Royal Oak Inn
18 Pepino's
19 The Globe
20 Pinocchio's Pizzeria

Where to stay

Campers should head out of Fishguard to the
Fishguard Bay Caravan Park (☎ 01348-
811415, 🖳 www.fishguardbay.com, Mar–
Jan, see Map 69) where a pitch for a small
tent will cost you £10 between two people.
It is situated two miles (3km) east of
Fishguard. The coast path goes straight
through it so it is hard to miss.

In town, budget travellers will appreciate
Hamilton Backpackers Lodge (☎ 01348-
874797, 🖳 www.fishguard-backpackers.
com, 21/23 Hamilton St, 18T). It's run by a
friendly Australian guy who keeps the place
ticking over in a very informal way and it's
open all year. It's a useful stop if you arrive
late in the day since there is no curfew.
Prices: £11 bunks, £13 doubles per person
and £14 singles. It lies just off Main St on
Hamilton St.

Cri'r Wylan (☎ 01348-873398, Pen
Wallis, 3T) has three rooms from £18 per
person, while the unimaginatively named
Three Main St (☎ 01348-874275, 1T/2D)
has rooms from £25. On the same road is
the ***Manor Town House Hotel*** (☎ 01348-
873260, Main St, 12T) which has B&B
accommodation from £24.

On High St, the ***Cartref Hotel*** (☎ 01348
-872430, 🖳 www.abergwaun.com/cartref.
htm, 15/19 High St, 4S/4T/2F en suite) has
rooms from £32 to £38. On Market Sq is
Abergwaun Hotel (☎ 01348-872077, 2S/
4T/4D/2F) with en-suite rooms from £26.

On Vergam Terrace, from the hill leading into Fishguard from Goodwick, is *Tara
Hotel* (☎ 01348-872777, 2S/2T/3D/3F) with
rooms from £20 per person. On the same
street are *Inglewood* (☎ 01348-873475, 13
Vergam Terrace, 3D) with B&B from £32
per person and *Camelot* (☎ 01348-872640,
22 Vergam Terrace, 3S/1T/2D) with single
rooms from £16 to £18.

Where to eat

The ***Old Coach House*** (☎ 01348-875429,
6–9pm) on High St is a lively pub specializing in Italian food. For something cheap but
filling try the ***Ship and Anchor*** (☎ 01348-
872362, 7–9pm). It's the big pink building in
High St and does bacon and onion baguettes
for £1 as well as more substantial meals.
Close by is *Taj Mahal* (☎ 01348-874593, 22
High St, 6–11.30pm Mon–Sun) for typical
Indian dishes. You can get take-away until
midnight.

Also doing food is the *Royal Oak Inn*
(☎ 01348-872514), a rustic pub on Market
Sq. Close by is *Pinocchio's Pizzeria*
(12–2.30pm, 6–10pm) with pizzas and pas-
tas from £4.75.

Pepino's (☎ 01348-875349, 5 Main St, 7–9.30pm) is an Italian restaurant with evening meals from £10.25, or lunchtime toasties from £1.55. Booking is advisable. Next door is *Three Main St* (see Where to stay, 7–9pm) a smart restaurant with three-course meals for £30. Booking is essential.

Opposite Hamilton Backpackers is the *Dragon House Chinese Restaurant* (5–11.30pm) for takeaway Chinese food. There are **fish and chips** in Main St and also in West St at *Jean's Diner* (75 West St) to sit in or take away. Opposite this is another Chinese takeaway, *The China Chef*.

A good place for a late night drink is *The Globe* on Main St which gets very busy at weekends largely thanks to their midnight licence.

On the way out of Fishguard heading east you pass the *Ship Inn* in Lower Fishguard, a good place for a pint though they don't do food.

FISHGUARD TO NEWPORT   MAPS 68–72

It's **eleven miles (18km, 4¹/₂–5hrs)** if you follow the entire coast path via the peninsula known as Dinas Island. Cheats, or those in a hurry, can take the short-cut, bringing the distance down to nine miles (14km, 3¹/₂–4hrs).

The pretty fishing village of **Lower Fishguard** with its colourful houses lining the quay below the hillside and boats bobbing in the harbour contrasts greatly with the bustling main town on top of the hill.

From the top of the steep climb up the main road the path passes through gorse bushes to the remains of the 220-year-old **Fishguard Fort**.

Another mile and a half (2km) and the path brings you directly into Fishguard Bay Caravan Park where it is possible to camp (see Fishguard). The path continues along the edge of steep, high cliffs all the way to the tiny sheltered beach of **Aber-Bach**.

At Pwllgwaelod you must decide if you want to include the peninsula of Dinas Island in your walk. If the answer is no follow the well-made straight path through the valley to Cwm-yr-eglwys. If the answer is yes take the easy to follow path which climbs steadily through heather and bracken all the way to the 142-metre (466ft) Pen y Fan, the summit of **Dinas Head**.

The path continues around the peninsula above high slopes of bracken before passing through bushes and trees to emerge at **Cwm-yr-eglwys** (Church Valley) named after the church which lies in ruins by the beach. This is a popular holiday spot with a caravan and boat park. With everything squeezed into such a narrow valley the effect is claustrophobic so it is a relief to escape by walking up the steep lane opposite the boat park.

After ten minutes or so of lung-busting ascent the path can be found sneaking between high hedges on the left next to a house. The path is well hidden by hedges and trees until you reach cliffs above the cove at **Fforest**. The cliffs along the next section are sheer and in places overhanging. The path can be very close to the edge so watch your step.

The next cove is a real beauty. The unspoilt nature of the area makes it quite a rarity. Unlike most of these coves there is no road and no houses, just woodland, a marsh and a stony beach. From here the path continues along the edge of precipitous cliffs to **Parrog** and the edge of Newport town where it briefly crosses the shingle, mud and sand on the seafront.

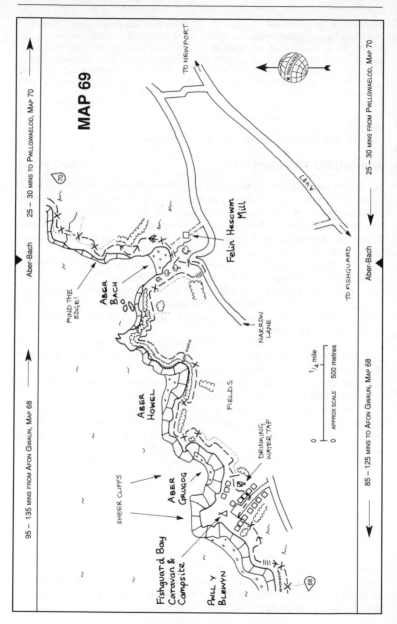

MAP 69

95 – 135 MINS FROM AFON GWAUN, MAP 68

Aber-Bach 25 – 30 MINS TO PWLLGWAELOD, MAP 70

85 – 125 MINS TO AFON GWAUN, MAP 68

Aber-Bach 25 – 30 MINS FROM PWLLGWAELOD, MAP 70

TRAIL BLAZER

TO NEWPORT

A487

TO FISHGUARD

Felin Hescwm Mill

NARROW LANE

FIELDS

MIND THE EDGE!

ABER BACH

ABER HOWEL

SHEER CLIFFS

ABER GRUGOG

Fishguard Bay Caravan & Campsite

PWLL Y BLEWYN

DRINKING WATER TAP

1/4 mile

0   APPROX SCALE   500 metres

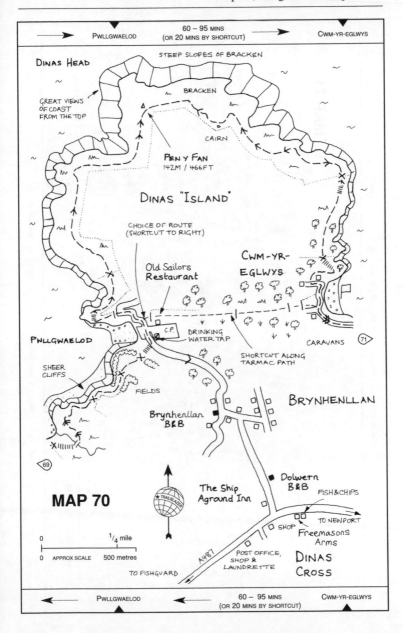

PWLLGWAELOD — 60 – 95 MINS (OR 20 MINS BY SHORTCUT) — CWM-YR-EGLWYS

DINAS HEAD

STEEP SLOPES OF BRACKEN

BRACKEN

GREAT VIEWS OF COAST FROM THE TOP

CAIRN

PEN Y FAN
142M / 466FT

DINAS "ISLAND"

CHOICE OF ROUTE
(SHORTCUT TO RIGHT)

CWM-YR-EGLWYS

Old Sailors
Restaurant

C.P.

DRINKING
WATER TAP

PWLLGWAELOD

CARAVANS

(71)

SHEER
CLIFFS

SHORTCUT ALONG
TARMAC PATH

FIELDS

BRYNHENLLAN

Brynhenllan
B&B

BRYNHENLLAN

(69)

MAP 70

TRAILBLAZER

The Ship
Aground Inn

Dolwern
B&B

FISH & CHIPS

0   ¼ mile

0   APPROX SCALE   500 metres

SHOP

TO NEWPORT

Freemasons
Arms

DINAS
CROSS

A487

POST OFFICE,
SHOP &
LAUNDRETTE

TO FISHGUARD

PWLLGWAELOD — 60 – 95 MINS (OR 20 MINS BY SHORTCUT) — CWM-YR-EGLWYS

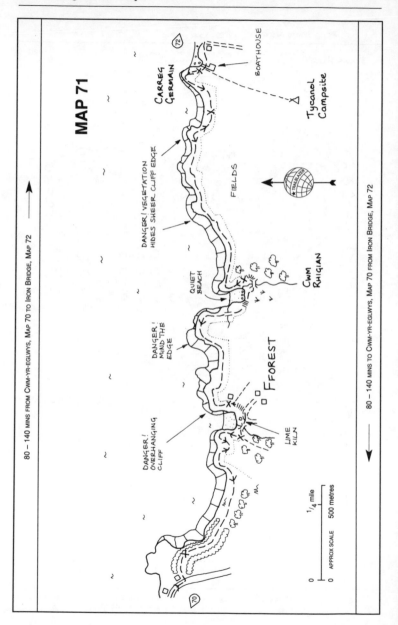

MAP 71

CARREG GERMAIN

BOATHOUSE

Tycanol Campsite

FIELDS

DANGER! VEGETATION HIDES SHEER CLIFF EDGE

QUIET BEACH

CWM RHIGIAN

DANGER! MIND THE EDGE

FFOREST

DANGER! OVERHANGING CLIFF

LIME KILN

TRAILBLAZER

1/4 mile

500 metres

0   APPROX SCALE

0

Where the path passes the salt marsh and some woodland there are two lanes, both of which provide access to the centre of **Newport**. The first leads up to the national park information centre, while the second takes you to the youth hostel.

AROUND PWLLGWAELOD AND DINAS CROSS   MAPS 69 & 70

The village of Dinas Cross is a short detour from the coast path. It can be reached by walking up the lane from Pwllgwaelod through Brynhenllan to the main road and turning right (20mins from the coast path). Here there is a service station with a mini **supermarket**, **post office**, **laundrette** and an **off-licence**. There is also a **fish and chip shop** (☎ 01348-811660, open daily); you can phone ahead to place your order. Next door is the *Freemasons Arms* where you can treat yourself to a pint.

Along the lane to Dinas you will find B&B for £17 at *Brynhenllan* (☎ 01348-811234, 2D/1F), while *Dolwern* (☎ 01348-811266, 1T/2D) is further up the lane closer to the main road. It has rooms from £17 per person. This is also where you will find the *Ship Aground* (☎ 01348-811261, 6.45–9pm) for good pub grub.

At Pwllgwaelod there is a **drinking-water tap** next to the public **toilets** in the car park. There's nowhere to stay but there is *The Old Sailors Restaurant* (☎ 01348-811491, daily 11am–6pm, booking essential Fri and Sat) with tasty lobster and crab lunches.

NEWPORT (TREFDRAETH)   MAP 72

Rising behind Newport are the Preseli Hills. This is bluestone country from where the stones for the inner circle of Stonehenge were transported. The hill directly behind the town is Carn Ingli rising to 319 metres (1046ft). From the top you can see the mountains of Snowdonia on a clear day.

The town itself is small and friendly. The **Norman castle** and church at the top were built along with the original town in the 12th century when the Norman invader Robert Martin chose the spot beside the Newport estuary to set up home. Unfortunately the castle is privately owned so visitors must content themselves with a view from the outside.

Newport is a surprisingly well equipped little town. Almost everything you could possibly need can be found in the compact centre. It's the perfect place to stay before the tough final leg of the journey to St Dogmaels.

Before you leave town check the *West Wales Eco Centre* (☎ 01239-820235, 🖳 www.ecocentre.org.uk, 9.30am–4.30pm, Mon– Fri, Apr–Oct) next to the youth hostel on Lower St Mary's St. It's home to the

smallest solar power station in the UK and has displays and demonstrations on renewable energy and conservation. Entrance is free.

Services

The **TIC** (☎ 01239-820912) is also the **National Park Information Centre** and is situated on Long St, which is the lane connecting to the coast path.

The **post office** is on the corner of Long St and the main road, Bridge St. There are two **banks**, one of which, on Bridge St, has a cashpoint. The best place for provisions is the Spar **supermarket** (8am–10pm, 7 days) on Market St. Alternatively there is the Newport Garage **mini-market** on Bridge St.

Dirty socks can be washed at the **laundrette** (9am–9pm, open daily) opposite the Golden Lion on the main road and there's a **chemist** (☎ 01239-820239) on Market St.

Remember to fill your water bottle before leaving Newport. The next stretch is a long one and there is no fresh water available until near the end of the walk.

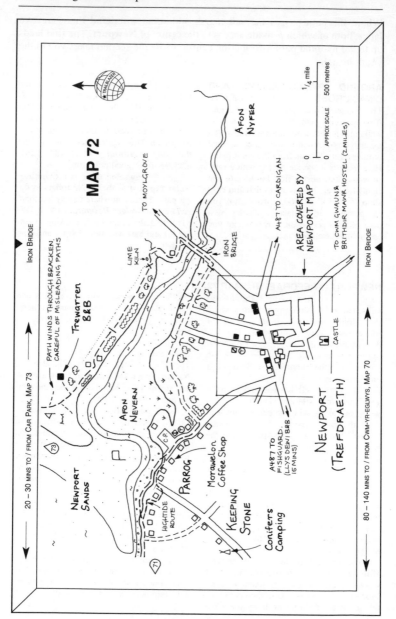

MAP 72

IRON BRIDGE

◄ 20 – 30 MINS TO / FROM CAR PARK, MAP 73 ►

PATH WINDS THROUGH BRACKEN.
CAREFUL OF MISLEADING PATHS

Trewarren B&B

LIME KILN

TO MOYLGROVE

AFON NYFER

IRON BRIDGE

A487 TO CARDIGAN

TO CWM GWAUN &
BRITHDIR MAWR HOSTEL (2 MILES)

AREA COVERED BY NEWPORT MAP

¼ mile

0   APPROX SCALE

0   500 metres

AFON NEVERN

Newport Sands

(73)

NEWPORT (TREFDRAETH)

CASTLE

A487 TO FISHGUARD (LLYS DEWI) B&B (16 MINS)

PARROG

Morawelon Coffee Shop

C.P.

KEEPING STONE

HIGHTIDE ROUTE

Conifers Camping

(71)

IRON BRIDGE

◄ 80 – 140 MINS TO / FROM CWM-YR-EGLWYS, MAP 70 ►

Where to stay

For **camping** there are a few places just before you reach Newport. *Tycanol Campsite* (☎ 01239-820264, Apr–Oct) is 200 yards from the coast path. Turn inland at the boat house by Carreg Germain. It costs £3 per person but there are also beds for walkers in the farmhouse at just £5 per person; a good option if it's raining.

For *Conifers Camping* (☎ 01239-820315, Apr–Oct) continue a little further along the coast path and turn right at Parrog. Follow the lane for 300 yards to Cippin Stone. The campsite is at the end of the line of houses on the right.

In the village itself is *Newport Youth Hostel* (☎ 01239-820080, Lower St Mary St, open all year), a converted schoolhouse with 28 beds costing £9.25 for members (see p11). From the coast path you can reach it by taking the second lane on the right where you see the YHA sign.

There are some good places to stay along East St. Recommended is the *Golden Lion* (☎ 01239-820321, East St, 11D) which has en-suite rooms from only £22 per person, and of course you only have to go downstairs for the nearest drink.

Further along the road is *Llysmeddyg Guest House* (☎ 01239-820008, 🖳 Penny @ipross.freeserve.co.uk, East St, 1S/1T/1D /1F) with some en-suite rooms for £25–£35. On the same road is *Cnapan* (☎ 01239-820575, 5D en suite) with beds at £31 per person. If they are busy there is a £7 single person's supplement.

Further up the road in Bridge St is another good pub with very comfortable en-suite rooms from £25 for a single: *Gwesty'r Castell* (☎ 01239-820742), or Castle Hotel. The owners are very welcoming and helpful.

Hafan Deg (☎ 01239-820301, Long St) near the TIC has en-suite B&B from £19 and *The Globe* (☎ 01239-820296, Upper St Mary St) has comfortable rooms at £25 single or £35 based on two sharing. Alternatively there is *Llys Dewi* (☎ 01239-820177, Fishguard Rd) which has three en-suite rooms from £18 per person. It's a bit out of the way, lying half a mile west of Newport along the main road. It's best

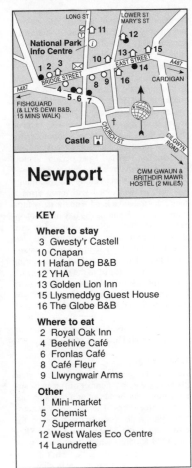

Newport

KEY

Where to stay
3 Gwesty'r Castell
10 Cnapan
11 Hafan Deg B&B
12 YHA
13 Golden Lion Inn
15 Llysmeddyg Guest House
16 The Globe B&B

Where to eat
2 Royal Oak Inn
4 Beehive Café
6 Fronlas Café
8 Café Fleur
9 Llwyngwair Arms

Other
1 Mini-market
5 Chemist
7 Supermarket
12 West Wales Eco Centre
14 Laundrette

reached by leaving the coast path at Parrog and following the lane up to the main road.

Moving along the coast path from Newport to the other side of the estuary is *Trewarren* (☎ 01239-820455) with two en-suite rooms. A sign by the coast path points you in the right direction.

Brithdir Mawr (☎ 01239-820164, Cilgwyn Rd, 12S, open all year) is a fascinating organic farm with **bunkhouse** accommodation two miles (3km) from Newport. It is run by a small international community working towards simplicity, sustainability and spirit. They welcome visitors by prior arrangement to their ecological hostel which has room for 12 people in two sleeping lofts and another family room. In the summer it can get booked up for weeks on end since many people come here and never want to leave so give them a ring to let them know your plans. It's a good idea to bring a sleeping bag although they do have some old sheets and blankets lying around. The cost is £5 per person. Visitors can take part in any of the music, dance and meditation activities run by the community and will be welcomed with open arms if they offer to lend a hand with the daily farm duties such as bringing the hay in and chopping wood. The whole place may feel as if it has one foot in the past but in reality has its eyes keenly focussed on a truly sustainable future. The only catch to this inspiring place is its distance from the coast path. It's a two-mile (3km) hike along the Cilgwyn road and all of it is uphill. However, if you do decide to make that extra effort you will be well rewarded. It's in a wonderful location and can be used as a base for a side trip into the Prescli Hills (see opposite).

Where to eat

Newport is completely spoilt with great places to eat with a number of fine pubs and restaurants. For breakfast or a snack try one of the coffee shops. The first one you come to as you walk towards the town on the coast path is the *Morawelon Coffee Shop* (☎ 01239-820565) which does a variety of snacks and light lunches. You can't miss it; it's on the seafront near the yacht club.

Many of the other coffee shops also do evening meals. On the main road is the *Beehive Café* (☎ 01239-820372) with big breakfasts for £4.95 and bacon butties for £1.50. For something more substantial they have chicken supreme at £7.90.

In the centre of the village is the very yellow and altogether continental *Café Fleur* (☎ 01239-820131, ✉ dianecafe fleur@hotmail.com, Market St). They do Greek, Italian, Thai and French theme nights. Try the very tasty panini toasted sandwiches.

Further up Market St opposite the Spar supermarket you will find *Fronlas Café* (☎ 01239-820351) which does breakfasts and afternoon snacks as well as evening meals (from 7pm, Wed–Sat, booking essential).

Look out for the *Golden Lion* (6.30–9pm) in East St which does very good food and has young, friendly bar staff.

Another good choice is the *Royal Oak Inn* (☎ 01239-820632, Mon–Sat 11am–11pm, Sun 11am–10.30pm) on Bridge St (near Newport garage). It's owned by a friendly Sri Lankan who really knows how to knock up a good curry. The traditional pub is an unlikely looking curry house but the chicken tandoori masala at £6.99 should be enough to convince you. Food is also available to take away.

Alternatively there is *Gwesty'r Castell* (see p183, 12–2pm, 6.30–9.30pm, 7 days, Bridge St) with local food, real ales and a roaring log fire, or you could try *Llwyngwair Arms* (☎ 01239-820267) for more Welsh food and real ales. For a straightforward restaurant *Cnapan* (see p183) on East St does high quality, if slightly expensive, evening meals.

NEWPORT TO ST DOGMAELS

MAPS 72–79

Nothing like leaving the best till last but there's always a catch. This is the toughest section of the entire walk. If you have come all the way from Amroth you will either be feeling fitter than ever or you will be feeling 30 years older and will find these last **sixteen miles (26km, 5½–7½hrs)** pretty strenuous.

The cliffs are bigger here, the distances longer, there is nowhere to get any food, nowhere to get any water and only one place to stay until you get to Poppit

❑ Walking in the Preseli Hills (Mynydd Preseli) and Cwm Gwaun

The Preseli Hills rise behind Newport, dissected by the deep Cwm Gwaun glacial valley. This little-known area is well worth exploring if you have time to spare as it provides some wonderful secluded walking away from the more popular coast. This is bluestone country. The rock here was transported all the way to Salisbury Plain for the construction of Stonehenge by some miracle of Druidian engineering. There are Iron-Age hill-forts and standing stones dotted all along the crest of the hills with fantastic views over the coastline and the sweep of Cardigan Bay.

The Preseli Hills are divided into three distinct parts. On the northern side is the lowest line of hills reaching 337m (1105ft) on Carningli Common above Newport. The higher Mynydd Preseli to the south reaches a height of 536m (1758ft) at Foel Cwmcerwyn, while the heavily wooded Cwm Gwaun valley separates the two. The circular walk outlined below starts in Newport and takes in the Cwm Gwaun valley before returning over the ridge of the lower hills via the distinctive peak of Carningli.

Safety Do not underestimate these hills. They may be relatively low but they are exposed and the weather can still change suddenly as with the rest of Britain's western hills. The ridge is a broad one with few distinctive landmarks making it very inhospitable in bad weather. Take the OS Outdoor Leisure Map 35 of North Pembrokeshire (yellow cover) and a compass in case the cloud comes down. Warm waterproof clothing and plenty of food and water for the day are also essential.

A circular walk (see map, p186) This walk is about **11 miles** (17.5km) and takes about **4–6 hours**, (please note, the times below are cumulative). From Newport follow the road up Church St with the castle to your right and the church to the left. Continue up the Cilgwyn Rd. After 2 miles (3km) is Brithdir Mawr (see opposite) an ecological farm which provides basic hostel accommodation. If you plan to stay leave any heavy packs here and take a light daysack for the rest of the walk.

Stay on the lane following the signs for Cwm Gwaun. The lane now heads downhill to a sharp right-hand corner. Continue up the hill, ignoring the left turn. The lane eventually meets another lane at a T-junction where you should turn right. After passing the tiny disused quarry on your left the road drops down with a fine view of the valley ahead. At the sharp right-hand bend it's time to leave the road and head along the woodland track through the gate to your left (1–1½hrs). This beautiful stretch of path passes through some impressive beech forest where red squirrels and buzzards can frequently be spotted. The path passes a number of ruined houses hinting at a time when the Cwm Gwaun was more heavily populated.

Keep to the path on the edge of the forest, passing fields on your right, eventually reaching the farm at Dan Coed (2–2¼hrs) where you have to rejoin the lane. It is a short walk along the road to the eccentric *Dyffryn Arms* (2½–3¼hrs) where you can get beer poured from a jug and passed through a hatch in what is effectively Bessie the landlady's living room. It's a good spot to eat your lunch, although the pub itself doesn't do food.

After a break it's time for the steep climb up to the hilltop. Turn right after the pub and climb the hairpin lane, reaching the bleak windswept moor at Bedd Morris where there is a car park and fine views of Dinas Head on the coast (3–4hrs). At the car park follow the track through the heather. In bad visibility a compass will be needed. Head directly east until you come to a fence. Follow the fence line, passing the rocks of Carn Edward on the right. From the end of the fence head up onto the 337m (1105ft) rocky top of Carn Ingli (3½–5hrs), an interesting little hill with views over Newport on an otherwise featureless upland moor. *(Continued on p186)*

❏ Walking in the Preseli Hills (Mynydd Preseli) and Cwm Gwaun

(continued from p185). Look out for the hut circles on the ridge leading to the top. If you are going back to Newport follow the obvious path north down the slopes and join the track which takes you back onto Church Rd (4–6hrs). If you are staying at the organic farm at Brithdir Mawr you must retrace your steps off the south-western end of Carn Ingli to join the small path that drops down through slopes of bracken. Keep the old stone wall to your right, cross the track at the bottom of the hill and follow the path to the gate. At the end of the short track turn left onto the Cilgwyn Rd. Brithdir Mawr is down the first track on the right (3¾–5½hrs).

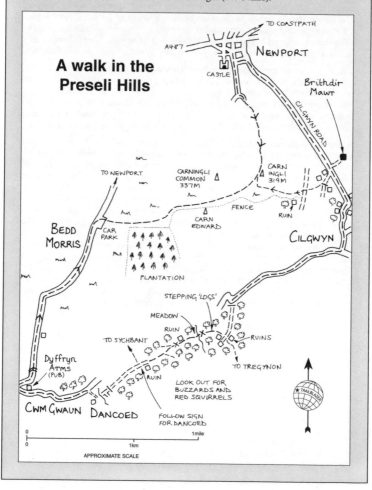

A walk in the Preseli Hills

TO COASTPATH

A487

NEWPORT

CASTLE

Brithdir Mawr

CILGWYN ROAD

TO NEWPORT

CARNINGLI COMMON 337M △

CARN INGLI 319M △

CARN EDWARD △

FENCE

RUIN

CILGWYN

BEDD MORRIS

CAR PARK

PLANTATION

STEPPING 'LOGS'

MEADOW

RUIN

RUINS

TO SYCHBANT

RUIN

TO TREGYNON

Dyffryn Arms (PUB)

LOOK OUT FOR BUZZARDS AND RED SQUIRRELS

CWM GWAUN DANCOED

FOLLOW SIGN FOR DANCOED

TRAILBLAZER

0   1km
0   1mile
APPROXIMATE SCALE

Sands. These are all ingredients for a tough day. Count on taking at least two to three litres of water with you and more if it's a hot day. That one place to stay is in the village of Moylgrove near Ceibwr Bay. If you intend to stay there you are well advised to book in advance (see p190).

After crossing the iron bridge over the **Afon Nyfer** the path follows the northern edge of the estuary, through bushes and bracken and across a golf course to a car park next to **Newport Sands**. Here there is a small **café**, **toilets** and a **drinking-water tap**.

This is where the hard stuff begins. The path climbs up onto high cliffs, passing through a beautiful heathland nature reserve. In the summer this area is alive with butterflies. The path continues above very high, steep slopes of bracken and around some spectacular bays sheltered by terrifying barren cliffs, climbing steadily higher and higher to reach a high point of 150 metres (492ft) where the hill of **Foel-Gôch** plunges into the sea.

Once past a couple of huge old landslips, which are no doubt still vulnerable to collapse, the path drops down to lower cliffs, eventually arriving at the spectacular formations around the **Witch's Cauldron**. A great wedge of rock lies just offshore trapping a finger of the sea below the cliffs. The path, rather worryingly, passes very close to the nasty drop down into this pool. Watch your step. Further on is the Witch's Cauldron itself, a sea cave where the roof has collapsed. The result is a beautiful cove with a natural bridge making it appear separate from the main body of the sea.

A little further on is **Ceibwr Bay** with its shingle beach; a good halfway point for lunch. The village of **Moylgrove** is about half a mile inland, along the valley road. The only accommodation for miles lies just beyond the village.

Ahead are wonderful twisted folds of rock dropping into the sea. After skirting around the flanks of **Foel Hendre** spectacular cliffs come into view. The impressive folding of the rock in these cliffs will have geologists drooling at the mouth. The path here begins to spasm in a series of excruciating descents and ascents. In places it climbs quite improbably steep slopes.

Once above the aforementioned cliffs the path swings to the east reaching the highest point of the entire coast path at 175 metres (574ft). The steep slopes of bracken that sweep down to the sea certainly make you feel a long way up.

Soon the path passes an old lookout building and drops down to the broad **Cemaes Head** before heading south to Allt-y-coed Farm where the track joins a country lane. The lane leads steadily downhill to the lifeboat station and car park at **Poppit Sands** and on to **St Dogmaels** where the coast path officially ends by the slipway. If you are after a celebratory drink you will find the *Ferry Inn* just down the road.

The main village is further still while the bigger town of **Cardigan** is a mile further east on the other side of the **Afon Teifi**. You can get to Cardigan by turning left at St Dogmaels following the B4546 road, or following the riverside path that leaves the road just south of the end of the coast path.

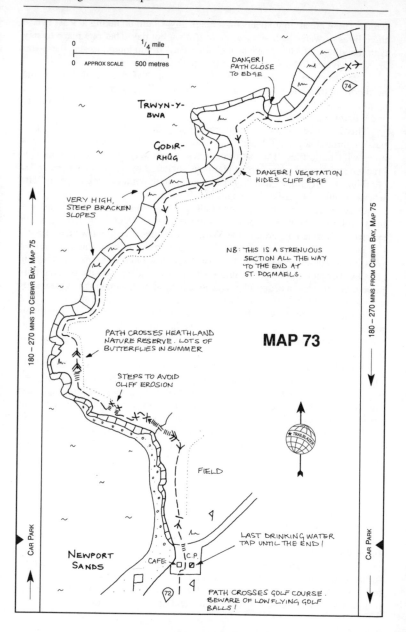

0   1/4 mile

0   APPROX SCALE   500 metres

DANGER! PATH CLOSE TO EDGE

TRWYN-Y-BWA

GODIR-RHÔG

74

DANGER! VEGETATION HIDES CLIFF EDGE

VERY HIGH, STEEP BRACKEN SLOPES

180 – 270 MINS TO CEIBWR BAY, MAP 75

180 – 270 MINS FROM CEIBWR BAY, MAP 75

NB: THIS IS A STRENUOUS SECTION ALL THE WAY TO THE END AT ST. DOGMAELS.

MAP 73

PATH CROSSES HEATHLAND NATURE RESERVE. LOTS OF BUTTERFLIES IN SUMMER

STEPS TO AVOID CLIFF EROSION

★ TRAILBLAZER

FIELD

LAST DRINKING WATER TAP UNTIL THE END!

NEWPORT SANDS

CAFE

C.P.

72

PATH CROSSES GOLF COURSE. BEWARE OF LOW FLYING GOLF BALLS!

CAR PARK

CAR PARK

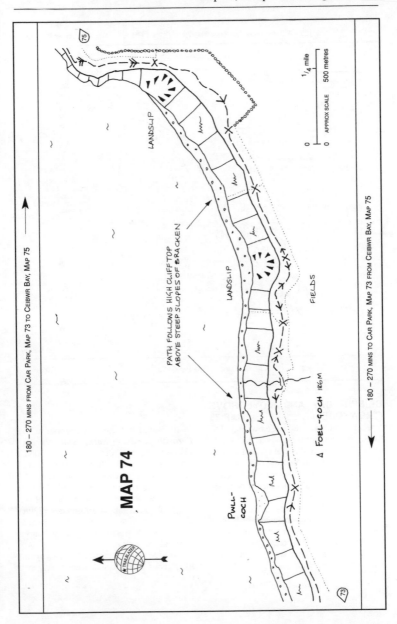

MAP 74

180 – 270 MINS FROM CAR PARK, MAP 73 TO CEIBWR BAY, MAP 75

180 – 270 MINS TO CAR PARK, MAP 73 FROM CEIBWR BAY, MAP 75

PWLL-COCH

△ FOEL-GOCH 186M

PATH FOLLOWS HIGH CLIFF TOP ABOVE STEEP SLOPES OF BRACKEN

LANDSLIP

LANDSLIP

FIELDS

0   APPROX SCALE   ¼ mile

0   500 metres

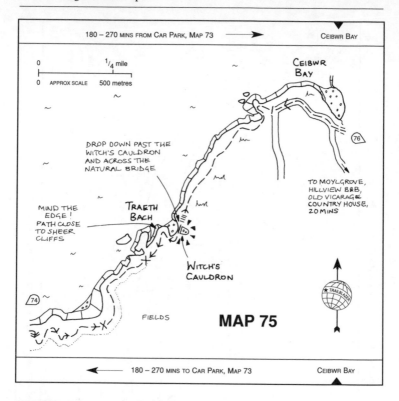

CEIBWR
BAY

0   ¹/₄ mile

0   APPROX SCALE   500 metres

DROP DOWN PAST THE
WITCH'S CAULDRON
AND ACROSS THE
NATURAL BRIDGE

76

TO MOYLGROVE,
HILLVIEW B&B,
OLD VICARAGE
COUNTRY HOUSE,
20 MINS

MIND THE
EDGE!
PATH CLOSE
TO SHEER
CLIFFS

TRAETH
BACH

WITCH'S
CAULDRON

74

FIELDS   **MAP 75**

TRAILBLAZER

CEIBWR BAY AND MOYLGROVE (TREWYDDEL)   MAP 75

You will find very little at Ceibwr Bay. The hamlet of Moylgrove lies about half a mile up the lane through the valley. Just beyond the village you will find the *Old Vicarage Country House* (☎ 01239-881231, 🖳 stay@ old-vic.co.uk, 1T/2D en suite). Prices are from £30 per person if sharing and £38 if you are alone. The only other B&B is *Hillview* (☎ 01239 881219) with beds from £22 per person. You'll find it up the road in the direction of Newport. Book well in advance because there are no alternatives until you reach Poppit Sands.

In the summer there is a tearoom at the *Penrallt Ceibwr Farm and Nursery* (Mon–Sat 9am–5.30pm, Sun 9am–4.30pm) where you can find light snacks, tea and coffee. You can reach it by following the track inland from the beach and climbing the path up the steep wooded nose of the hill in front. It sits at 100 metres (320ft) above sea level so you might want to hide your rucksack in some bushes at the bottom to avoid carrying it.

There are occasional buses from Moylgrove to St Dogmaels and Cardigan.

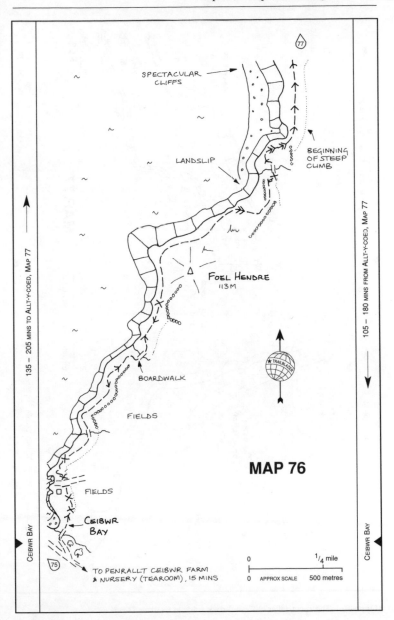

SPECTACULAR CLIFFS

BEGINNING OF STEEP CLIMB

LANDSLIP

FOEL HENDRE
113M

BOARDWALK

FIELDS

MAP 76

FIELDS

CEIBWR BAY

TO PENRALLT CEIBWR FARM & NURSERY (TEAROOM), 15 MINS

135 – 205 MINS TO ALLT-Y-COED, MAP 77

105 – 180 MINS FROM ALLT-Y-COED, MAP 77

CEIBWR BAY

CEIBWR BAY

TRAILBLAZER

0   1/4 mile
0   APPROX SCALE   500 metres

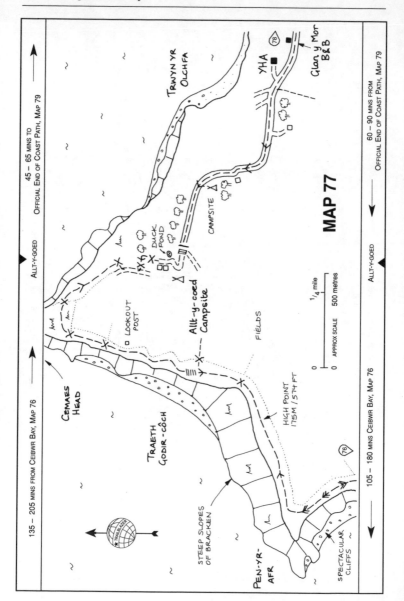

ALLT-Y-GOED

45 – 65 MINS TO
OFFICIAL END OF COAST PATH, MAP 79

135 – 205 MINS FROM CEIBWR BAY, MAP 76

TRWYN YR OLCHFA

YHA

Glan y Mor
B&B

MAP 77

DUCK POND

CAMPSITE

Allt-y-coed
Campsite

LOOKOUT POST

FIELDS

¼ mile

500 metres

0
APPROX SCALE

0

ALLT-Y-GOED

60 – 90 MINS FROM
OFFICIAL END OF COAST PATH, MAP 79

CEMAES HEAD

TRAETH GODIR-CÔCH

HIGH POINT
175M / 574 FT

STEEP SLOPES
OF BRACKEN

PEN-YR-AFR

SPECTACULAR CLIFFS

105 – 180 MINS TO CEIBWR BAY, MAP 76

(Opposite): The spectacular cliffs and rock folds at Cemaes Head.

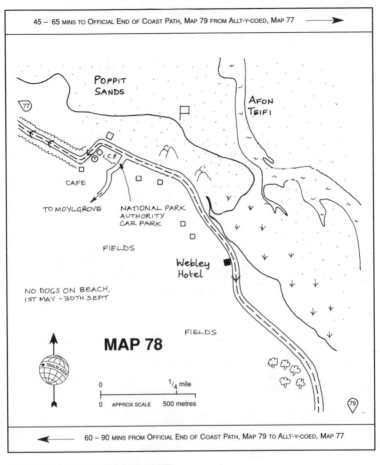

POPPIT
SANDS

AFON
TEIFI

77

C.P.

CAFE

TO MOYLGROVE

NATIONAL PARK
AUTHORITY
CAR PARK

FIELDS

Webley
Hotel

NO DOGS ON BEACH,
1ST MAY – 30TH SEPT

FIELDS

MAP 78

★ TRAILBLAZER

0   ¼ mile
├─────────────────────┤
0   APPROX SCALE   500 metres

79

POPPIT SANDS (DRAETH POPPIT)
MAP 77

Poppit Sands refers to the scattering of houses that stretch from Allt-y-coed Farm all the way down the lane to the car park and lifeboat station next to Poppit Sands itself, an enormous beach that fills the mouth of the Afon Teifi estuary. There's a **phone** by the car park and a **café**.

The official end of the path is still a mile and a half (2km) from Poppit Sands but there are plenty of places to stay along this stretch leaving very little to do the next morning. The first place you come to after rounding Cemaes Head is *Allt-y-coed Farm* (☎ 01239-612673). The coast path runs right through the farmyard. Just up the

---

(**Opposite**): Access to the secluded beach at Pwllcrochan (see p167) and its cave is by rope down the cliff.

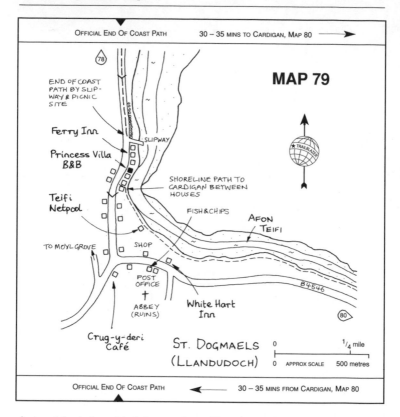

78

END OF COAST PATH BY SLIPWAY & PICNIC SITE

MAP 79

Ferry Inn   SLIPWAY

Princess Villa B&B

SHORELINE PATH TO CARDIGAN BETWEEN HOUSES

★ TRAILBLAZER

Teifi Netpool

FISH & CHIPS   AFON TEIFI

TO MOYL GROVE   SHOP

POST OFFICE

† ABBEY (RUINS)   White Hart Inn

B4546

80

Crug-y-deri Café   ST. DOGMAELS (LLANDUDOCH)

0   ¼ mile

0   APPROX SCALE   500 metres

slope past the duck pond is their **campsite** offering pitches all year for £1.50 per person. From the farm the path joins the narrow Poppit Sands Lane. A short way after Rock Cottage is another small unofficial **campsite** in a small field on the right hand side. There are no services here but a pitch will only cost you £1 per person.

Half a mile further on is *Poppit Sands Youth Hostel* (☎ 01239- 612936, open all year) overlooks the Sands less than an hour short of the end of the trail. It has 30 beds at £6.75 for members and gets very popular in the summer. You can also **camp** here for half the normal bed price with full use of the hostel facilities. A little further down the hill on the left is a white house called

Glan-y-mor (☎ 01239-612329, 1S/1D), the B&B with 'a loo with a view'. A bed costs £15 per person. It's home to a friendly basket weaver who is also a dab hand at making big breakfasts.

If you hadn't already noticed that you are now in the Welsh speaking part of Pembrokeshire you will if you go to *Webley Hotel* (☎ 01239-612085, 12–2pm, 6.30–9pm, no credit cards), about half a mile down the road from Poppit Sands. B&B is £31.50 per person with room for 16 people in single, double and twin rooms. There's reasonable food including lasagne for £5.95. Their chubby goat certainly likes the leftovers and has also been known to join the locals at the bar for a pint of Guinness.

ST DOGMAELS (LLANDUDOCH)
MAP 79

St Dogmaels is stretched along a dog leg in the river estuary. The coast path ends at the northern limit of the village but the main centre is further south. Before rushing through on your way to Cardigan it's worth taking a look at the old **abbey ruins** which can be found in the main part of the village. Head down the hill and look behind the **post office**.

There are a few small **shops** here but Cardigan, on the other side of the river, has far more to offer. There are **buses** into Cardigan from The Square roughly every hour. Alternatively you can phone for a taxi: **Cardi Cabs** (☎ 01239-621416).

For a place to sleep look in the northern end of the village where the coast path finishes. *Princess Villa* (☎ 01239-612224, 1T) is close to the end of the coast path and offers B&B at £15 per person. Far more accommodation can be found in Cardigan.

Right by the end of the path the *Ferry Country Inn* (☎ 01239-615172, food 7–8.45pm) is the perfect spot for a celebratory pint and slap-up meal. In the main village further south is *Crug-y-deri* (☎ 01239-613118, 6.30–10pm Tue–Sun) with good food such as trout (£7.95) and rabbit (£7.50). It's just to the right, across the road as you reach the junction in the middle of the village. *Teifi Netpool Inn* (☎ 01239-612680, 7.30–9pm) is another good place to kick the boots off and congratulate yourself with a pint or two. It has typical pub food and does a good plate of fish and chips. There is a *fish and chip shop* next to the post office and a little further down the hill is another good pub, the *White Hart Inn* (☎ 01239-612099, 7–8.30pm) with decent pub grub.

CARDIGAN (ABERTEIFI)   MAP 80

Cardigan is a mile (2km) beyond the end of the coast path. If you are using public transport to get home then Cardigan is the place to go.

There are a number of places to spend the night and recover before heading home the next day.

To get to Cardigan follow the riverside path which continues on from the official end of the path in St Dogmaels. This takes you to the bridge across the Afon Teifi and into Cardigan. Alternatively, just follow the road. If, after 186 miles (299km), you just can't bear the thought of walking then you can always catch the **bus** (see services).

To let your hair down after the long walk the best place for a drink is the very Welsh *Red Lion*, tucked behind Finch Sq at the end of Priory St. The friendly bar staff are only too happy to welcome strangers despite this being very much a locals' hangout. Be prepared for some strong Welsh singing once the beer starts flowing.

Services

The **TIC** (☎ 01239-613230, Bathouse Rd) is inside the theatre building. There are plenty of **banks** and all the **shops** you need along High St. Down Quay St, off High St at the river end, is a Somerfield **supermarket**.

The all-essential **bus stop** is on Finch Sq. There is an hourly bus to and from St Dogmaels. If you have left your car in Kilgetty or Amroth you will need the Tenby service which passes through Kilgetty. It is a limited service which runs two days a week only. There are also buses to Newport and Fishguard for connections elsewhere (see public transport map, p37).

Where to stay

A very friendly place to stay is *The Highbury* (☎ 01239-613403, Pendre, 2S/10D) which can be found by continuing on along High St. They have comfortable en-suite rooms with big breakfasts in a sunny conservatory. Prices start from £17 per person. Opposite this is *Llys Peris* (☎ 01239-615205, 4S/1T) with rooms from £20 per person.

There are more affordable B&Bs along Gwbert Rd at the far end of the town. *Brynhyfryd Guest House* (☎ 01239-612861, Gwbert Rd, 2S/1T/3D/1F) has

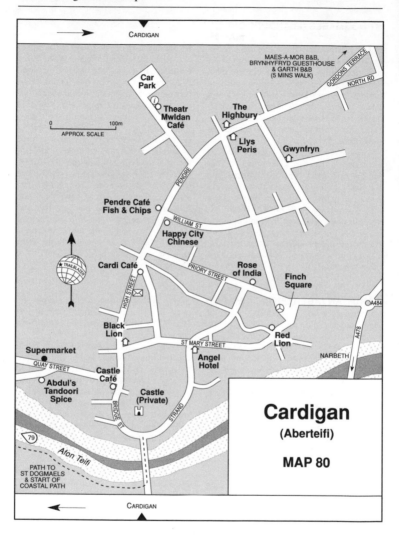

CARDIGAN

MAES-A-MOR B&B,
BRYNHYFRYD GUESTHOUSE
& GARTH B&B
(5 MINS WALK)

GORDONS TERRACE

NORTH RD

Car Park

Theatr Mwldan Café

The Highbury

Llys Peris

Gwynfryn

0   100m
APPROX. SCALE

PENDRE

Pendre Café Fish & Chips

WILLIAM ST

Happy City Chinese

TRAILBLAZER

Cardi Café

PRIORY STREET

Rose of India

Finch Square

A484

HIGH STREET

A478

Black Lion

ST MARY STREET

Red Lion

NARBETH

Supermarket

QUAY STREET

Castle Café

Angel Hotel

Abdul's Tandoori Spice

BRIDGE ST

Castle (Private)

STRAND

79

Afon Teifi

PATH TO
ST DOGMAELS
& START OF
COASTAL PATH

CARDIGAN

Cardigan

(Aberteifi)

MAP 80

prices from £18 per person, or £20 for en-suite rooms; *Maes-a-Mor* (☎ 01239-614929, Gwbert Rd, 3T) which has en-suite rooms from £16; and then there's *Garth* (☎ 01239- 613085, 2S/2T/2D) with beds at a similar price.

The *Black Lion* (☎ 01239-612532, 3S/5T/5D/1F) in High St has rooms from £30 per person. In Napier St there is basic en-suite B&B for £15 per person at *Gwynfryn* (☎ 01239-612489, 1D). On St Mary St the *Angel Hotel* (☎ 01239-612561, 2S/5T/1D/1F) does rooms from £16 per person, some of which are en suite.

Where to eat

Abdul's Tandoori Spice (☎ 01239-621416, 5–11.45pm, 7 days) is hidden down Quay St by the river, opposite the Somerfield super-market. This is an award-winning restaurant with very friendly waiters and a menu that takes a good half hour to read. Book your table in advance because it is very small and the locals like it a lot. They do takeaway as well. There are also good curries at *Rose of India* (☎ 01239-614891, Priory St).

The *Black Lion* (6–9pm) has an extensive menu while the *Angel Hotel* (12–2pm, 6.30–9pm) also does food for non-residents. For something quick and easy there are a number of takeaway places and coffee shops along High St and Pendre. Try *The Castle Café* on the corner with Quay St, or *Happy City Chinese* on Pendre. Good fish and chips can be found at *Pendre Café*. At the old theatre, which also houses the TIC (see p195), you will find the *Theatr Mwldan Café* while The *Cardi Café* on High Street is well worth hunting down for the excellent toasties for £2.15 and all-day breakfasts for £3.50.

Map key

		$\boxed{\$}$	Bank	$\triangle$	Camping Site
⇧	Place to stay	🏛	Museum	●	Other
O	Place to eat	📖	Library	⏲	Public Telephone
✉.	Post Office	⤢	Internet	⊕	Bus Station
ⓘ	Tourist Information	⊘	Public Toilet		

Route map key

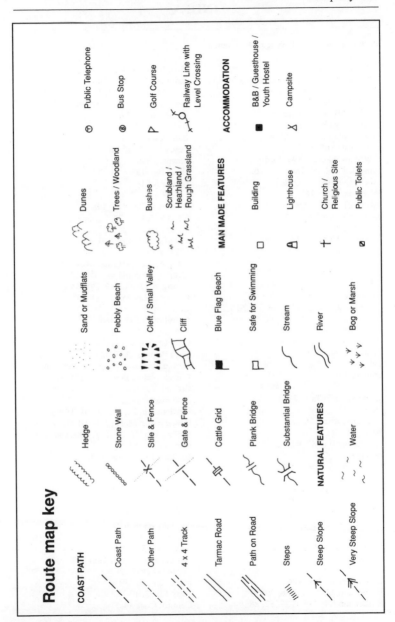

COAST PATH

Coast Path

Other Path

4 x 4 Track

Tarmac Road

Path on Road

Steps

Steep Slope

Very Steep Slope

NATURAL FEATURES

Water

Hedge

Stone Wall

Stile & Fence

Gate & Fence

Cattle Grid

Plank Bridge

Substantial Bridge

Sand or Mudflats

Pebbly Beach

Cleft / Small Valley

Cliff

Blue Flag Beach

Safe for Swimming

Stream

River

Bog or Marsh

Dunes

Trees / Woodland

Bushes

Scrubland /
Heathland /
Rough Grassland

MAN MADE FEATURES

Building

Lighthouse

Church /
Religious Site

Public Toilets

Public Telephone

Bus Stop

Golf Course

Railway Line with
Level Crossing

ACCOMMODATION

B&B / Guesthouse /
Youth Hostel

Campsite

INDEX

Page references in bold type refer to maps

❏ TRAILBLAZER GUIDES

Adventure Cycling Handbook	1st edn late 2004
Adventure Motorcycling Handbook	4th edn out now
Australia by Rail	4th edn out now
Azerbaijan	2nd edn out now
The Blues Highway – New Orleans to Chicago	2nd edn out now
China by Rail	2nd edn Feb 2004
Coast to Coast (British Walking Guide)	1st edn early 2004
Cornwall Coast Path (British Walking Guide)	1st edn out now
Good Honeymoon Guide	2nd edn out now
Inca Trail, Cusco & Machu Picchu	2nd edn out now
Japan by Rail	1st edn out now
Kilimanjaro – a trekking guide to Africa's highest mountain	1st edn out now
Land's End to John O'Groats	1st edn late 2004
The Med Guide	1st edn mid 2004
Nepal Mountaineering Guide	1st edn early 2004
New Zealand – Great Walks	1st edn Jan 2004
Norway's Arctic Highway	1st edn out now
Offa's Dyke Path (British Walking Guide)	1st edn Jan 2004
Pembrokeshire Coast Path (British Walking Guide)	1st edn out now
Pennine Way (British Walking Guide)	1st edn early 2004
Siberian BAM Guide – rail, rivers & road	2nd edn out now
The Silk Roads – a route and planning guide	1st end out now
Sahara Overland – a route and planning guide	1st edn out now
Sahara Abenteuerhandbuch (German edition)	1st edn out now
Ski Canada – where to ski and snowboard	1st edn out now
South Downs Way (British Walking Guide)	1st edn early 2004
South-East Asia – The Graphic Guide	1st edn out now
Tibet Overland – mountain biking & jeep touring	1st edn out now
Trans-Canada Rail Guide	3rd edn out now
Trans-Siberian Handbook	6th edn out now
Trekking in the Annapurna Region	4th edn Jan 2004
Trekking in the Everest Region	4th edn out now
Trekking in Corsica	1st edn out now
Trekking in the Dolomites	1st edn out now
Trekking in Ladakh	3rd edn mid 2004
Trekking in Langtang, Gosainkund & Helambu	1st edn out now
Trekking in the Moroccan Atlas	1st edn out now
Trekking in the Pyrenees	2nd edn out now
Tuva and Southern Siberia	1st edn late 2004
Vietnam by Rail	1st edn out now
West Highland Way (British Walking Guide)	1st edn out now

For more information about Trailblazer and our expanding range of guides,
for where to find your nearest stockist, for guidebook updates
or for credit card mail order sales (post-free worldwide) visit our web site:

www.trailblazer-guides.com

ROUTE GUIDES FOR THE ADVENTUROUS TRAVELLER

Europe
Trekking in Corsica
Trekking in the Dolomites
Trekking in the Pyrenees
(and the British Walking Series)

South America
Inca Trail, Cusco & Machu Picchu

Australasia
New Zealand – Great Walks

Africa
Kilimanjaro
Trekking in the Moroccan Atlas

Asia
Trekking in the Annapurna Region
Trekking in the Everest Region
Trekking in Ladakh
Trekking in Langtang
Nepal Mountaineering Guide

Trekking in the Pyrenees *Douglas Streatfeild-James*
2nd edition, £11.99, Can$27.95 US$18.95
ISBN 1 873756 50 X, 320pp, 95 maps, 55 colour photos
All the main trails along the France-Spain border including the GR10 (France) coast to coast hike and the GR11 (Spain) from Roncesvalles to Andorra, plus many shorter routes. 90 route maps include walking times and places to stay. Expanded to include greater coverage of routes in Spain.
'*Readily accessible, well-written and most readable...*' **John Cleare**

Trekking in Corsica *David Abram*
1st edition, 320pp, 74 maps, 48 colour photos
ISBN 1 873756 63 1, £11.99, Can$26.95, US$18.95
A mountain range rising straight from the sea, Corsica holds the most arrestingly beautiful and diverse landscapes in the Mediterranean. Among the many trails that penetrate its remotest corners, the GR20, which wriggles across the island's watershed, has gained an international reputation. This guide also covers the best of the other routes.
'*Excellent guide*'. **The Sunday Times**

Trekking in the Dolomites *Henry Stedman*
1st edn, 224pp, 52 trail maps, 13 town plans, 30 colour photos
ISBN 1 873756 34 8, £11.99, Can$27.95, US$17.95
The Dolomites region of northern Italy encompasses some of the most beautiful mountain scenery in Europe. This new guide features selected routes including Alta Via II, a West-East traverse and other trails, plus detailed guides to Cortina, Bolzano, Bressanone and 10 other towns. Also includes full colour flora section and bird identification guide.

Kilimanjaro: a trekking guide to Africa's highest mountain
Henry Stedman, 1st edition, 240pp, 40 maps, 30 photos
ISBN 1 873756 65 8,£9.99, Can$22.95, US$17.95
At 19,340ft the world's tallest freestanding mountain, Kilimanjaro is one of the most popular destinations for hikers visiting Africa. It's possible to walk up to the summit: no technical skills are necessary. This new guide includes town guides to Nairobi and Dar-Es-Salaam, excursions in the region and a detailed colour guide to flora and fauna.

The Inca Trail, Cusco & Machu Picchu *Richard Danbury*
2nd edition, 288pp, 45 maps, 35 colour photos
ISBN 1 873756 64 X, £10.99, Can$24.95, US$17.95
The Inca Trail from Cusco to Machu Picchu is South America's most popular hike. This practical guide includes the **Vilcabamba Trail** to the ruins of the last Inca capital, plus guides to Cusco and Machu Picchu.
'*Danbury's research is thorough...you need this one*'. **The Sunday Times**

Sahara Overland – a route & planning guide *Chris Scott*
1st edition, 544 pages, 24 colour & 150 B&W photos
ISBN 1 873756 26 7 £19.99, Can$44.95 US$29.95
Covers all aspects Saharan, from acquiring documentation to vehicle
choice and preparation; from descriptions of the prehistoric art sites of
the Libyan Fezzan to the ancient caravan cities of southern Mauritania.
How to 'read' sand surfaces, using GPS – it's all here along with 35
detailed off-road itineraries covering over 16,000kms in nine countries.
*"THE essential desert companion for anyone planning a Saharan trip on
either two wheels or four.'* **Trailbike Magazine**

Tibet Overland – a route & planning guide *Kym McConnell*
1st edition, 224pp, 16pp colour maps
ISBN 1 873756 41 0, £12.99, Can$29.95, US$19.95
Featuring 16pp of full colour mapping based on satellite photographs, this is a
guide for mountain bikers and other road users in Tibet. Includes detailed information on over 9000km of overland routes across the world's highest and
largest plateau. Includes Lhasa-Kathmandu route and the route to
Everest North Base Camp. *'...a wealth of advice...'* **HH The Dalai Lama**

The Silk Roads *Paul Wilson & Dominic Streatfeild-James*
1st edition, 336pp, 50 maps, 30 colour photos
ISBN 1 873756 53 4, £12.99, Can$29.95, US$18.95
The Silk Road was never a single thread but an intricate web of trade
routes linking Asia and Europe. This new guide follows all the routes
with sections on Turkey, Syria, Iran, Turkmenistan, Uzbekistan,
Kyrgyzstan, Pakistan and China.

Trans-Siberian Handbook *Bryn Thomas*
6th edition, 432pp, 52 maps, 40 colour photos
ISBN 1 873756 70 4, £12.99, Can$26.95 US$15.95
First edition short-listed for the **Thomas Cook Guidebook Awards**.
New sixth edition of the most popular guide to the world's longest rail
journey. How to arrange a trip, plus a km-by-km guide to the routes.
Updated and expanded to include extra information on travelling
independently in Russia. New mapping.
'Definitive guide' **Condé Nast Traveler**

Trans-Canada Rail Guide *Melissa Graham*
3rd edition, 256pp, 32 maps, 30 colour photos
ISBN 1 873756 69 0, £10.99, Can$24.95 , US$16.95
Expanded 3rd edition now includes Calgary city guide. Comprehensive guide to Canada's trans-continental railroad. Covers the entire
route from coast to coast. What to see and where to stay in the cities
along the line, with information for all budgets.

The Blues Highway New Orleans to Chicago
A travel and music guide *Richard Knight*
2nd edition, 304pp, 50 maps, 30 colour photos
ISBN 1 873756 66 6, £12.99, Can$29.95, US$19.95
New edition of the first travel guide to explore the roots of jazz and
blues in the USA. ❏ Detailed city guides with 40 maps ❏ Where to
stay, where to eat ❏ The best music clubs and bars ❏ Who's who
of jazz and blues ❏ Historic landmarks ❏ Music festivals and events
❏ Exclusive interviews with music legends Wilson Pickett, Ike Turner,
Little Milton, Honeyboy Edwards and many more.
'Fascinating' – **Time Out**

West Highland Way *Charlie Loram*   **Available now**
1st edition, 192pp, 48 maps, 10 town plans, 40 colour photos
ISBN 1 873756 54 2, £9.99, Can$22.95, US$16.95
Scotland's best-known long distance footpath passes through some of the most spectacular scenery in all of Britain. From the outskirts of Glasgow it winds for 95 miles along the wooded banks of Loch Lomond, across the wilderness of Rannoch Moor to a dramatic finish at the foot of Britain's highest peak – Ben Nevis. Includes Glasgow city guide.

Cornwall Coast Path *Edith Schofield*   **Available now**
1st edition, 192pp, 81 maps & town plans, 40 colour photos
ISBN 1 873756 55 0, £9.99, Can$22.95, US$16.95
A 163-mile National Trail around the western tip of Britain with some of the best coastal walking in Europe. With constantly changing scenery, the footpath takes in secluded coves, tiny fishing villages, rocky headlands, bustling resorts, wooded estuaries and golden surf-washed beaches. It is an area rich in wildlife with seabirds, wild flowers, dolphins and seals.

Offa's Dyke Path *Keith Carter*   **Available Jan 2004**
1st edition, 208pp, 86 maps & town plans, 40 colour photos
ISBN 1 873756 59 3, £9.99, Can$22.95, US$16.95
A superb National Trail from the Severn Estuary to the north Wales coast following the line of Offa's Dyke, an impressive 8th-century earthwork along the English/Welsh border. The ever-changing landscape – the Wye Valley, the Black Mountains, the Shropshire Hills and the Clwydian Hills – is steeped in history and legend providing 168 miles of fascinating walking.

Coast to Coast *Henry Stedman*   **Available Feb 2004**
1st edition, 256pp, 95 maps & town plans, 40 colour photos
ISBN 1 873756 58 5, £10.99, Can$22.95, US$16.95
A classic 191-mile (307km) walk across northern England from the Irish Sea to the North Sea. Crossing three fabulous National Parks – the Lake District, the Yorkshire Dales and the North York Moors – it samples the very best of the English countryside – rugged mountains and lakes, gentle dales and stone-built villages; country lanes and wild moorland; sea cliffs and fishing villages.

South Downs Way *Jim Manthorpe*   **Available Mar 2004**
1st edition, 192pp, 50 maps & town plans, 40 colour photos
ISBN 1 873756 71 2, £9.99, Can$22.95, US$16.95
This 100-mile (160km) footpath runs from Eastbourne to Winchester through East Sussex, West Sussex and Hampshire. It follows the chalk downs through several Areas of Outstanding Natural Beauty.

Pennine Way *Ed de la Billière & K Carter* **Available Apr 2004**
1st edition, 288pp, 130 maps & town plans, 40 colour photos
ISBN 1 873756 57 7, £10.99, Can$22.95, US$16.95
Britain's best-known National Trail winds for 256 miles over wild moorland and through quiet dales following the backbone of Northern England. Crossing three National Parks – the Peak District, the Yorkshire Dales and Northumberland – this superb footpath showcases Britain's finest upland scenery, while touching the literary landscape of the Brontë family and historical legends along Hadrian's Wall.

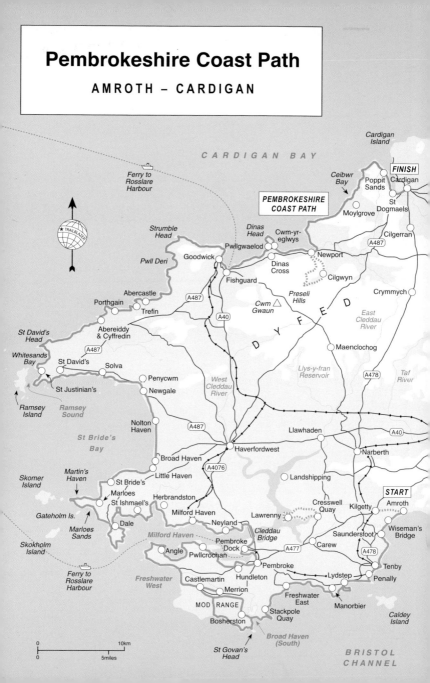